INDIGNANT HEART
Testimony of a Black American Worker

by
Charles Denby (Matthew Ward)

Pluto Press   London

First published in 1979, in Great Britain by
Pluto Press Limited, Unit 10 Spencer Court,
7 Chalcot Road, London NW1 8LH; and in the U.S.A.
by South End Press, Box 68, Astor Station, Boston,
Massachusetts 02123.

Copyright © 1978 by Charles Denby
ISBN 0 86104 088 0
Library of Congress Catalog Card No.: 78-65368

Cover design by Terry Seago
Photos by permission of Charles Denby
and *The Detroit News*

Printed in the U.S.A.

"...whether his voice cheered the starving Hindoo crushed beneath British selfishness, or Hungary battling against treason and the Czar; whether he pleaded at home for bread and the ballot, or held up with his sympathy the ever-hopeful enthusiasm of Ireland,— every true word spoken for suffering man, is so much done for the Negro bending beneath the weight of American bondage. It is said that the earthquake of Lisbon tossed the sea in billows on the coast of Cuba; so no *Indignant Heart* is beating anywhere whose pulses are not felt on the walls of our American bastille."

—Wendell Phillips, November 26, 1850

This book is dedicated to my son who I trust and hope will not have to go through what I went through when he becomes a man.

CONTENTS

Foreword
1. Childhood in the South 1
2. North to Detroit 27
3. Back to the South 37
4. My Wife, Christine 44
5. Work in the South 50
6. Work in the South II 69
7. Work in the North 87
8. Detroit Riots 1943.......................... 110
9. The Left Wing Caucus of the UAW 120
10. Jed Carter, the Foreman 124
11. South With My Son 135
12. In the Plant 138
13. Christine in the Plant 142
14. UAW 146
15. The Communist Party 163
16. The Trotskyist Party 166
17. Visiting Montgomery 181
18. Little Rock, Greensboro, Oxford 190
19. The FBI Does Nothing: The Murder of Viola Liuzzo,
    The Bombing of the Churches 202
20. Stokely Carmichael in Lowndes County 212
21. The Anti-Vietnam War Movement
    and the 1967 Detroit Uprising 226
22. Watergate and the Communist Giants 238
23. Challenging the Bureaucrats 245
24. DRUM, ELRUM, FRUM, and the Stinger 262
25. With the Wildcatters 272
26. Worldwide Struggle for Freedom 282
    Afterword   295

FOREWORD

There are differences in Part I and Part II of this book that I believe are important to explain. In Part I, the original *Indignant Heart* published in 1952, I wrote that I was born and raised in Tennessee, and used the name Matthew Ward. The names of other people and places were also changed.

The reason for the changes was to protect individuals from the vicious McCarthyite witch hunt then sweeping the country, which resulted in the persecution and literal destruction of many people. Few who did not go through that experience of national repression of ideas can fully understand the truly totalitarian nature of McCarthyism and the terror it produced. It is interesting to me that McCarthyism was destroyed at the same time that the Montgomery Bus Boycott developed—1955-56.

The changes in Part I, however, do not take anything away from the truth of the experiences described. What I wrote about my early years in Part I could be true of almost all Blacks living in the whole of South, USA.

I was born and raised in Lowndes County, Alabama, and the fact that this area will be forever recorded in American history as the place where some of the most important Black revolts occurred in the 1960s is because Black oppression was probably as complete and total there as almost anywhere else in the South.

Some who read the manuscript of this book commented on the difference in writing style of Part I and Part II. It could hardly be otherwise. It isn't only that 25 years separate Part I from Part II. More importantly, the great events of the 1960s that gave birth to a new generation of revolutionaries could but give a new direction to my thoughts and actions as a Black production worker who became the editor of a very new type of newspaper— *News & Letters*.

Charles Denby
Detroit, Michigan
September 1978

PART I.

1.
CHILDHOOD IN THE SOUTH

I WAS BORN in Tennessee in the southeast part of the state. I would like to put the name of the county in too, Leavitt County. I lived on one of the largest cotton plantations in the county with about two hundred or three hundred tenant renters and halfers. This is a halfer: a man is working, and makes six, eight or ten bales of cotton. Everything is divided equally between him and the landlord. Out of his half the halfer has to pay for tools, stocks and rent of the land. He practically never comes out with anything. He's always owing the landlord.

The Berger plantation was divided into sections called Barnes Place, Field Place, Old Gardner and Gaines Place. Berger was the complete boss of the county. What he said, that was it. In fact, he was the only man some whites have said, who ever put a fence across a public highway. Everybody had to get out and open and close the gate as they drove past his place. It was said that he was the wealthiest landowner in the state at that time. My father was one of the renters on Field Place when I was born.

My grandmother and her husband were renters too. Grandmother wasn't able to tell me how she got on the Berger plantation but she had been a slave. She could remember her mother screaming when she was sold off as a girl of twelve. That was in Georgia. She often used to tell us incidents of her life in slavery. On some places Negroes could have churches. But five or ten years before the Civil War began they weren't allowed to hold meetings. They couldn't visit other plantations without a pass. My grandmother said that they used to slip out in the woods. The men would walk around the edge of the woods to keep lookout. She said that many people used to slip away and escape from the meetings. I don't know if she meant the Underground Railroad. I was in Detroit when she passed. It was about 1925 and they all were sorry that I couldn't be there. The last words she said were, would Matthew get there in time.

When we visited her she always gave us food in a bag to eat on the way home. We lived about a mile from her house. There was an old oak tree in her yard with wooden pegs all up in it. We hadn't any idea what they were for. It was a whipping ground. During slavery the whites took a woman, pegged her dress over her head and whipped her.

I remember asking my grandmother, "Where is the whipping ground for men?"

She said, "Any place."

She used to sing and pray and talk about the Lord. I asked where was the Lord, what did he say about those things? She said many of them used to wonder about the same thing. She said it seemed like John Brown and Abraham Lincoln did more for our people, but that it was the work of the Lord.

On the plantation most of the tenants were close relations. The majority had foster children. My grandmother's husband wasn't my mother's father. There was not much difference shown to foster children. The father acted like they were his, or the woman acted like they were hers. The kids were never told anything about the married life of the grownups. We just couldn't be too inquisitive. They would say, so and so was your brother, or your father, or the father of another family. It was all like one big family.

My mother's father owned one hundred acres or more. During the Civil War a few of the Negroes were given land. Some of them, the baddest Negroes, never gave their land back. That land is in the hands of the family today. It was deeded from child to child so that it couldn't be sold. We lived in a frame house, in fact, all the houses were put up of rough lumber. Our house was one room with a shed for the kitchen. There were a lot of log cabins. Mud was dabbed between the logs to close up the spaces. The houses didn't have a ceiling. The women would take magazines and newspapers and glue made of flour and cover the walls and up under the rafters to keep out the rain and cold. Roofs were tin and a few houses had shingles. Most of the kitchens had dirt floors. Five to seven kids lived together in one room. Many of the children didn't have beds, just quilts on the floor. In winter it was cold and they had to pack up in bed.

All of us worked in the field. My mother, father, three boys and one girl. Before daylight the men were in the field. The women were in the house cooking food to take to the men, washing, milking and cleaning. After they finished work in the house they came to work in the field. When food was brought we'd sit right on the ground or on the stump of a tree to eat. My mother told me this story. Mother had to take us in a wagon to the field. It was at least a mile or a mile and a half away from the house. She spread a quilt at the end of a row and put us under a tree while she worked. We'd scream and she would run to us. We'd be covered with red ants. She'd pick them off and cry but she had to go as soon as she was done or the cotton wouldn't get picked. Everyone had to pick a hundred pounds or more per day.

Just before night everyone had a clean place made in the center of the field. The seed cotton would be gathered up and packed in bags and weighed. After it was weighed and checked it was put in one pile. The wagons were loaded and we would start home. We had to cross creeks to get back. The road turned sharp and the pitfall was so steep the mules had to run real fast and hold back. On one occasion we got turned over in the water underneath the cotton. They called and counted. Mother went to screaming. My sister was missing. My brother ran down and scratched and pulled the cotton and got my sister. She had almost drowned. To this day, if you try to put clothes on her she will almost have convulsions. Mother often cried all night at the condition of her children.

My father was a tenant farmer from my birth to my tenth year. When I was around ten he moved to the east end of the plantation and bought forty acres of his own. He was the only one on the plantation of three hundred to buy land from Berger. How did he do it? That's what I've wondered. He worked at the sawmill. He slipped away and chopped cord wood and saved everything. But what really did it was World War I. Cotton went up to forty cents instead of three to ten cents a pound. My father made his best crop one year of the war. He made around eight bales. He made a bid for the land. It was a surprise to Mr. Berger. At the end of the war he was through paying for it.

Father was a small man, five feet five, weighing about one hundred and forty-five pounds. Mother was a large woman weighing two hundred pounds. She had a light brown complexion, father was dark. Mother was known to be the leading Negro woman on the plantation in arranging church socials and affairs.

She was known through the county and part of the state. We were all happy together. Somehow or other, I was the only one who seemed different from the family traditions and ideas. My father seemed very close to me. But I asked questions leading into arguments about whites and questions about the hard life for the Negroes. It was hard for me to accept that sometime we'd be happy after death. It kept a controversy going between me and the rest of the community. My mother and the rest talked. My father was mostly silent. The tradition of my father's family was that they were the meanest Negroes that ever lived.

Father said, "About the law: you have to take what they do but only to a point. If anyone hits you then you're not to stand silent but fight them back." He wouldn't have us kids take a kick or a beating from anyone without fighting back. He used to say, "I worked for the farm so that we could live as free as everybody should."

At the age of five my mother told me about the school in the center of the plantation. She made me a book satchel of colored cloth and bought me a book. I was never so glad to get anything in my life. My brother set me in his lap and taught me the alphabet. I could read in the Primer and do the alphabet long before going to school. My brother would kid about the times we would have in school. He was fifteen and in the third grade.

The first day of school I was waiting for my brother outside our house.

Mother said, "Go ahead to school."

"I am waiting on Buddy. I want to wait 'til he comes."

Mother insisted, "Go alone, brother is not going. He had to go to the field."

I asked if I could wait until he would go again but she said that she doubted that he would ever go.

She said, "Go, or you will get a whipping."

I cried all the way to school. I felt I was crying because if the big kids jumped me I wouldn't have my brother to help. I always felt he would have been my protection. When I got to school I was shocked. The children knew my name. Some said, "I'm your first cousin."

I knew some but most of them were strangers. They said for me not to cry and not to worry. The teacher had gone to the sixth grade. I never had a white teacher in my life. Everyone called the teacher cousin Marthie. The school was so full of cracks that a child could raise a plank in the floor and slip away without the teacher knowing.

School ran five months. It opened in November and the date depended upon how well the crops had been gathered. School closed early March or on the first of April. Sometimes there were enough children left by closing day for commencement services. The subjects were spelling and arithmetic. Sometimes we had a little geography. I went to school that year until closing day. On closing day the women cooked up baskets and trunks of food. There were baseball games and the children went through examination demonstrations. The highlight of the school closing was the spelling game. The last one to sit down was the winner. Everyone would talk about him in the field for months. He was the hero, he could sit the school down in spelling. The one who could work the quickest answer in arithmetic was another hero of the class. In the evening, before night, we would give speeches and dialogues. The men would miss the celebrations because they would be working in the fields. Sometimes we would ask the owner if we could have commencement again so that the men could come. They very seldom said yes.

The girls in the school were from five to sixteen. Most of the boys were up to twelve or thirteen. That age was the end of their school career. Planting the cotton and corn, and chopping and hoeing, was what they had to do then. The girls generally missed one or two days a week to wash the clothes for the family. Out of four or five months of school we missed at least a month. When it rained we couldn't get over the creeks and ditches and on the coldest days there wasn't enough fire from the stove to keep us warm.

After a year my school was torn down and I had to go to what was supposed to be the finest school on the highway. There I had a man teacher who lived on Jerome Place. The teacher got caught buying cotton soon after I went to that school. Some renters would steal cotton and sell it cheaper than the set rate to a buyer. This was called night communications. The wagons would be loaded up at night and the cotton sold before daybreak. The teacher got caught by the riding boss. Berger told him to get out of Tennessee as quick as he could. Two things Negroes could not do on the farm:

Mess with white man white cotton,
Mess with white man white woman.

Berger had a huge barn with two or three hundred horses and mules. Every year he bought fifty to a hundred new mules. The tenants would kill out the mules, they rarely lasted more than a year. The tenants felt that they were working for nothing. Since the stocks belonged to Berger they felt that the crueler they were, the more money he had to spend. They would plow real deep. They would put all the strain they could on the animals especially if they were using a good pair of mules. Man to man they kept those mules going until they couldn't go any more. The mules would stop and lay out in the field. It gave everyone a chance to rest and play around until they brought out new mules.

Berger lived away from the plantation. His first wife died before I can remember. When I was ten or eleven he married a fourteen year old girl who was one of the poorest whites in the county. Berger was at least thiry-five. After four kids were born Berger bought Barnes Place. He owned several plantations throughout the state. On Barnes Place he had a space clear in the middle of some briars and built a village. His house had fifty rooms. There was a three story brick store and the streets were paved. He had an artesian well bored right through a hill. The house itself cost about one hundred thousand dollars. Berger's oldest daughter became president of the bank in Seldon. Berger always wanted to be advisor to the Negroes. He was nice to tenants on other farms. He would let them borrow or get food on credit. They would get in debt to him and have to move on to his place. He insisted that the girls marry boys on his place so they wouldn't move away. Many were related who married.

Berger came to our plantation once or twice a week. He kept a riding boss to see about his business. The riding bosses were always white men. If the riding boss, or overseer, carried his gun visibly, some of the Negroes carried theirs the same way. If they had concealed their guns before, they took them out as soon as they saw the riding boss coming. It took the overseer one or two days to ride through the plantation to see if everyone was working. Sometimes it would be two weeks before we saw him. If the riding boss hit anybody the tenants would make a commotion and tell Berger they were going to leave. Berger always fired the riding boss; they never worked over one year on his farm.

One Saturday my brother was at the mill waiting to grind the weekly corn. There was a dispute as to who was first. There was a loud commotion and the riding boss, a relative of Berger, came in. He told my brother to shut up or he wouldn't grind his corn. My brother said he didn't care who was first; he was going to grind his corn. The riding boss started to hit him, but before he did my brother pulled his gun. Berger came in but my brother kept his pistol at his side while they talked.

My brother said, "I'll die before one of you will hit me a lick."

Berger came to our house the next morning. He told my father to get my brother in order. He said he was mannish and carrying a revolver.

Berger said, "I'm not afraid of a machine gun. I won't let any Negro pull a revolver, or think I'm afraid, or that I will back down on anything that I've said."

My father told Berger that he could handle his boys as long as no one attempted to hit them. Berger talked for half an hour. He said my father was a good Negro, that he had bought the farm but that he still wouldn't have anyone pull a gun on him. Father didn't say one word to my brother.

Something else used to happen to Berger. At least three or four times, in my childhood days, his huge barn was completely destroyed by fire. Hundreds of mules, horses, cows and hogs got burned to death. The last time his barn was burned one Negro said that he was rich and could afford it.

A young boy said, "Yes, but this sure knocks a hole in his check."

Berger never found out who set the fires. Most of the older Negroes would have a whispering campaign. They'd say it was a certain Negro that Berger had tried to hit, but no one ever knew. It was really good, no one was ever punished. There was never any evidence.

We worked from dawn to dusk, Monday to Saturday. Our amusement was a picnic or a baseball game with the Negroes on other plantations. They would kill a pig, or something, and pile up a table with food. We'd go to the picnic and buy something to eat. We'd have a guitar or a harmonica, but mostly a guitar. There would be wonderful singing and music. The frolics were held under the trees. Many religious women would slip up close enough to hear the singing but they didn't want to be seen.

On Gerson Place the halfers and renters complained and said they wanted a fifty piece band. The owner said that he would buy the instruments and each Negro would be charged for the one he chose. The day the band came each man took the instrument he wanted. No one had ever held an instrument before, except the guitar or harmonica. They held the instruments and played such music that people came from all the plantations. At the end of the month they were known, and had engagements to play all through the southern part of the state. They played by ear and could hear anything once and play it. There was only one man who ever had music training in that part of the county. He'd played in the band at Tuskegee. The others played better than this man by the end of the month. The way those people could play was known all over. You could find people in many leading cities who would tell you the same story.

It was very difficult for me to go to the Saturday night picnics. I was always worrying and hoping to go. I had a friend who could go. We arranged for him to ask me to go with him to see about some business for his folks, or to go possum hunting. We had the best possum dogs around and my father would always lend them. After mother and father went to bed we'd run the dogs home and go to the party. One party was at my pal's home. I asked my father if I could spend the night with my pal. He said yes and when he found out about the party he had already given his word.

Practically every riding boss went with a colored woman or lived with one. Usually she'd been with a colored man before him. If the riding boss was going with a woman he would be at the parties. He'd stay off a short distance or try to use some Negro to tell her he was there. The time of the party at my pal's place I was twelve or thirteen. Curtis Gordon had been going with a light mulatto woman. He was talking to her with his arm around her shoulder.

The riding boss came up and said, "Take your arm off her. She's mine."

Curtis swore and hit the riding boss. He knocked him down.

The riding boss got up and said, "Stay here, I'll take care of you."

I was excited; it was the first time I saw a white man get hit. Blood was running from his face. I ran home. My father was excited and I asked him what would happen to Curtis. Father told me that whatever happened to Curtis would happen to a lot of other Negroes if we sat and did nothing about it.

I said, "But he hit a white man, I'm scared."

My father was mad, "I'll whip you if ever I hear you say you're afraid of a white man. I won't own you for a son if you ever say it again."

Nothing hurt me so much as his saying that. Dad took down his shotgun and we went over. About two hundred Negroes were waiting but the riding boss didn't show up.

Curtis said, and let it be known everywhere, "I'm going with this woman. If I ever meet that white man it means death to him."

Berger fired the riding boss and he and his family had to move off the plantation.

At another party two white men came. One drove the truck which brought people from another plantation. The other was a deputy sheriff of the county. A young man was sitting talking, and the truck driver asked him for a match.

The fellow said he didn't have one.

The truck driver asked again.

The fellow said, "No, I haven't a match."

The driver walked away and the sheriff said, Did he say, no, or no, sir, to you?"

The driver went back and asked, "Did you say, no, or no, sir?"

"Why?"

"Don't ask, say what you said."

The truck driver took out a gun and threatened to shoot everyone who was there.

The Negro said, "I said, 'No, I don't have a match'."

The truck driver told him, "You know what you're supposed to say."

The Negro answered, "Say whatever comes into my mind."

All the Negroes were standing around. The driver told them to get in the truck. He drove as fast as he could. One Negro grabbed the wheel and the truck went in the ditch and overturned. Everybody jumped off leaving the driver in the cab. They set a match to the carburetor but the truck driver escaped. The Negroes rushed to Berger and told him that the truck driver had run his truck into the ditch trying to kill them. He was fired the next day.

Ten or fifteen days a year we had to work on the county road making repairs. This was the way the taxes of the plantations were paid. But it wasn't our plantation. The riding boss was always there to see that we kept working putting in our time. One riding boss claimed that he could do anything that any Negro could do. He had a lot of physical strength. He was the meanest riding boss and a relative of Berger. Hamp Hodman, who every Negro and many whites said was crazy, and ready to fight anybody, was working the road. The riding boss got in an argument with Hamp.

Hamp said he'd better not hit him because anyone who hit him he'd hit back.

The riding boss told him to watch his language and to say, "I'll hit any Negro who hits me."

Hamp looked at him, "I didn't make any mistake in what I said. Anybody who hits me, I hit them."

The riding boss asked, "Would you hit me?"

"Anybody hit me I hit them back."

The riding boss said, "I've been hearing about you. Now, I'm going to see."

He got down from his horse, got a stick and hit Hamp on the shoulder with the big end. Hamp snatched the stick, drew back and hit the white man square on the head. He was unconscious and blood was flowing all around. The Negroes laid him aside and continued to work until he revived. He got up on his horse and went to the store. His wife took him to the doctor. By night everyone knew about it. When the riding boss told Berger, he said that he thought everybody in Leavitt County knew Hamp Hodman. Anybody who fooled with him ought to have better sense. He said he was a good working Negro if left alone. But if anyone fought him they'd better plan to kill him.

Hamp got in many incidents. The last time he came to my father he told about all the fights and shooting scrapes with whites. He said that he'd been lucky to have come off alive. But he said he was getting old and was going off by himself somewhere.

"I can't continue carrying on a battle all my life to let the white man know he isn't any better than I am."

Every year in November and December was settlement. Everyone had to sit before Berger; he had two books, cash items and bigger items. He'd tell us our debts and the interest. Then he'd tell us how much cotton we had baled, what he paid us for it and then he'd say, "You still owe me ——." We had no record and nothing we could keep. It was always what we owed him.

Then he'd say, "What clothes and food do you just have to have for Christmas?"

He'd tell the storekeeper to charge it and then we owed for that too. This would go on all through the years. I have some relations who from the time I can remember owed Berger until they died. It was twenty-five years or more. They never once paid out of debt.

We charged everything at Berger's store. One Negro who worked in the store always gave us anything we wanted whenever we came. Every tenant shed tears when he got fired. He was an old man, so when Berger asked him about the missing stuff, he said that he was old and that his memory was going. He said maybe he'd made some mistakes. Another man worked in a store in Gardena. He stole enough to buy a plantation of his own.

All the churches on the plantations were wooden churches, painted white on the outside, but just rough lumber on the inside. There were long wooden benches made by some carpenter on the plantation. Each one seated between fifteen and twenty people. The churches could accommodate about two hundred. Sometimes a church would be built right facing the highway, but usually they were far back on the plantation. High up in a tree, on the church property, a large steel bell would be hanging which was rung only on Sundays. We never had church service in the morning, but always in the afternoon. On our Revival Sundays, our Big Day, we called it, we would start gathering at the church about one o'clock, and continue through the day until dark. Before the Big Day, someone would go to town and buy up things to sell. He would set up a stand about a hundred yards from church property. He would get there early and have his table all fixed before the crowd got there. Some hundred yards in the opposite direction there would be men with cards and dice. These were the sinners. They cleared off a place in the woods to have their game going all day. The well where we got our water to drink for that day was some distance from the church. All day long there would be a regular going and coming from the church to one of these places while the service would be going on.

On the Sunday beginning the revival the people of one church would make all the preparations for it. They would go into debt and buy new clothes and food. They killed hogs, goats and chickens, and cooking went on two or three days in preparation. Sometimes toward the end, the women would be cooking all night long. There would be huge trunks filled to the top, large boxes, baskets and shoe boxes of food. There was always enough food to feed everybody from two hundred to one thousand people. Food was served in real plates which the people brought. All the food was given away. There was special interest in giving it to members of other churches. Seventy-five percent of those who came didn't even go inside the church but they would be there at the side. It was their holiday too. They did as much preparing for the holiday as the deacons, the sisters or the preachers of the church. It was a chance for everybody to socialize.

For the Big Day, the boys my age and myself would wear box coats, made of blue serge or French serge, with fifteen or twenty buttons on the pockets. We wore peg-top full English pants with five or six buttons on each hip pocket, and high Cuban heeled shoes with hard toes that pointed inwards. We would try very hard to have on a white silk shirt with large red or blue stripes, and a detachable collar. The last thing was a John B. Stetson hat, usually brown. Our girl friends at the church all admired us. All day long we would be walking our girls to and from the well, not to get water but to walk and be seen by the others. We would take our girls to the stands and buy ice cream and soda water, and maybe a souvenir. The young girls served the food and the "courting girls" saved special plates for their boy friends. There was no eating until after the sermon which lasted until about three o'clock.

The kids sat in the first seats facing the preacher. He'd preach and then go into the special part about converting. If some kids didn't get up and shake the preacher's hand he would worry them for an hour or an hour and a half. He'd say they might die, and things like that. The preacher would ask the congregation to pray over them. When you were coming through religion you were supposed to see a white baby. That's supposed to be an angel. The only picture they ever showed me in the Bible was a white angel.

I spent five years on the mourner's bench. My brother spent fifteen. I never did see the white baby. Some kids would come out jerking and I knew I never would feel like that. When I was twelve I joined four Baptist and three Methodist churches. At the first church the preacher said I was an infidel. I didn't know what that was. Then he said I was a reprobate. So I talked with some boy friends and we said we would join. Another time my mother took me to visit friends. On the way home we stopped at a revival. At this church the people rocked like with the blues. I said this sounds good. My mother looked away for a minute. When she looked around I was on the mourner's bench. My mother couldn't get me away from the bench. She called but I wouldn't look. I shook the preacher's hand. There were some old men sitting on the bench who wouldn't join. They said it was a privilege just to sit on the mourner's bench. On the bench were also some women who were called blues singers and rowdy women. They would go through the screaming and a conversion motion but it wouldn't stick. They'd let their names stay on the membership book but they went on in the same life. My father had my name taken off and I stayed in the church where he and mother were members. At that time he was a deacon and he said he wanted us in the same house.

After the revival closed there would be the baptizing. It would be in a creek where the water was deep enough to come under our arm-pits. These were mostly holes where cows and mules had been bathing and urinating. It was muddy and smelly. We were led up until it was deep enough and then dunked under the filthy water. We were dressed in long white gowns. The last baptism was when I was fifteen. There was a boy in the group called Teddy. He was always hitting and throwing and was just an antagonistic kid. He was very afraid of snakes. After half of us were baptized they led Teddy up in the water. As he was walking he saw a black snake swimming toward him on top of the water.

As the preacher started to pray he said, "Reverend, look at that snake!"

The preacher ignored him. Teddy kept screaming, "the snake!" and the preacher kept trying to pray. The snake kept coming and Teddy jumped out of the water and ran all the way home in his long white robe.

He said, "They are not going to baptize me in that creek if I never go to heaven."

When he ran away the other kids wouldn't go in. Each one

turned around and said, "No, I've already been in."

Everybody would talk the whole week in the field about the time they had at the revivals. Our feelings were intense because we knew that after the Big Day we wouldn't see our girls again until the following Sunday. We would all be too busy working on the farm. This routine would be part of our life every year, from July until October. There were two other times a year when we looked for this kind of enjoyment, Christmas and the Fourth of July. Many people came from the cities and some in the North would time their vacations for the revival period.

A leading member of one church in Gardena was Bill "Devil" Jones. All the people gave him that name. He was able to pray the best in the church. He was a devilish type. He kept everyone laughing. He wouldn't work in the field but was always walking around telling the Negroes what happened in town. He would collect food at the revivals and take it home to eat for the week. The work he did was piddling; he'd tell jokes, true stories and sometimes chop a little wood.

In Gardena there were four stores. One of the stores had a bar where poor whites and Negroes hung out. Bill Devil signed up to work one year with the owner of the store. In turn the owner gave him a little plot to work in his spare time. Bill worked hard and made one bale on the small plot. At the end of the year he went to settle up for what he got out of the store to eat. The owner got out the cash book. It had "Bill Devil, cheese and crackers. Bill Devil, stage planks and sardines." Stage planks were a hard cracker we used to eat. The whole cash book with about eight or ten pages was this way all through. Bill Devil didn't have but one dollar coming out of his bale. The Negroes made a song out of it. "Bill Devil and cheese and crackers, Bill Devil and planks——" He didn't sign up to work with anybody after that. He walked around the town and fields.

Sally Bradley and Ben Bradley had a farm in Gardena. They were white. One of Miss Sally's sons was living with a Negro woman. The son had three children, Dickie, Buster and Locket. Their mother died when the oldest child was ten but the father stayed and took care of his children. He passed when the oldest was fifteen. Miss Sally took the children to live in her house and when they were grown she sent them to Birmingham to work in the office of a cousin.

Ben Bradley wasn't a Christian. His wife was the most religious white woman in Gardena. Bill Devil always talked to her about religion. He would chop some wood and she would feed him. She always complained about her husband going to the bar every Saturday, getting drunk and fighting. She wished he'd get religion. Every Saturday Bill Devil would go to Gardena to take Mr. Bradley home when he got drunk. He'd wake up Miss Sally and they would put him to bed. Miss Sally and Bill Devil would talk religion. The whites started a revival in Gardena and Ben Bradley joined one Friday night. The next morning Bill Devil passed the Bradley house and Miss Sally called to him.

"Come, come, I have good news for you. Bradley has come to religion. We're the two happiest people in the world."

Bradley came out and said to Bill, "Bill, if you had told me religion was this sweet I would have joined long years ago."

He told Bill he had seen an angel. Bill asked if Bradley was going to hold his religion.

Miss Sally said, "Yes, he is serious. Don't you believe he will hold it?"

Bill said, "If he holds it a month I'll chop wood a whole day. If not, you must cook me a meal big enough for three days."

She said she would do it.

In a few days Bill Devil was walking by and stopped at Miss Sally's. They could watch Bradley plowing in the distance. The horse stepped out of the traces and he was trying to get it to step back. He was getting mad. He unhooked the horse and it stepped back. As he was hooking it, a sharp point stuck in his finger.

He yelled, "Whoa horse! God damn your soul! I ought to take this off and kill you."

Sally heard him and said to Bill Devil, "Let's go ask him if he remembers what he said a week ago."

The blood was dripping from Bradley's finger.

As they come up he said, "Don't come near me. Go back, God damn! God damn this horse! I'd cuss him if I was plowing in the streets of paradise!"

One time Bill Devil borrowed some money from some whites and didn't pay it back. The whites carried him into the woods for a beating. He asked if he could pray.

He got on his knees and said, "Oh Lord, I know you rule and control the heavens and all there is above, but Lord these white folks rule and control the South and all that is down here below——."

One of the whites touched him on the shoulder and asked him to repeat what he had said. He repeated the prayer.

The whites told him, "We won't beat you and you won't have to pay your debt if you promise to tell this to every nigger wherever you go."

Many of the kids used to say that they wished they were like my family.

They'd say, "You're in the boat, you can sail."

I never could see it. We owned our place, that was true. Actually we had to do the same work as everybody. We worked in the field, our clothes were just like the rest and besides, I never could see that people were different. This couldn't fit in my mind. It was something I rejected very strongly. It made me a very difficult boy for anybody in that community or around the county. When I went to training school I stayed with my cousin. He owned three hundred acres and had his own gin mill and barn and several tenant farmers. I had to eat at the table with him because I was a relative. The tenants had to eat later. My friends were tenant farmer's kids and I wanted to eat with them. My cousin whipped me and told my father. Father said that this was one thing about me they couldn't change. He said my cousin had better let me be like that if I insisted.

Among the Negroes there was no distinction along the color line. My foster brother's mother was practically white. Throughout the county it was like that. It is different in the North. Some of the light skinned feel that they are better than dark skinned. In the South the distinction was among tenant farmers or renters, and those who owned their own place. When I was fifteen I was supposed to go with girls whose families had their own equipment and their own stocks or cotton around the house, I couldn't agree with this idea.

Seldon, Tennessee, was twenty miles from the plantation. It took two nights and a day to go and return. There were no trucks or automobiles. We'd hook up a wagon and leave Friday night. We'd carrried crates of chickens and pigs to sell so we could get food and clothes. We always carried along the shotgun. When I was six years old father said I could go to Seldon. We drove until three in the morning until we came to Soap Stone Creek where everybody camped. The wagons sat around on each side of the creek and we slept there until almost daylight. Sometimes there were five to twenty wagons. Some people didn't know each other but we would get acquainted. I always wanted to see daybreak, just how night come to day. Baby brother and I made an agreement; one of us would stay awake to see the night change to day.

The farmers could walk around all day in Seldon but they had to carry their guns unbreeched and they had to be out of town by night. Many Negroes were forced to buy what they didn't want. They would ask to see something, the store owner would show it and then refuse to take it back. Uncle Tim and father went to a store together. Tim's wife wanted some cloth and asked to see a piece up on the shelf. The storekeeper got up on a ladder and took it down. Tim's wife didn't want the goods.

The storekeeper cursed. "Why in hell didn't you tell me before I got it down that you didn't want it?"

While they were looking around the store, the storekeeper rolled the cloth very tight and slipped it into a bag my aunt was carrying. We got out on the sidewalk, ten or fifteen feet away, when the man ran out.

He caught hold of my aunt and said, "Where is that cloth you stole?"

Uncle Tim slipped two shells into his gun, and raised it to his shoulder and cursed the man.

"Get the cloth out of my wife's bag or I'll shoot your brains out. My wife didn't steal it."

If the white man's pal hadn't helped him he'd have been dead.

He ran out hollering, "Don't shoot, don't shoot. You can keep the cloth or give it back or whatever you want to do."

Father told Tim to hold it and gave back the cloth. We walked around town all the rest of the day but the police didn't come. Uncle Tim couldn't talk very well, he stuttered badly. But it came out very plain what he meant to the storekeeper. I have no doubt he would have shot those men where they stood.

I'm forty-four the twenty-fifth of this month. That would be that I was born in 1907. I was seven years old when the war broke out. All the farmers talked about the war and the Germans. We wondered if the young Negroes eighteen to twenty, would have to go to war. Every Negro on the Berger plantation, but one, was strong against going. One woman said, "Go be a brave soldier."

All cursed and abused her.

The story came out that if they didn't go the money in the United States wouldn't be any good. They said: we never have any. What difference does it make.

The next circulation that came out was that if the men went they would have complete freedom. All wanted this but they asked why they couldn't have it now.

One of the first three drafted was my first cousin. The night before he left every Negro on the plantation had a reception. It lasted all night long. There was singing, praying, drinking. All were trying to feel they'd see each other again. When they left, many of us went behind them on foot for miles. The families were screaming the whole night and practically the whole week.

Uncle Tim's son, Oscar, was bad like his father. He loved action. He said he wasn't going to war, cross his heart and hope to die. This was a saying we would never back down on. Oscar said he'd cross both his hands before he'd go to war. He went over and sharpened the axe, laid his hand down on the chopping block and chopped off his shooting fingers. He was rejected. They had to hold Oscar when his brother got drafted. He swore he'd kill him if he went to the war. They sent Oscar to relations so that he wouldn't be home when his brother left.

Only the preachers were stimulating about the war. They didn't go very far, just said you had to go and left it at that. My brother was eighteen and he was always asking the preacher how to go to Mexico. Every day he took some kind of chemical so it would affect his health. When they examined him an organ was affected. They put him in the lowest class of the draft.

We got a letter from my cousin Elwood from Camp Dodge, Iowa. No one had ever heard of it. We all visualized it as in the war zone in Europe. Someone on the farm composed a song that we sang all the time:

> *This war has everybody troubled now.*
> *Not only me and you.*
> *Not only one and two*
> *The rich and the poor*
> *The white and the black*
> *Every nationality*
>
> *Lord we don't know what to do.*

> *Some left home and left the mother crying*
> *Some left home and left the wife crying*
> *About this war*
> *Got everybody troubled now*
> *This war, this war.*

    Some sang, hoping the Kaiser would soon get over here. They wouldn't care if conditions were bad if the whites were in the same category as they were. If anyone knew he was going he would go to the next plantation and pile up tremendous debts. He'd take home food and clothes for his wife. All would know but the boss. He would come around trying to find the fellow but everybody would say that he had gone to war.

    After the war, when testing out the freedom, many boys were killed before they could get home. Dixon, a plantation owner, killed a Negro soldier in sight of his own home. The fellow had stopped to talk to his friends. Dixon couldn't stand the sight of a Negro in a uniform and shot him.

    At least ten or twelve boys from Berger's place came home. They wanted to give a picnic to demonstrate what they had learned, marching and such. They all had their guns. The whites said they couldn't show the others. The Negroes said they had liked to shoot before they left home. They had gone to war to save the country and they were going to march to show their friends. Six whites came. Two hundred Negroes were watching the demonstration.

    This man, Dixon, was so mean that if a Negro from his place went to the city and got in trouble, the police would let him go. The police were afraid of Bob Dixon. He would as soon shoot them as speak to them. My friend and I were riding one night in a car without a taillight. A cop started after us. We told him we were from Dixon's place and he let us go and said to hurry home. Before I left for the North two Negroes from Birmingham just about beat Dixon to death. He had tried to beat them with his pistol. It was such a shock to all the whites in the country that Dixon had to make the excuse that he was getting old.

    There was the Harvey Place; the father was the sheriff of Leavitt County at one time. All Negroes tried to stay away from that plantation. The Harveys would insist that Negroes borrow money or get credit and then they would have to live on the

Harvey farm. If they wouldn't the Harvey's would force them. The Harveys didn't allow any law enforcement on their place. They had to settle everything on the farm themselves. This farm was the farm of slavery. Everyone said slavery had been abolished everywhere in the United States except on the Harvey Place. We called them the bad white people. It was said that old Harvey would shoot a white man as quick as a Negro. If Negroes came to Berger to escape from Harvey he would send them to a plantation two hundred miles away. Old Harvey had many Negroes working for him who had committed both minor and serious crimes. He'd go to court and tell the Negro he'd get him off his offense if he'd come and work for him. But this meant he could never get away from Harvey again. Harvey never tried to murder a Negro who ran away, he would capture and bring him back. One time Harvey got a Negro out of jail who had shot his wife. The man went back to the Berger plantation. Harvey came with a revolver and threatened to kill Berger but Berger wouldn't give the man up to Harvey.

On the Harvey plantation it was slavery and this was true. There were two brothers. One was six feet seven. He was Eaton. He was talkative and liked to carry on jokes at all times. The other was Russell, about five feet and he weighed a hundred and thirty pounds. He didn't talk at all. The word went out for them as the meanest white men there ever were. They were middle class. The other middle class owners were afraid of rich owners like Berger, but these weren't afraid. It was the only plantation where there wasn't a church or a school. When someone would pass, the Harveys would decide who could go to the funeral. Sometimes they would make the immediate family work when the body was being buried.

Old Harvey always said to anyone who got in trouble: "Always get your feet on the line of my place and you're safe."

Russell, the little one, was married to a white woman and had two or three children. He had a Negro maid and built her a house close to his house. He would spend one night with her and one night with his wife. The maid had two children for him. He told his wife the children by the maid had to spend as many nights in the bed with her own children as he wanted. She'd have to see to them without any resentment at all. One day his father's wife's brother was paying a visit. The brother started playing around with the Negro maid. At the table he hit the maid on the butt side while she passed the food. Russell Harvey shot and killed him while they were all eating.

On the Harvey Place they were never allowed to invite the others for a picnic or a frolic. There was not one Negro on the Harvey Place who had any type of religion or pretended to have any. The Negroes resented it and whispered that some day they'd come out from under.

There were three brothers and a father on another plantation. Richard Manton, Richard Manton Jr., William Manton and George Manton. (George Manton was the riding boss who hit Hamp Hodman.) Everybody had trouble getting away from the Mantons but not as much trouble as with the Harveys. Old Harvey would get you back if it meant killing a white owner who tried to help. But the Mantons were bad like the Harveys.

I had never gone up on the Harvey Place until I was about twelve. One day I, and two other boys, decided to go up to the mill. It was said that the Harvey mill ground the best corn in the county. Eaton Harvey was at the mill when we came. He cursed the Berger Place and said why didn't we all come to his place to live. He wanted me to sell him the corn I had brought to grind. I told him that my father would whip me.

He said, "Money in your pocket is worth a whipping. How old are you?"

I said, fourteen, but I was twelve.

He said, "If you sell me your corn I'll take you over to my plantation and give you any woman you see that you want."

We said, no, and got away.

On our way out a little boy came up and said he knew something serious. Cross our hearts not to tell if he told us. It was concerning white folks and we would get killed if we mixed in white folks' business. The Negroes were slipping from the Harvey Place to the Manton Place to live, and then from the Manton Place to the Harvey Place again. Usually it was a different individual each time but sometimes the same one would go back and forth. It had got so serious that Harvey and Manton were threatening that one more Negro better not go. The little boy said that it was no accident that the Negroes were moving back and forth. They felt this was the only way out of their slavery. They hoped it would lead to the Mantons and the Harveys killing each other out.

My uncle was in on it. He moved to the Mantons in the heat of the argument. He slipped back in the middle of the night and said he had been forced to go at gunpoint. He said that if Harvey wanted to get a Manton, one was riding horses to Brewton the next day. Russell Harvey said he'd plant himself between a certain oak tree and the road. Uncle went back to the Mantons and the next day they went on the trip. As they came near the tree my uncle saw Harvey behind it. He hit his horse and it jumped ahead. Harvey shot Richard Manton Jr. and killed him and the horse. My uncle pulled around and raced back to the Manton Place. He spread the news to the other brothers and the father that Russell Harvey had killed Richard Manton. Manton had shot Russell in the groin before he died but Eaton Harvey took him to the hospital before the Mantons could get him.

In the midst of this the Negroes continued to transfer from one place to the other. It was about a month before Russell was back home. The Mantons made a threat that they would kill both the Harveys. The Harveys said they'd kill the Mantons or be killed themselves. The Negroes transferred the news. The Mantons, at this point, were the aggressors. They were always passing through the Harvey plantation. Richard's father, Richard Sr., was acting insane walking up and down on the Harvey plantation. He died during this period. It was not known for certain how he died, whether natural or killed, but the word was passed by the Negroes that Russell Harvey had shot the old man.

The Mantons tried to make a deal all through the county with the Negroes to fool the Harveys out. They offered two hundred dollars. They said if the Negroes wanted to move out of the state it would be all right. But no one would take the money or make a plan with them. I can remember the day a Manton came to our house. He tried to get my mother to talk to a relative of hers on the Harvey Place, to fool Russell Harvey out for him.

Mother told Manton, "I haven't anything to do with white folks' business. It's too serious a business."

One of the Harvey houseboys, their closest boy, slipped away to the Manton Place. After staying on the Manton Place a month, he said that he'd come back to fool Harvey out. He would go ask Harvey protection from the Mantons. This is where discrimination comes in, and Harvey died for it. The houseboy, along with two Manton brothers, went to the Harvey Place around two o'clock in the morning. They planted a bucket in the road of the pass that led up to the house. This was arranged as the signal to the Mantons if Harvey could be fooled out. The Negro boy would get him outside for a talk and kick the bucket and lie flat on the ground leaving Harvey standing. This was carried out. The boy knocked on the Harvey door and said he was running away. He said he was afraid the Mantons would kill him. Could he stay close to the house and not be harmed? Because he was a Negro they couldn't let him sleep in the house, so Eaton told him he'd take him down to the barn. The boy walked a step ahead and came to the bucket. He kicked it and pinned himself to the ground. Harvey was killed by crossfire from the weed part of the road. That left only Russell Harvey.

All this time the Harvey children and the Manton children were riding the same bus to school. The school had to hire a different bus to take them to school separately. They were fighting and wrecking the buses every day. During the feud the state troopers didn't do anything. They weren't supposed to come on those plantations for *nothing*. The Mantons and the Harveys were the law of their land.

Manton sent a communication to Harvey that if he wanted to live he'd have to move out of the state. Harvey said he wouldn't move and that he could have killed Manton the week before when he passed a certain spot. But Manton's wife had been with him and out of respect for her, he hadn't shot. That time Manton sent word that at a certain time and place *he* could have killed Harvey but his wife was with him. He wanted to respect Harvey's wife. They decided to let the court decide the feud. On the date of the hearing, Harvey's wife insisted on going along with him. He told her, no, that he was tired of taking her around to save his life. One day it had to happen, one of them would die.

The ward filled up with Negro and white spectators an hour before the court opened. Harvey walked up to the stand and put his hand on the Bible. When he raised his hand bullets started to whistle. Harvey had two revolvers, and was shooting wildly, but he was dead when he fired the last bullet. Berger was the first one back to the farm with the news.

He went shouting all through the plantation, "They got the tiger cat! God damn, they got the tiger cat!"

When the news came, the Negroes shouted and screamed like they had after the war came to an end. A frolic was held on the Harvey Place that night and the spirit was never so high. It was a frolic which was known all over the county. From then on the Harvey Negroes were known as the best frolicking Negroes that ever lived. The plan to get rid of the Mantons and the Harveys took a year to carry out: 1922 until 1923. Not one Negro got hurt or was killed or in trouble. Today, Negroes in that plantation own their own land and automobiles, are sending their children to college, and are ginning and selling their own cotton.

The majority of white men where I lived went with Negro women. Some lived with Negro women and raised families with them. McQuarter was a rich white man who lived with a Negro woman until he died. He bought her a home and could have bought a mansion. The Ku Klux Klan threatened to burn him out. He had one or two of his brothers sit on the porch of the woman's home. He openly stated that he would die there. McQuarter and Fanny raised five daughters and saw them married. When he died the brothers took everything except the house. Fanny still has the home and lives there today. One day Fanny sent one of the children to town. The little girl saw McQuarter and ran to him, calling, "Daddy, daddy." McQuarter turned and ran down the street. That night at home, he told the children not to call his name or come to him in public.

Negro boys would go to visit McQuarter's daughters on Sunday afternoon. He and Fanny would be in one room and the girls and boys would be keeping company in the next room. McQuarter warned his girls not to marry those boys because they would be put to work on a farm. A friend of mine went with one of the girls. He hated white folks. He hadn't planned to marry the McQuarter girl but when he heard what McQuarter had told his girls he swore to marry her. He didn't intend to live on a farm but he said he would do it for a year to show McQuarter that a man does what he wants with his wife after he gets her. He married McQuarter's daughter and made her do the most rugged work of any Negro woman. She dug ditches, drained the land and cut logs. After a year they moved to the city.

One of the biggest things that ever penetrated me in my childhood days was a white funeral. When anyone passed they had to be buried the next day. There was no embalming. They'd go around and get six or eight friends to dig the grave. Sometimes the ground was very hard. When a white person would die they'd ask Negroes to dig their graves. One day I went with some Negroes to dig a white woman's grave. After my friends dug the hard dirt they sat off to the side to see the burial. People who dug always stood by until the pastor said, "Ashes to ashes—" then one would take a shovel and shake a little dirt in the grave. One young Negro had no reason not to believe they did the same as with Negroes. When the pastor opened the book he started to shake a shovel of dirt over the grave. A white man asked what he was doing. He said he was helping with the burial. The white man told him to put down the shovel.

"You are all done, go on home."

We didn't think we were done, we stood there with our shovels.

The man said, "Look, nigger, you're not that much of a damn fool. As long as you live you're not going to throw dirt on a white person's face."

This was shocking to everyone of us. One said, "That's crazy. How we can hurt someone after they're dead, I can't understand. I can't understand the whites. They say we're crazy and ignorant but if they're not crazy then I don't know what crazy means."

In my early days, many of the white barber shops in the South had Negro barbers. No Negroes could go to them, only whites. This is still true in some parts of the South today. A friend of mine used to tell of the insults they would get from whites who were sometimes sober and sometimes half drunk. One day a white man came into my friend's shop and sat in the chair. He had long whiskers, and bumps all over his face.

"Nigger, you see I have bumps on my face. Several times I have been cut. I find blood on my face after I am shaved. I get mad when I see my own blood. I get mad especially if it was a nigger caused me to bleed. I want a shave. Now, if you think you can't shave me without blood appearing, then say so right now. I'll shoot hell out of you if you shave me and I find even one drop of blood on my face." He pulled out a pistol and put it in his lap.

My friend shaved the man. When he had finished, the man went over to look in the glass. There was no blood. The man paid and said, "You have a lot of nerve. You didn't cut any bumps but what would you have done if you had? I would have shot you."

My friend said, "I wasn't worried. I had you laid back in the chair, I was holding your head with my arm and I had the razor in my other hand."

    The man looked upset and nervous and walked out of the shop real shaky. My friend told the other barbers that if he had cut any bumps he would have cut the man's throat before he'd let him shoot him. He said the man was crazy to get in his chair and threaten him with a pistol.

2.
NORTH TO DETROIT

THE FIRST TIME I went North was in 1924. My pal then was Hines, a young man about eighteen. He was from a farm in Texas. We were hoping we'd get to see the Mason-Dixon line. I thought in my mind that it would look like a row of trees with some kind of white mark like the mark in the middle of the highway. We were hoping day would break before we got to the line. The train stopped in Covington, Kentucky just as the sun was rising. Someone said the bridge ahead was the Mason-Dixon line. We were North. We didn't have to worry about sitting in the back, we felt good. We walked around staring at all the buildings.

Hines and I met a boy from Columbus we had known in school. We agreed that if there was one white man on the train with a seat beside him, we'd sit there to see what he would do. All the things we'd heard before was like reading in the Bible. When I get to heaven I have milk and honey and pearly gates. I wanted to see was I there. We walked through the train feeling shaky. We thought any minute they would tell us to sit in the Negro coach. We found a seat for two. Hines and the boy from Columbus sat down. I continued to walk until I saw a seat by a white man. I was very uncomfortable for the first hour. Hines seemed very surprised that I continued to sit by the man. I relaxed some. He was reading a paper and when he finished half, he pushed it to me and asked if I wanted to read. He wanted to know where I was going and said, "Detroit is a nice place." This was the most relaxing time I had.

When we reached Detroit each of us had an address of the people where we would live. Mine was the Gordon house on 30th Street. I looked at that number so many times before leaving home I had it perfect. I put it in my trunk thinking surely the trunk would be there when we arrived. Hines did the same thing. We got off the train and at that moment our memories snapped. Both Hines and I could remember the streets but not the numbers. We took the checks and went to the trunkroom. There would be no trunks until the next day. We had money but we'd never slept in a hotel. We didn't know how, we didn't know just nothing. We decided to take a cab and ride to the streets and look at the numbers. We thought the addresses might come to us this way. We thought if we asked someone on the street they would surely know our friends just like we knew everybody in the country. We rode a cab to 30th and McGraw. The cabdriver said colored people lived north of McGraw. We walked slowly and spoke to people. They didn't stop or look around at us. We were amazed. People speak back in the country. We started again at one end of 30th. We would knock on two or three doors on each block. The train arrived at five and we were still walking at nine. We began to get real worried. Would we sleep in the street? Were there any parks? One side of 30th was completely white. But hearing so much about equal rights and complete freedom, and that North was heaven, we didn't realize any difference. One white woman said that our friends couldn't possibly live on her block because no colored lived at that end of 30th. We walked off her porch wondering why. We didn't want to believe in discrimination up North but it kept going around in our heads.

Someone advised us to call the police and spend the night at the station. We said to each other, "Hell, no, we aren't going to write home and say we spent our first night in the city in jail." I had never been to jail at that time and I sure wasn't going to start then.

Every main street we came to we would say, "This is the center of town." Around eleven-thirty, a Negro man said we could sleep in his house. We were so hungry we were practically dead. His wife fixed a lovely meal and right afterwards we went to sleep. That night in bed I dreamed of the numbers of the Gordon house. They came out just as clear. The people asked us to stay for breakfast but we were anxious to get to the address. When we told them what it was they laughed and laughed. The address was in the next block down. We had been standing right across from the Gordon house when we met the man the night before.

Mr. Arthur Gordon was light-colored and his wife was dark. They were very nice people. They charged us ten dollars a week to sleep, eat and do our laundry but at that time it seemed terrible to me. We had heard at home that you could make twenty-five or thirty dollars a week in the factory. I thought I'd be rich. On the farm if you had five dollars you'd carry it around for six months. Ten dollars seemed impossible. I felt five dollars should be right and I would deposit the rest. After a few years I would have several thousand dollars. I always planned to send money to my mother and father. I wanted them to build a home like the white people had. I was afraid to tell anyone how much money I had with me. We had always heard that they pocket-pick and slip you out of your money in the city.

The next big plan was to get a job. Hines and I got work at Graham Paige. It was an independent factory then as were Dodge, Chrysler and DeSoto. We were very happy to get the jobs. It was a welcome thing: we could be here the rest of our lives and never go back to the South, on any condition, except in the case of death in the family. I met a friend from home and asked him if he would ever go South again.

He said, "No, it's too many ups."

I asked, "What do you mean, it's too many ups?"

He said, "The first thing in the morning, before day breaks, you have to wake up. Then you have to get up, then you have to feed up, gear up. You go to the field before the sun is up and hitch up, the first words you say to the mules is 'git up.' And you start to bedding up. When night comes you look over how much of the earth you have turned up. After you plant up, you start getting ready to round up. When you're through rounding up, you start chopping up. When you get through with that it's time to go to the hayfield and start baling up. When that is done you come back to the field and start gathering up. Then you start to hauling up to the white man to have your settling up. And you don't get a damn thing in return, but a big mess up. No, I'm not telling a mule 'git up' no more, if he's sitting on my lap. I'm not planting any more cotton, and I'm not planting any more corn. If I see some mules running away with this world I'm going to tell them to keep going, 'go ahead on.' "

My job at Graham Paige was in the foundry shaking out the oil pan that fits under the motor. Hines got a job just outside the foundry, chipping motors. I was very much surprised when I was hired. I asked the man if there were any jobs. He said, yes. I told him I preferred somewhere else when he told me to work in the foundry. I had worked in a foundry in Anniston. I knew what the work was like. He said there were no other jobs open. When white men came he told them about other jobs and hired them. I started looking and wondering, How could he say, to my face, there were no other jobs when he told a white man ahead of me about polishing and put another in the carpentry shop. Hines' job was worse than mine. They led us out to see where we would come to work the next morning.

As I looked around, all the men were dirty and greasy and smoked up. They were beyond recognition. There were only three or four whites. These were Polish. Negroes told me later they were the only ones able to stand to work. Their faces looked exactly like Negro faces. They were so matted and covered with oil and dirt that no skin showed. Hines and I went home discussing how it was that they could say everyone was free with equal rights up North. There was no one in the foundry but Negroes. We didn't believe those men wanted to be in the foundry.

At the end of the week they said we'd get no pay the first week. They held it in what they called abeyance. The job was very rugged. I had to work continuously, as fast as I could move. The heat from the cubulos, which were round furnaces for melting the iron, was so hot that in five minutes my clothes would stick with dirt and grease. We'd walk through on our lunch period to talk to a friend. We couldn't recognize him by his clothes or looks. The men working in his section would tell us where he was or we could tell a friend by his voice.

My job paid five dollars a day. The first foreman was quiet, he didn't do much raring or hollering like the other foremen. They would curse and holler. They would pay us off right there if we looked back or stopped working. Workers passed out from the heat. The foremen rushed a stretcher over and two workers would take the man out, give him fifteen minutes to revive and then he would have to go back to work. When a man passed out, the foreman would be running out to see if the guy was conscious. He would be cursing all the time. If the worker took too long, he'd shake him. They never mentioned a wound serious enough to go to first aid. Workers would get a layer of iron from the cubulo, bring it to the iron pourers, fifteen to twenty men with long ladles. These would be filled with hot iron running like water. As their ladles filled up, the men had to straighten their arms out level and pour the iron down a little hole the size of a milk bottle. All the time they had to turn slow, like a machine. If they poured too fast, the iron would explode the mold and burn the other men. The iron would drop on a wet spot and hit the men like a bullet and go into the skin. The man getting hit still had to hold the ladling iron level to keep from burning the other men. They would wait their chance and pick out the balls of iron, and sometimes the foreman picked it out as the men went on working. A man would sit a half hour after work too tired to change clothes and go home.

When I had worked for a month the foreman came and said they were going to change the standard of the job and put it on piece work. We could make more money. I got a nickel for each pan I shaked out. I was glad for the money but I was sorry we were on piece work. We had to work just like a machine. Take a mold, knock it out, set it back. Over and over for nine hours. It was never under nine hours and sometimes ten, eleven and twelve hours a day. We never knew how many hours we were going to work. If they wanted to send us home at ten, ten we went. If a machine broke down we waited an hour for repairs. The money was taken out of our weekly pay even though it wasn't our fault. We cursed every minute of the day. The main curse was against the foremen. The foremen would say, "God damn it. Do it. If you can't do it there are plenty of men outside who will." No women worked in the plant except one little section. They put in seats or something like that.

In four months I was laid off. After being off for some weeks we finally felt we were rested and could go around to see the city. Everything was different in Detroit in 1925. Relations between Negroes and whites were close then. Negroes and whites boarded in the same homes many times. There were Negroes and whites walking around together and nobody even looked up. Every Sunday you could see mixed couples and Negro couples and white couples on motorcycles. Gangs of kids were often mixed. If a white and a Negro got in a fight in the plant it was just between them. Whichever one got whipped we laughed. One night, near Hamtramck, a white man stepped on a Negro's foot. The Negro cursed him. The white guy ran, and caught him, got him down and beat him up. There were seven of us, and two or three whites watching. The Negro guy said he'd had enough. All the way home he was laughing and saying he'd gotten whipped by that white man. But the jobs that whites had were in different places from

Negroes. We didn't know whites in the shop. There was no such thing as going to a white person's home. There was no reason for a white to invite you. The only whites around us in the foundry were Polish and their language was different.

We got laid off from the foundry, got called back and then laid off again. I left Detroit and went to Pittsburgh with a friend. We hoped to work steady. We got a job in a steel mill. It was rough work but there were other Negroes doing it. We could take it only three weeks. We came back to Detroit and went to work for the city. I had a laborer's job, I cleaned drains, repaired sidewalks and dug holes. We worked way out in the Polish neighborhood near West Warren. The foreman was an old man who slept most of the time. Many times we'd hide the shovels and run off for awhile. We weren't there more than three days until we felt a strong resentment from the Polish who were working for the city. We talked it over; we said they didn't want us, but we sure were going to work there. One of the Polish men was reporting to the foreman that we were doing something or other wrong in the neighborhood. We sat on the sidewalk to eat dinner. We kept to ourselves and the Polish sat to themselves. Violence broke out in a month.

I sometimes played mumble-peg with two Polish kids in a bank of dirt. One day I won eighty or ninety cents. Just before the whistle blew, the Polish kids went in back of a Polish home to get a drink of water. I told them that I would like water too. They said the woman of the house couldn't speak English. They repeated some Polish words for me to say so that she would give me a drink. I could say them pretty good and went on back, cleaning my knife as I walked. I said the words to the Polish woman. She stretched her eyes and said something in Polish. I wiped my knife and put it in my pocket. I repeated the Polish words. She stomped, and said something for three minutes then shook her finger in my face. I turned and went out, it wasn't the place to get water.

The woman came out of the house and went across to the Polish leader. He went in the house with her. Pretty soon a police car came up. Both policemen jumped out with revolvers in their hands. The Polish leader got in the car with the cops and they drove up to where we were sitting. I was in the midst of the men telling them what had happened.

My friend, Charles Herbert, said, "That son of a bitch told those cops you were in there raping that woman."

The cops brought the woman up and said for her to point out the man. There were about twenty of us sitting around. She pointed her finger at another man.

I said, "I'm going to tell them, Herbert." I said, "What's wrong?"

The cops said, "This man attempted to rape this woman and threatened her with a knife."

"Nobody attacked this woman. He wasn't even back there. I was."

The cops looked confused and asked why I tried to rape the woman. I explained what the two boys had told me to say in Polish. One cop looked real mad and the other kinda broadened his face.

The boys denied that they had told me anything. One boy claimed I was lying. The Negroes crowded around; the whites crowded around. The Polish said, "Take him in." One policeman was vicious. He started to handcuff me and got one cuff on my wrist. The Polish ringleader was behind me and Herbert knew he was going to hit me. He struck me behind my neck. At the same time, Herbert knocked him down and cursed. I didn't know what had happened. I fell up against the cop and he let me loose. When I looked around, the Polish guy was lying on the ground. I started hitting him in the face with the handcuff. One cop snatched me up.

"That's how niggers get killed. They start to break and run."

The other cop said, "No, we're supposed to protect anyone we have in our custody. That guy had no business hitting him in the neck."

They told us they'd have to take us both in. But the foreman was crying and begging them to turn us loose. He was afraid he would lose his job. They turned us loose and said, "Don't get in any more trouble or you won't work for the city again."

We worked on out the city. The tension was very strong. There were outhouses for us to use. One day the Polish ringleader went in. I saw my chance to get him. He was sitting down when I came in. He started to beg and plead that it wasn't his fault, he thought the kids had told the truth. I went back on out.

One fellow, from Mississippi, named Holly, cried when he

heard about the fight. He said he wished he was God. "I'd destroy this damn world today, the way whites treat Negroes for nothing."

He told me he wouldn't have taken it if he had been there the day it happened. We worked on one side of the street and the Polish worked on the other. One day a young Polish kid came up on a motorcycle. Holly borrowed it to try it out. He rode around and then rode up to where the whites were working. The first time, he slowed when he went by them. The next time he came back slow, until he got near the ringleader. He turned the handlebar, put the gas on hard and ran into the man. It split the Polish fellow's lip, burst his ribs and knocked out his teeth. The ambulance and the police came. Holly told them he didn't know how to ride very well. His hand had slipped on the handlebar and fell on the gas and the motorcycle got out of control. They didn't do anything to Holly. They separated the Negroes and the Polish; we were transferred downtown.

I went to work again at Graham Paige. I worked off and on for them from 1924 to 1925. I got fired in 1925 and the way I got fired was like this: Many workers would pass out. The boys would say, "The bear has got you." When we got real hot, we'd see little dots in front of us. We worked on a swing shift. We'd get through, after a continual half-running pace all day, fifteen minutes before the whistle. If we sat down we often caught the cramps in our legs and all over. We couldn't move, sometimes we had to wait fifteen or thirty minutes before we could get up and go home. One day, I told a pal that I felt a case of cramps coming on. I said I would get in a hot bath and try to keep them away. My pal said he would cover for me if the foreman came before the whistle blew.

The foreman came in. I was sitting on the bench in the washhouse and he said, "God damn it, get in your clothes and go back to work."

This was a few minutes before the closing whistle. If I had changed back into my clothes they were so dirty that I would have needed another bath. I went to my locker real slow. He cursed me and said if I didn't get dressed, and get on the job before the whistle blew, I wouldn't have a job. He cursed me some more. I stopped and stood there.

He said, "God damn, get out of those clothes."

I said, "These are my clothes. I'm going to keep them on." I had tried to talk nice in the beginning, but I got mad when he cursed me. The whistle blew and I went on home. The next day, a note to see personnel was in place of my time-card in the rack. They told me that the foreman had said to pay me off.

I said, "Let me tell you what happened."

They said, "We don't care what happened. If the foreman said you're out, you're out."

I did mainly construction work for a while. In about a year I went back to Graham Paige because they were hiring men who had worked there before. About one hundred workers came out that day. They hired all the men in the line ahead of me. I got to the desk and gave my name. He said he was sorry but that I had been fired and I could never again work for Graham Paige. I went out and watched him hire more men. I switched caps and shirts with a fellow in the line. I got in the same line as before and said I hadn't worked for Graham Paige. I gave a false name and got a job. I worked there until the Depression. It always bothered me working under the wrong name. If I had got killed, my mother and family wouldn't have gotten anything out of it.

I never wanted to work for Ford. And I never did work there. Everyone talked about it, they said it was the house of murder. There was a big rumor all over the city that other men had to take care of Ford workers' sexual home affairs. Everybody always asked about a Ford worker's wife, "Who is her boyfriend?" If a man would see a woman and she would say that her husband worked for Ford he would make a big joke. He would pretend to take a pencil and a pad and ask her for her telephone number. They were all so worked down they couldn't have sexual relations. Mr. Gordon's wife had to help him up the steps, bathe him and feed him in bed. Where he laid on a sheet at night he didn't move from that spot. Every worker could identify Ford workers on the streetcars going home at night. Every worker who was asleep was working for Ford. You'd see twenty asleep on the cars and everyone would say, "Ford workers." Many times the conductors looked over the car and shook a man to tell him it was his stop. On Sunday Ford workers would sleep on the way to church.

Sometimes some people tried to cover it up. They would say it was working in a foundry that made the men sleep. They said it was the fumes. But everybody knew Ford was a "man-killing" place. That always frightened me. I tried to stay away. But during the Depression, everything closed down once for two or three months. The paper came out asking for men for Ford. The next morning there was a stampede at Ford of two thousand men at five a.m. They were only hiring fifty or a hundred men. The agent came out and told us they were not hiring but nobody would leave. We thought it was a line to send us away and give jobs to those who remained. We stayed, pushing and shoving. The police rode up on horses and ran at the crowd hitting us with sticks. This didn't disperse the workers. The police called the Fire Department and they hooked up their hoses and shot cold water on us. It was the middle of winter. While we waited for the streetcars our clothes froze on us as hard as bricks. That's the first and last time I went to Ford to look for work.

3.
BACK TO THE SOUTH

THE FIRST TIME I went back to the South was during the Depression in 1930. There was plenty of work on the farm but no pay, no money, no clothes. A friend had written me in 1927 to ask if I would ever come back South. I wrote that when all the roads were paved and there was electricity and water in every house, then I would come back to visit. That's how I felt. But I was laid off in 1929 and the little money I had saved was soon used up. In 1929 no one was working. People ate stale, thrown away food picked out of the garbage around stores and restaurants. All winter I walked the streets, I saw families sitting out in the snow with their furniture. It got to the point where the city had to do something. They gave families with children enough food on which to exist. The city officials put in the paper that the city would pay the fare of anybody who had any place to go. City workers were paid by slips of paper instead of money which could only be used for trading. Workers stole food and other things. The police didn't do anything, they said they couldn't afford to feed everybody in the jails. A friend of mine stole a truckload of tires from in front of a department store. He sold half of them to a big cab company and the other half to some police. Many people, including myself, had to wear a coat in the house, to hide their pants. Our trousers were completely worn out in back. A friend of mine cut off rubber boots and wore them as shoes a whole winter.

Another friend and I used to catch flies and kill them. We'd go to a restaurant and order a big meal. Half-way through, my friend put the fly on his plate and called the waitress. He acted as if he were getting sick and was going to call the Board of Health. The manager would beg us not to call and we wouldn't have to pay. We'd have our one meal for the day. There was another way we'd eat. We'd pool whatever we had, a dime, nickel or quarter, with several friends and cook together. The next night we'd go to another friend and do the same thing. The soup lines were as long as the lines of workers waiting at the plants trying to get work. We'd wait one and a half hours for a dish of soup and a cracker. My mother sent me the money to come home. They had plenty of food but not much money.

I was sick for three months after getting home. I dreamed of Detroit every night. I thought I should have stayed there and died there. I went to the store with my mother and the owner asked me a question. I said, "Yes."

He walked around the counter, "What did you say?"

I said, "I must have made a mistake. I mean, yes, sir."

"Don't think just because you've been up North you can forget you were raised here."

I was sick. If you've been away they gave it to you even worse than if you stay. I told mother I'd rather be in prison in Detroit than to be free in the South. She cried and felt bad.

Another thing that bothered me was that I couldn't walk around in the dark at night. The average person could walk all around and visit at night. But I'd go out and fall, or bump into things. Everybody kidded me. People in the South could sit on their porches at night and hear somebody go past on a horse and say who it was. The girls looked different from the girls in Detroit. They couldn't go to the beauty parlor or dress up in the afternoon. They were mostly barefooted. I didn't think they'd ever impress me enough to be happy, along the lines of being with a girl. My father gave me a three acre farm and told me everything I made on it was mine. I tried to do my best but I always knew I'd leave as soon as I could get a job outside the Southern cities. I wrote to friends every day but they wrote that things were worse in Detroit than when I had left.

Berger had died a year before I went home. A man named Rambert took charge for Mrs. Berger. He was driving many Negroes away from the farm. It was called "breaking them up." If they couldn't pay, Rambert would take over everything they had. My father had some relatives, three brothers named Perryman. They were double jointed and known to be the meanest Negroes that ever lived in Leavitt County. Rambert said that they owed Berger money and that he was going to break them up. He got a wagon and some Negroes to help and went toward the Perryman's farm. The Perrymans heard that Rambert was coming and armed themselves. When Rambert came he cursed and tried to get his helpers to go in the house. Nathan Perryman came out to the wagon. Rambert told him he'd come to break him up. He said he had heard that they had some fine cows. He said he was taking everything: hogs, corn, house-furnishings, everything.

Nathan said for him to wait a minute. He went in the house and came out with a rifle. He told Rambert, "I never heard of cows growing up out of land. I never heard of hogs growing up out of land. I raised the corn in my crib to feed my children. I'll open the door for you to go in but none of you will come out."

Rambert told the Negro helpers to go in. They said, "After you." Nathan raised his rifle and pointed it at Rambert. Rambert went to town and got the deputy sheriff. On the way back, the sheriff asked who they were breaking up.

When he heard who it was he said, "The safest thing for us is to stop right here and go back. These are the craziest niggers in the county. If you make one mad you'll have to kill every one on the settlement. When we have to arrest a bad nigger we try to deputize a Perryman to go with us."

Nothing was ever done to the Perrymans. The youngest one, a son, is a deputy sheriff in Leavitt County today.

A law was passed saying that a farmer could only make so much cotton on a given amount of land. All over this amount had to be divided between the farmer and the government. I was working my three acres; I worked hard and I felt that everything on the farm was mine. The three acres made three bales of cotton but I was only allowed one bale. Rambert came to ask me where I was going to gin my cotton. I told him I might gin it at his place. We paid five dollars a bale to gin the cotton. I told him I didn't want to give the government my cotton. He said that a lot of farmers on the plantation were not making their quota, and he could put it on the allotment and I wouldn't have to give anything to the government. I had to gin with him if he did me the favor. I left the cotton with him for a day and it was sent to the market. Rambert came and told me what grade it was and reached for his check book. I told him I hadn't said who I was selling to.

He got mad and said, "You think I'm lying?"

"You're not necessarily lying but I want to sell it myself."

He had only figured two bales and I asked him about the third. He said the third goes to the government. I told him I thought he'd figured it so that I wouldn't have to give any to the government. We had a sharp argument.

He said, "Why didn't you stay up North and not get to be such a bad nigger?"

I went to the market and sold the cotton myself. I got twenty-five dollars more than Rambert had offered. He never liked me after that and I stayed away from him.

The following year tragedy struck my home. Everything we had was destroyed by fire. Rambert tried to get my father to mortgage our land in order to build another home. Father wouldn't do it. It was good land and we knew Rambert wanted it. My mother was active in church. In five or six months she raised enough money to build another home. As soon as the house was completed my mother passed. My mother was different than anyone in the family. She was the leader. She took care of any business transactions for my father; he felt lost when she passed.

While I was South two lynchings took place in the same year. Joe Bush was a Negro administrator of the Gerson plantation. The plantation was owned by an insurance company in the city. He was the most well-lived farmer around, that's why he was appointed. He had complete charge of the plantation. He rented the land, sold the timber and collected the money. He dealt directly with the company. Most of the land was lowland, and very rich black soil. It was noted for growing corn. Even those who lived on small plantations with bottom soil would rent some of this fertile land for growing corn.

There was a group of whites six miles from the Gerson plantation. Two of the men were Al Brooks and Fred Beale. Brooks and Beale went to rent some land from Joe Bush but they wanted him to charge them less than the other renters. He refused and they came back two or three times.

The last time they told him, "We'll get you, nigger. You black son of a bitch."

Some few months later the farmers began to plant. When the crops are being planted the stock is rounded up so it won't destroy the new plants. Many times cows would get mixed with someone else's stock. The cows always had a brand and the owner was notified to come for his stock. One cow came in with Joe Bush's cattle. It had a G brand. G didn't stand for either Brooks or Beale. Joe Bush sent word around that he had a strange cow. Brooks and Beale sent a Negro to say that it was the Brooks' cow.

They didn't go to look at it but sent word they wanted to talk to Joe.

When Joe went to their place they put their guns on him, tied him up and took him to a dairy barn five miles away. They beat him for two hours, taking turns beating. When he was unconscious they took him to a doctor who examined him. Both kidneys were beat clear loose from his back. The doctor cursed them and told them to take Joe out of his office. He said they should go to jail. He said he couldn't do anything for Joe and he was going to die. Brooks and Beale put Joe in a wagon and on the way home he died.

The insurance company made a big fuss. They swore they'd see justice done. A few months later they went through a trial. There were several Negro witnesses but in five or ten minutes Brooks and Beale were "Not guilty." Brooks lived with a Negro woman all his life. I always had a sharp resentment about Negro women going with white men. Every time a lynching happened, it sharpened my hate toward white men and to the Negro women living with them.

The second lynching was of Willie. Willie used to buy standing timber off of Negro farms. He'd sell it at a mill. He borrowed money from some white people and couldn't meet a payment. The whites threatened to whip him up. He was working near me. It was rare to see a Negro with a shotgun every day in midsummer but Willie said he was carrying it to keep from being beaten.

One Saturday night Willie went to the store to pay the whites. Another white man was there and they tried to whip him. He wounded two men slightly and was wounded himself. The report went out that he had broken into the store and wounded two white men. He knew the woods and hid in the swamp. Our mailbox was on the highway and one of us went for mail each day. I got the mail two or three days after Willie had hidden in the swamp and coming back I saw three or four cars speeding on the dirt road to the swamp. As I reached the road I heard shooting, like I'd heard many times when I was hunting in winter after birds, only it lasted longer than this type of hunting. A Negro came along and said they were going to hang Willie and shoot him. I stood for a half hour until they returned with Willie in the car. He'd been shot everywhere. Blood streamed. He was asking for help: he hadn't passed. He kept calling the name of one of the white men. Before he was shot so bad he probably saw the man's face and it was still in his head. It didn't appear to me that he could recognize anyone now. Faber, a white man, was with them. He was living with a Negro woman and had five children with her.

"We should have finished him there. What if he lives?"

"If this nigger lives he's better than a cat and they're supposed to have nine lives."

They said they would take Willie up the road and finish him. They threw his body into the car. I felt a wave of humiliation and shame come over me. I was humiliated that I was part of a race that could be dealt with like they would deal with a ferocious animal. Then I was shamed by a government. This happens year after year and they're helpless to do anything about it. I had one hundred and one thoughts. How they would stop the Germans but they wouldn't stop a few whites from breaking Negroes like a few sticks to have fun out of them. As I started away it didn't feel as if my feet were touching the ground. I was floating along. It was like I was in a cloud, a dream.

I heard shots and met some Negroes, "They finished lynching Willie."

The next day I talked to Mary, the woman who lived with Faber. She said that Rambert had come for Faber and had told him they had guns and ropes to lynch Willie. She asked Faber if he was going. He said he had to go. That if he didn't, it would be rough on her. The whites would think he was taking her side and come wipe them both out. When he came back he said he was sorry it happened. This put hate in me. My deepest hate was for her. I wanted to go with her and be cruel. I was hating every Negro woman in the South who was part of the white man. I asked Mary how any Negro woman could live with a white man. Did they feel they weren't part of the Negro people?

Mary said that no one understood. She told me that when a Negro woman got tied up with a white man she couldn't break. Only he could break or put her down when he wanted. I knew a Negro woman who tried to leave a white man. She was killed in Dallas County. Mary said that every Negro woman knows, not at first, but after she gets stuck with a white by accepting clothes or money, that she may be killed. She has sold her complete life to a white man. Mary said she didn't know one Negro woman who ever got away from a white man if he wanted her. Once Faber beat Mary all night. She ran away to her folks. He had her put in jail for stealing until he could come for her. Mary used to sleep with every Negro in the place. She had four children for Faber and one for a young Negro. After the baby's birth Faber met the young Negro in the road. He told him that the state of Tennessee was too small for both of them to live in and he was not planning on leaving. The Negro left his home for eighteen years and came back after Faber's death.

4.
MY WIFE, CHRISTINE

My wife, Christine, comes from my neighborhood. Here she tells of her early life.

I WAS BORN in Rainsville. My parents were farmers. I have six brothers and four sisters all living now. Dad owned two hundred and eighty acres. My grandfather left one hundred and fifty acres to my father. My grandfather was a farmer and had his own gin mill for awhile, his own peanut thresher and hay baler, and his own stock. He had three sons and my daddy. Two sons went to the city; they didn't want anything to do with the farm. Another son had a blacksmith shop, and my father saw about the farm. My father grew everything that could be raised. He had eight people working for him. He'd make, in a good year, twenty-five or thirty bales of cotton. I worked right in the field and I didn't let anybody beat me. I was fast at all the work. I didn't start in the field as early as some, but waited until I was twelve. I went to the County Training School and finished the twelfth grade. I had to do the same work as the rest but we were close to the school and that's why I got to go for so long.

The white man next to my father's place was Mr. Gard. He had thirty or forty people working his place. Mr. Gard's riding boss was my cousin. Mr. Gard didn't like white men. He didn't even like his brother-in-law. He said he didn't want him to pass his door, and that's the highway. The only white person he liked was his sister's third boy. The state was going to throw up a highway through his place and he went to court and said he hated white people. They slapped him down. He wanted to put a gate across the highway but they wouldn't let him. They had stopped owners from doing that when I was a girl.

Mr. Gard had a riding boss, before my cousin, who was white. His daughter, Millie, fell in love with him. Gard fired the man. He said he couldn't stand white people riding over his land. He got a Negro to beat up the riding boss. Miss Millie, Mr. Gard's daughter, went with my cousin after that. If his people were hungry she would slip him hams and meat. Mrs. Gard knew about my cousin, but Mr. Gard didn't know. No other white people knew. Miss Millie was real hateful, she was prejudiced against all colored people but this one Negro. But her mother was friendly.

Gard was going with two colored women. He would catch them in the field late in the evening. He wouldn't be with them in a house. On the farms, the white men had the most relations with colored women. In the city, if a white man stayed with a colored woman, and he wasn't known or friendly to colored, the Negroes would kill him or burn him out of his place.

My mother was real religious but my dad didn't believe in the Bible. He only went to church two times in his life. One time he went he didn't go in. He just sat in front in a car and listened to the preaching from outside. He didn't join the church until he married and was twenty-nine years old. There was a Christian Church on my father's place but he wouldn't go. Daddy said the church didn't do any good. He said the Bible was written by a white man and couldn't anybody go by that Bible and act like the white people act. He said no white person ever went by the Bible, they were hypocrites. He asked my mother how she could believe it. Grandfather did get money from daddy to give and he always made us go to Sunday School. Almost every day my grandfather and daddy would argue and argue about religion. Thomas Peterson, a relative on daddy's side, went to church. But he went to see the women. He wouldn't go inside. He didn't believe in the Bible either but he liked to look at the ladies.

Mr. Gard called my father a "biggety-nigger." He said if my father's cows ever got in his pasture he was going to kill every one. My father fixed the pasture so our cows couldn't go out. Mr. Gard's cows came to our place but my father didn't kill them. Gard just hated my father. If a white man can't work you like a dog, like slavery time, he hates you. He didn't hate grandpa. Grandpa always kinda talked to him. My father wouldn't have anything to do or say to Gard. The two biggest families were the Welchs and the Donaldsons. We were Welchs. The Welchs owned their own homes. The Donaldsons were mostly on Mr. Gard's place renting. Mr. Gard could stand the Donaldsons but he didn't like the Welch folk.

Another white man who hated my father was Jack Dutton.

He had a big plantation but he was poor. He had a lot of people working on his place but he was a bad manager. He always had to pick at my father. He'd borrow from father, a mow or hay cradle or something; then he would never return it. He offered to shoot my father and said he was too independent. If he could have gotten a lot of white men around him he would have killed or beaten daddy. But there weren't that many whites around. There were only three.

Mr. Gard wouldn't beat anybody. He'd get a white man or a Negro to kill someone he didn't like. He got a white man to kill my cousin. He killed him on his own place because my cousin wouldn't let him sell his cotton or anything else for him. My cousin wanted to sell it for himself. If you didn't gin at Gard's place he'd get someone to kill you. This was about 1939. Mr. Gard and all other white men wanted to sell the cotton and then give you whatever they wanted and keep the rest.

They wouldn't let a colored person drive a Dodge or Oldsmobile in the South. They'd never let him drive a Cadillac. White men used to beat up a friend of mine who had a Dodge. He got two beatings for driving "a white man's car." They always said a Buick was a "nigger car." Another thing in the South: the women could always get away without saying, "sir." My cousin always said, "yes," or, "no." She didn't care who it was, she wasn't going to say, "yes, sir." But if a man says "yeah" to a white man he's going to die or get sentenced.

I met Matthew when I was real small. The girl he was going with was large and she was carrying me to school. After a year when Matthew came back from Detroit I started going with him. When his mother died he wanted us to marry. We got married a year after she passed. We moved to Memphis and roomed for a year, then my son was born and we got a house. A girl from home, real nice looking, gave a big party one night. We sold the drinks and that was against the law. The police came in and the whiskey bottle was sitting right on the table. One cop arrested the man of the house and took him out to the police car. Then he came back inside. The other policeman took the pretty girl, Inez, into the bedroom. He told Inez she was a nice looking girl and that if she would go out with him he would let her husband go free. Inez said she wouldn't go.

They came back into the room where we were waiting and the police said, "Neither of you gals going with us?" One girl said she would go if they would turn her husband loose. Inez said she would go too.

The policeman said, "Okay, let's go."

Inez said, "No, let's go tomorrow night."

The girls said they would meet the cops the next evening at a certain bar. The police let the man go.

The next night the police came back to the house looking for those two women. They went up and down the street kicking at the doors and trying to find them.

In one house a real rough colored man said, "What are you looking for?"

The police told him they were looking for a man. They wouldn't tell they were looking for those girls. The police walked in and pulled the covers off the beds looking. They started to pull the covers off the man's daughter. The rough colored man told them to stop.

"God damn it. You see long hair? That's a girl, that's my daughter and don't pull those covers down. You're looking for a man so go on back and look at my boys."

The police got mad but they went in the back and pulled the covers off the boys. The man told them, "You're not looking for a man, you're looking for trouble."

They came kicking at our door. Matthew said, "Who is it?"

The police didn't say anything, they just hit on the door.

Matthew said, "I'll take my gun and come asking who it is."

They called out, "Police. Open up."

When Matthew went to the door they asked him if he hadn't heard them knocking. "You weren't knocking, you were looking for trouble."

"No, we're not looking for trouble. We're looking for a man."

Matthew told them, "If you kick at our door again I'm liable to open it with my pistol."

The police were nearly crazy. They went up and down the street half the night looking for those two women but they didn't find them.

When Matthew, Jr. was about three years old I went to work in a shirt factory. I was a pocket setter. Mr. Green was the manager. He liked colored women too. If they were nice looking and talked to him he'd go with them sure. You had to go with him or be a good worker to stay there.

Jessie, the girl sitting next to me, told me, "He tries to go with anybody. If it isn't you're a fast worker or go with him you can't stay. Honey, you got to do some work to stay here."

Matthew's cousin worked there and she was so fast that she could make forty or fifty dollars a week when everyone was making twenty. The only machine Mr. Green showed to the white people was her machine. I was supposed to put out eight bundles a day, one hundred and forty-four shirts in a bundle. I had to put two pockets on each shirt. You had to jump to do that too.

After I was there for two or three months, Jessie told me, "He's getting ready to ask you to go out with him."

I told her I sure wasn't going with him.

He came to my machine and smiled, "Girl, how're you getting on? You need to pick up more? Can you make some extra?"

I told him, no, and he didn't like it. The girl told me I should have said, "I'll try." He carried me into his office and asked me if I couldn't do better. Jessie had told him I wouldn't go with him. I told him I was doing as fast as I could. He let me go.

I took another cousin's job for a few weeks. It was cooking for white folks. I never liked that. I had to clean eight bedrooms, and cook two meals a day for seven dollars a week. I also had to wash diapers for the woman's grandchild. The woman complained about paying seven dollars. She wouldn't feed me, she wouldn't give me anything to eat. I had to carry my own lunch. She wouldn't let me taste the food to season it while I was cooking. She always stayed to watch.

I told her I had friends who were fed, paid more and worked less.

She said, "We're not able to feed. We haven't enough money."

I told her that I thought she was rich.

She said, "That's my husband, not me." She asked me where my husband was living. When I said, Detroit, she said, "Oh, that's why you think this is too much work."

The woman next door told me why they wouldn't feed me. A girl who had worked for the neighbors on the other side of the street, sat down and ate a big steak one day. It was during meat rationing. The two white employers tried to jump her, they were so mad. The girl quit but she sure was going to eat.

Many colored women in the South, and especially in my home town, are planners. They have a set salary they work for and they cook in private homes. Sometimes they cook in small hotels or large rooming houses. This type of Negro woman demands her salary before going to see the job. I can't say if they have organization or not, but they all get practically the same salary rating. One planner knows another one wherever they meet. A planner is a cook who plans all the meals on her own time. At no time can any of the family tell, or know, what they will eat at the next meal. If the white woman she is cooking for asks what they will have at a meal, the Negro cook is mad and won't tell her. She says, "Wait and see."

Hundreds of whites in my home town will sit down to eat in their own homes and not know from one day to the next what they will eat for breakfast, dinner or supper. This type of cook controls the kitchen and cooking of those homes. Many of these cooks never allow anyone in the kitchen, not even one of the members of the homes. They don't do any other work in that home, just cooking, serving meals and cleaning the kitchen. They get out or go somewhere until it is time to start preparing for the next meal. They mostly work for rich white people and they all meet in the parks every day to discuss their work and their lives. In this sense they are organized.

When I got ready to go to Detroit the white woman where I was working wanted me to get someone to work for her. I carried my girl friend to see. When she saw the house and the work she wouldn't take the job.

When I was a little girl at home, my father would say, "Where will you live when you are grown?"

I always said I would go to New York and work in a factory. He said he thought I would be a farmer. I said, "Not me!"

Now, I was going North with Matthew, Jr. to meet Matthew in Detroit.

5.
WORK IN THE SOUTH

WHEN CHRISTINE AND I lived in Memphis, I got a job in a machine supply company. There were seventy-five to eighty Negroes, and the same number of whites, working there. The machine shop was very clean where only whites worked, except for one Negro who lifted and transferred heavy material. The rest of us worked in the foundry or the yard. After a week's work we got our pay. The old foreman, Mike, would get in the company truck and draw a sack of money out of the bank. Our pay was eleven dollars and seventy-five cents. We worked from six a.m. to seven p.m. six days a week. The Negroes would go into the building near the foundry to have their checks cashed. I always went home and gave mine to my wife, but Christine had trouble cashing the checks, so one time I went to the foreman. He took the check of a man in front of me, looked at it, looked in a book, said, "Okay," and gave him some money. He took my check and looked in the book. Then he looked at me mean and hard and threw it back.

"You don't owe me nothing."

A fellow asked me: "You don't owe him nothing?" Then he told me I'd better owe him something or I wouldn't have my job much longer. "All of us have to borrow whether we want to or not. We have to give him twenty-five cents on each dollar. We don't have to pay the full amount as long as we work here. But every week we have to give him the interest."

That made me sick; I never thought I'd have to pay anybody anything to keep my job. I worried all week. I started talking with the foreman and asked him if I could borrow two dollars. That meant fifty cents interest each week. I didn't use the two dollars but kept them for two months. It made me sick every week I cashed my check when he'd give me eleven dollars and twenty-five cents. Sometimes he wouldn't lend to workers unless they borrowed large amounts like six dollars or more.

One day I asked to get off work to go hunting on my father's farm. The foreman asked if he could go with me. I carried him down and had my father charge him for riding my horse. Anybody else that came it was a pleasure for me to let them ride. I never charged before. The foreman paid fifty cents to ride each time he went hunting with me, the same interest I had to pay each week on my loan. One day I told him I wanted to pay back the two dollars, I told him while we were hunting. He said it would be okay as long as I didn't tell anyone else. From that time on the foreman gave me breaks. I could be off for days and he wouldn't say anything.

He'd say, "It isn't out of my pocket, it's out of the company's pocket."

One of the hardest days I had was unloading steel. I was just beat. After work I caught the bus and got on downtown. Two Negroes were standing and I was one. The bus company had a system. As the bus would go away from town toward the Negro neighborhood, and the whites would get off, the remaining whites would move toward the front and the Negroes could sit down. This afternoon there was a white woman sitting beside another woman near the back. Her husband was up front near the bus driver with a little girl about five years old. The seat ahead of the woman had only one woman in it. After two stops the woman next to her got off and the stop after that the woman in front, sitting alone, got off too. I thought the woman would move up as she was supposed to do and I could sit down. Instead she called to her husband to push the little girl back. She put her in the empty seat but she didn't move up to sit with her. This meant she, her husband and child were enjoying three seats in the bus while we were still standing. I was tired and getting madder. I thought she'd get off at the next stop. There were fifteen whites in front and the same number of Negroes in back. I said to myself if she didn't move up by the next stop I would sit in front of her. It looked as if she was deliberately making me stand up because she saw me there. She didn't get off at the next stop and I sat down in front of her. When I sat down I kinda eased my knife out and snapped it open and kept it down by my side.

Her husband jumped up and said, "Nigger, get up. You're sitting in front of my wife. Get out of that seat or I'll knock hell out of you."

I stood up, "Come on, knock hell out of me. Your damn wife had every chance to move up there with you. If you come back here I'll cut your damn throat."

He got about a foot toward me and stopped. His wife yelled, "Don't come honey, don't come. He's got a knife." She knocked me kinda soft on the shoulder and said, "Let me by. Please let me by."

I brushed her off and told her, "Stay back there. You should have moved before."

Her husband said, "I'm not afraid to come back there."

I said, "Damn it. Come on. I don't want you to be afraid. Just come within my reach. Just let me reach you."

The bus driver got up and said, "Let me go get him."

I told him, "Come on. You look just like the other man. As long as you're white. I'll do the same to you if you just get in reaching distance."

"We didn't guarantee you a seat."

"There was no guarantee that I would stand up either when seats are empty."

"If you don't move back I'll call the police."

"Call everyone in the city. I won't move. I got on here to get home and I don't intend to get off this bus until I reach my stop. If I go off this bus it will be my dead body going off."

The majority of the Negroes stayed on the bus encouraging me. A middle-aged Negro woman came up the aisle and said, "Don't move back one inch." She pulled a razor and opened it: "I'll cut every one of them in two as fast as they come. They won't come at you in a gang. I'll send every one of them to hell. I carry this razor every day and I'll keep on carrying it. No one is going to mess with me."

The white woman and one or two Negroes yelled for the driver to open the back door so they could get off. They got out. The driver said he was going to take me to court and wanted the passengers to sign a paper saying what they'd seen. He got the white people to sign. Then, from his seat, he asked me to sign the paper.

"I didn't sign when I got on this bus and I'm sure not going to sign to get off. Why didn't you ask any of the people in the back to sign?"

He said, "I'll ask them, I'll ask them."

There was an old Negro named Mr. Eastley, a kind of Uncle Tom who had been trying to pacify me all the time. He kept telling me to keep quiet and let them go on and not to make trouble. The bus driver had heard him and asked him to sign. He signed.

Then the bus driver said, "There, I got a Negro to sign. Now will you sign?"

"No. If you're going to drive the bus you can go ahead drive it. You can stop fooling with me to sign. I'm not going to sign and if you ask me again I'm coming up there to you. I'm staying on this bus until I get home."

He said he was going to call the police at the next stop. I said he could do whatever he liked. The bus passed my house and I was going to stay on it until I got there. There were only six or seven whites still on the bus.

One white woman said, "Mister, I signed that paper. But if I go to court I'm going to tell what I saw. That woman should have moved, she did it deliberately. You could have been sitting ten minutes ago. The bus driver didn't tell her to move either. It's his fault too."

The bus driver got excited and said he didn't see the woman. I told him he saw everything else. He asked me to sign again and I told him we'd settle it right there if he mentioned signing any more. The white woman kept talking, saying it was a damn shame and that the woman's husband must have been nervous and wanting trouble to talk to me that way.

The bus driver went to a filling station and stayed for awhile. When he came out he stepped in with a halfway pleasant look and asked, "Did that fellow run who was making trouble?"

I said, no, and the woman with the razor said, "There are no damn rabbits on this bus."

The bus driver said, "Well, I'm not mad with you. I just called the manager of the bus company instead of the police. He asked me if I had asked the woman to move up front and that if the woman hadn't moved, then you had a right to sit in front of her. So I don't think anything else will be done."

"I don't care what happens or is done. I'm riding this bus home."

At the next stop almost everyone was gone. There were two or three Negroes left. One said, "Let's ride to the end of the line and teach that bus driver a lesson. Let's beat hell out of him."

The bus driver pleaded with us. He said he hadn't done

anything and that we'd only get in trouble. We were afraid to do anything to him because the old man, Mr. Eastley, was still on the bus. We were afraid he'd get off and report us to the police.

My second job in Memphis was for Peter Lynn Randall from 1936 to 1943. He was a lawyer from a large family of lawyers. They owned a building called the Randall Building. The father was a doctor with an office in the building and there was another brother who was a lawyer and another who was a doctor. I was surprised to work for P.L. Randall because I was supposed to get a job with the old man, the doctor. He met me downtown and stopped me and my cousin and asked where we came from. We, knowing the situation of whites, said we were from the country. This type of white wants the most backward kind of Negro. They think they can make him their boy, give him a line. We said we wanted work.

The doctor said, "I need a chauffeur. Come by my office in the Randall Building."

I went up to Dr. Randall's office. Three or four Negroes were waiting in line and I assumed he had told them all the same thing. He took them one by one into his office. He told me to leave my address, that he wanted to try out some others who had references first. Dr. Randall wanted me to do some painting on his farm. He sent me a letter to come in. When I went back this time he talked freer, not feeling around, he said:

"I sent for you because I think you are the boy that fits the job. I haven't any work for you but my sons need a boy. The other boy they had was too lazy. Go back, tell P.L. I sent you."

I went on back and P.L.'s secretary said he'd be out in a minute. The Negro maid of the doctor walked in and said to tell P.L. the doctor sent me. The secretary sent me in to see Robert Eric Randall because he wasn't busy. I walked in and this man looked so young, I couldn't imagine that he was a lawyer. In fact, later, the Randalls showed me some clippings from a well-known newspaper, telling that Robert Eric was the youngest man ever to get a law degree.

Robert Eric talked about the job and then buzzed for his brother. P.L. came in and began to tell me that if his father said all right, it was all right with him. He asked if I was married. I said, yes, and that I had a kid. He said he didn't think that the job would suit me. There wasn't much work and the pay was too small for a family man. The main task was to keep the office clean, sometimes drive the family out of town for weekends, deliver things, move desks or furniture. I hadn't been working for two months so I said I'd take the job. Randall said the pay was seven-fifty a week and that I could start work the next morning. He gave me the keys to his office and asked for my references. I had never worked around white people in the South before, that is, in their homes. I'd been working in the machine shop so I gave the name of Mike and his brother. I also gave Mr. Berger's wife's name. Each time I said the men's names Mr. Randall said, "Are they white men?"

I washed floors and windows all the next day. They didn't pay any attention. I had to make my own job. There was nothing specific to do. One main errand was to pay bills and go to the bank. P.L. got so he trusted me with money.

In the beginning he asked, "Do you steal?"

Robert Eric said, "You steal from us you'll get put in jail."

When I was hired I asked P.L. if the office work was all I had to do or if I would have to work around his house.

He asked me why I wanted to know.

I told him I never liked being a butler.

He said, "What's the matter? Don't you agree with women?"

I said, yes, but that I'd rather work with men.

He told me that sometimes I'd have to wash windows or lift something heavy at his house, but that his wife could hire her own boy for anything else.

After my first week of work they asked me to go on a hunting trip. The main objection to this was that I didn't know when I'd get home. It was on a Saturday and P.L. didn't say anything about pay. He came that night and gave me eight dollars. He said I had done a good job all week. In a month he gave me fifty cents more and the next month another fifty cents raise. P.L. and the other big shot doctors and lawyers would often go hunting out of season. P.L. would lie to people about where he was going. He would have me lie for him. I always went with him, and had to stay some distance away from where they were hunting to watch for the game warden. I usually stood on a hill where I could see all the roads, and I always stood close to the car. One time his young brother was with him on furlough from the Navy. We arranged that I would shoot the gun several times, fast, as a warning to them if I saw the game warden and they would run for cover. I would pick them up later in the car. This time P.L. said that he and his brother couldn't afford to get caught. I was standing guard and went to sleep. When I woke up I saw that a white man had passed me going in the direction of P.L. It was not the game warden but a white farmer looking for his turkeys. I began shooting the pistol because I was not to take any chances if the man was white. This happened at nine o'clock in the morning and I didn't locate P.L. and his party until four o'clock in the afternoon.

Since the brothers had been in law practice, only one secretary stayed more than a year. Some stayed only six months. The Randalls just didn't like one of their fastest typists. They would talk about her in the car. To me the truth about it was that we were supposed to close at five-thirty in the afternoon. The sceretary would start getting ready to go home and we'd be closing the office when P.L. would say, "Miss Betty, will you get out some letters before you go?"

He'd call me and tell me the letters had to be mailed that night. I'd sit beside the secretary and as she finished I would stamp and seal the envelopes. It would make both of us curse to do this after closing time. I think P.L. knew Miss Betty didn't like it.

A young girl, Victoria Brian, worked across the street in an Abstract office. She kept coming to apply for the job with the Randalls. The Abstract office wsn't paying as much as Randall. He was paying twenty-five a week. She was very friendly and asked me if I could help her get the job. She was sure that we would get along. She had brown hair and was about five feet two or three. She was pretty, with a lovely complexion and a wonderful personality. After about four months, another secretary left and they hired Miss Brian.

Many of the stenographers would ask me to do things for them like getting coca cola. Sometimes they gave me a nickel or a dime, or, most often they'd just say thanks. Miss Brian always got a coca cola and tried to pay me twenty-five cents.

I took the-Pittsburgh *Courier*. It was delivered to the office and left on the desk. The Randalls had some objection and Miss Brian would hide the paper for me. She would slip it to me and I'd go to a little room across the hall and read. Many times she asked to see the *Courier*. I would answer the door and watch, while she read. She asked me what I thought about the paper. I said it was news, true news. Some I didn't agree with but most I did agree with. She said she thought the same thing.

One day the police walked into a house on the west side of town.

The woman of the house asked them, "What do you want?"

The police said, "We had a call for a disturbance."

She told them there was no disturbance, "No one is here but my child."

The police turned and started out. The little girl laughed. The police said, "What the hell are you laughing at?" and shot the child in the head.

When I told Miss Brian she said, "What's wrong with this police force?"

The other secretary, Miss Parson, walked in and asked why the police acted that way.

Miss Brian said, "You know how the police are."

She asked me what happened to the little girl. When I said she was in the hospital and that she might always be a mental patient, Miss Brian said, "That policeman should have a bullet so he would be a mental patient."

Miss Brian and I could talk freely. She told me secrets. She was always saying, "I can talk this way with you."

I told her I had been to Detroit and that I was going back. She said she hoped that as long as she was working for P.L. I would be there, and that she didn't work so well with anyone as with me. The lawyer was away three or four days, sometimes a week. When he was away we worked an agreement. She'd be in the office and I'd stay away and the next day she'd be away. We'd rotate and laugh about the time we had and say this is how people should always work.

In the summer the lawyer always planned a two week vacation in Florida or on the Gulf of Mexico. I asked to go because I had never been there. He said I could go but that I would get only half of my salary. Miss Brian said it was a God damn shame that he would pay only half my salary when I was only getting ten dollars a week. P.L. took his wife, maid and children down first. Then we took one of the other cars, the Ford. The only work in Florida was to go fishing sometimes with P.L. After we came back he wrote a check and gave me my full salary.

I was interested in the job and in the family. I would stay and clean the office before going home at night and not go in so early the next morning. By this time I had my own keys to the office and house, and had in all, about seventeen keys. I never did have to work around the house any more than I wanted to. If I didn't want to do it I'd say so. Because his wife couldn't get me to work we had many difficulties. She would tell the maid that P.L. had ruined me, that I wouldn't do what she wanted, and on like that. We would always work it out because P.L. said my job was at the office and told Mrs. Randall to "go hire your own boy."

The maid was named Catherine and we were very close to each other. She would fix meals for me.

Mrs. Randall said, "Have your meals downtown where you work in the office."

But Catherine would call me to lunch when Mrs. Randall left the house. Mr. Randall would come in but we both felt happy. No slipping or ducking with him.

One weekend the Randalls were away. I called at the office. Miss Brian didn't have much work to do. She asked me to keep the office while she went across the hall to read the *Courier*. When she was through she asked me if Josephine Baker was colored. I told her, yes.

"Is she married to a white man? I was just reading in your paper where some white man committed suicide about her."

I told her, "I have heard of several doing the same thing."

Miss Brian said, "As much as I have been hearing about her and as much as I have read about her, I had no idea she was a colored woman." Then she called me close to her desk and said, "Matthew, I have something very confidential to ask you, but I want to have your confidence. If, deep down, you don't feel confidence in me, then just walk away."

"Is it true Negro men and white women marry up North? Do you know of any, personally, who are married?" She asked very slowly and surprisingly, "Matthew, I hope you never think I would ever try to get you in trouble. I wanted to know. I heard talk but when I hint to any white man they always tell me that it's a damn lie. Just how do white women act with Negroes for a husband?"

"Same as any other people."

"Did you ever see any children from a Negro man and a white

woman?"

I told her a child with a Negro father and a white mother was always darker than a child with a white father and a Negro mother. I compared it to the olive complexion of some gypsies on the corner near the Randall Building.

She said, "I just imagined it would be that color, that's the most beautiful color in the world."

I said, yes, that I thought the child was more beautiful than from a Negro woman and a white man.

"How do they feel?"

I could not answer.

She wanted to know how much time I had spent with any mixed couple. I told her my cousin in Long Island had a white wife and that I had stayed with them for some time. Miss Brian had a broad smile. She said she hoped to come North one day to see some white woman who was the mother of a Negro child. She asked me could I give any reason why the baby was darker with a Negro father than with a white father. I never did know, but some people used to say the pigment of the man is stronger than in the woman.

I think Miss Brian would have gone with a Negro man but we were friends in another kind of way. She was just someone I got to know very well. One day a Negro came and asked where was "P.L." and she told me it made her mad that he didn't say "Mr. Randall." I never could place her in my mind after that. A white man in the building used to make passes at her. He told me to tell her he liked her. She said she knew he did but that some day she would be getting married. She knew she would go overboard with a man, so she would stay on the safe side until she married. After she married she invited me out to her place. There was something funny about those white people. I went out and she invited me in the front door. We ate together and sat in the living room.

That reminds me of something about P.L. I could go in the front door most any time. I did it just to see. His wife didn't mind if there wasn't company. But if I drove up and saw lots of bridge parties that was the time I really opened the front door and came right in. Once she told Catherine to tell me to go in the back door. The maid told me in a jokified way she was glad I did it.

"Mrs. Mamie sure gets mad when you come in that front door."

Mrs. Randall would tell P.L. and he would say, "Many times I send Matthew in a hurry and he does things as quickly as he can when he knows I'm waiting."

One afternoon I came in just after Mrs. Randall had a bath. It was a hot day and she was walking around without clothes. When she heard the door open she started to run. "Catherine, who just came in?"

Catherine said it was Matthew.

When she heard it was me, she just took her time walking out. In the South they always acted like Negroes were tree stumps or something.

Catherine had one afternoon and evening off a week. The day fell sometimes on Randall's day off. Mrs. Randall liked to go dancing. Once she wanted to go in the worst way. She was wondering and hoping to go. She had four children, four, six, eight, and two years old. She was almost crying after she left the office. I gave her a ring and said she could get ready to go out with P.L., that I would come over and keep the children. This surprised and tickled her because I always refused to do anything at the house. Even at parties they had to hire outside butlers. I only served one time, just special, for P.L. on his birthday. She was very nice to me for four or five months after I stayed with the children.

White kids around ten or twelve talk very freely to Negroes working in their homes. They tell all about what their folks do and say. The Randall's oldest boy, who was about ten, used to talk to me. Mrs. Roosevelt stayed one weekend and all the whites hated her. They called her a Negro whore. The Randalls called her that. They said she went to Tuskegee to sleep with some Negro men. They discussed her all one night. Social equality was burning them down. The day after Mrs. Roosevelt's visit, Randall's ten year old son talked to me strongly.

"Matthew, I have something to ask you. Don't tell anybody. How would you like to marry a white woman?"

"I'm married and I'm married to a Negro woman."

"I know, but how would you like to be married to a white woman?"

"But I'm married and I wouldn't divorce my wife for any movie star that plays in California."

The boy looked shocked. He said, "I heard dad and mother

talking about Mrs. Roosevelt wanting white women to marry Negro men. She wants a brown race. Would you like to have a white woman?"

"I'm only interested in one woman. That's plenty for me. I don't know how Negroes who have no wife feel about it."

He said he didn't think Mrs. Roosevelt's plan would work. He used to ask me all about how babies were born. They never told him anything. I told him about sexual relations one day and he said his mother and father never did anything like that.

I said, "Yes, they did, there are four of you children."

He said, "Well, but I don't think they got us like that."

Christmas was a big day for Negroes in P.L.'s office. Two days before, we would go to every office paying and collecting bills. All the stores gave me from two to five shirts, socks, and shoes, and I collected fifty to seventy-five dollars in quarter and fifty cent pieces. P.L. always gave me two weeks salary as a present. I had ten or twelve suits. The way I got them, was whenever P.L. bought a new suit I'd tell him half a dozen times it looked awful on him. I'd say that I hated to see him in it. In a day or two he'd send me up to get it to take home. My father and brother-in-law still have three or four of those suits.

P.L. was tall and skinny with brown hair, weighed about one hundred sixty pounds and was six feet five inches tall. He had a pleasant personality and smiles for practically everyone he met. He liked to tell jokes and kid around with tricks and novelties. Everyone in town, both white and Negro, had a high respect for him. Many leading whites would say, "you are lucky to be working for a swell man."

I think he was the nicest white man I ever knew in the South. His brother, Eric, was small, weighed about one hundred fifty pounds, five feet five inches tall with blond hair. He was mostly silent. His general attitude made him not too well liked by some of the people in the cities. Some whites stated to me that many people respected him only because he was P.L.'s brother, and some said they didn't like him at all.

The first two years I worked for Randall, Adam Brown and a man named Warren Peters ran for Governor. The Randalls campaigned for Brown. Brown was a lawyer and lived in a small town of about two thousand population. The Randalls put up a strong campaign for Brown for some political reason I never could get. None of the Negroes knew about politics. It didn't mean anything to us, none of us could vote.

I went to the City Clerk's office one day and the white clerk asked, "Who are you going to vote for?"

I told her I didn't care who won, that I couldn't vote anyway. She said, "If you could vote, who would you want to win?"

I told her, "I'll wait for someone who'll help us vote. I'll vote then."

The other candidate, Peters, had been an aviator in World War I. He'd been shot down and wounded by the Germans. He had a wooden leg. Peters won by a large majority. The Randalls had a discussion after the election. They said they were sure to get Brown in the next time. Miss Brian gave me an indication that she didn't like Brown. She said she was glad the s.o.b. didn't win. I didn't go into it for it might have led into something. I just walked away.

On Inauguration Day for Peters they had floats and a parade with a band from the University. I listened to Peters that evening. All the Negroes walked away saying he didn't say anything about us. Most were in sympathy with the former governor. He had passed on before the peak of the campaign. He'd been governor four or five times. He built bridges, roads and schools, even Negro schools. I knew all of these people very well personally. I didn't know Peters at the time of his election but I knew his private secretary. I had to run errands to the business places downtown. Once or twice a week, I had many errands to the Capitol. Sometimes I was in the Governor's office two times a week. I'd have words with his secretary and see the Governor at times. Mr. Randall finally became friends with Peters. They had a date to go to Randall's lake. It was a huge lake with two or three houses, boat houses and small cabins. He and the big shots would go there to have a good time and outing away from the public. I always went because I would make as much in tips as my salary for the week. I could give my wife my whole pay for food. Saturday we closed the office at twelve o'clock and as soon as I ate dinner I drove up to the Capitol to get Governor Peters.

One or two Negroes would be at the lake waiting at the boat house to paddle the boats. We all would decide who we wanted to take in our boat. Sometimes we'd pick by the expression on the face. Sometimes we'd think one would tip the best. We always tried to avoid the cheap-skate. I insisted on paddling the Governor's boat on this outing. Mr. Randall asked me why I wanted to paddle the Governor. I told him I wanted to have some fun. Peters had only one leg and he couldn't swim. I said I was going to get him out in the middle of the lake and ask him to parole a relative I had in the penitentiary. If he wouldn't, then the boat was going to capsize. P.L. said if that was my plan I could take the Governor out. The Governor asked me all about my life.

He yelled to his secretary and said, "Here's a man from your birthplace."

It was mostly jokes they wanted to carry on. But I did mention a relative in prison. He said to come to the Capitol to see him the next week.

On Monday I told Miss Brian what the Governor had said. She told me about the racket in the parole with Negroes and some of the poor whites. In the Randall Building there was a lawyer named Martin. Martin had a wife who was a stenographer for the Governor. She would always know when the governor was discussing a man for parole. She would hear the decision and when the date of parole would be. She would take down the prisoner's name and his next closest kin's address. She gave the copy to her husband and the next day he would would write the prisoner's relatives saying he could help get the prisoner released. The relatives would come to Martin hoping for help. He would tell them to get money and on a certain day the prisoner would be freed. He drained all the money from the poor people. The prisoner would be paroled already anyway. Miss Brian thought it was the worst thing ever done. One day I saw someone I knew going up to the lawyer. Miss Brian said that his son was probably being paroled. She went to the Capitol to find out. It was true, just as she had told me.

I used to clean other offices, run errands for other places as well as my own. Mr. Randall knew it and as long as I was around when he needed me he didn't care. The Randalls used to dictate on the dictaphone at night and leave the wax rolls on Miss Brian's desk. One roll would tell me what to do. This worked up to the point where sometimes I wouldn't see them for two days. Friends dropped by and I'd go away with them. Randall couldn't find me but he wouldn't say anything.

I knew practically every one of the bankers in Memphis. I

knew all the cashiers, the president of the First National Bank and all the people in the Bank Building. Mr. Randall came to be executive officer of Union Bank and Trust Company, the second largest bank in Memphis. A relative, or cousin of his passed, and Randall took up the job. What used to puzzle me was the amount of money paid into P.L.'s office. Every day I deposited from two hundred to two thousand dollars. He had a few criminal cases when I first went to work. But after two years he had only large insurance cases or railroad accident cases. The minor cases, Negro and white, were referred to a young relative, Victor Randall.

P.L. had a cousin, Harry Randall. He ran for Senator and won office. I never was fully acquainted with him but knew him. He knew me as working for his relation. The relations between him and P.L. broke off completely with World War II. P.L.'s young brother was to be drafted. Practically all big shots went in the army with big commissions. After the brother found he was going to be drafted, P.L. drove to Washington to talk to Harry about getting him deferred or to arrange a commission. Harry said he couldn't do anything. The Randalls felt he could, or should, and they really talked about him in the car as we were going home. P.L. told his sister that cousin Harry was commissioned in World War I and didn't go overseas until after the war was over.

"God damn. He didn't want to get shot any more than anyone else. He thinks he's big, now he's up there. He thinks he's getting so close to Roosevelt he's important. But just let him wait. Sometime chickens must come home to roost."

After a long try the brother was accepted in the Navy as a lieutenant junior grade. Randall hired the cashier of the bank to help his brother clear away his business before leaving.

Shortly after I started to work for Randall, a Negro who lived next door to me got into trouble. He got into a fight with a white man. The white man was his friend. He was a worker and he and the Negro often went on drinking bouts together. Often they would stay away for one or two days on a drinking bout. The misunderstanding had happened when they were both drunk. The Negro beat the white man and the white man said the Negro had taken his money. He was lying but the white man sued the Negro. Randall defended him.

When the Negro testified that he and the white man had been drinking Randall said, "Gentlemen of the Jury. You see the kind of case this is. When a white man starts eating and drinking with a Negro he gets to be just like one. There is no difference, only one has a white skin. The defendant should be freed."

In twenty minutes the jury returned a verdict of "Not Guilty."

Another case had to do with me. Many middle-class whites would contact me and ask me to try and arrange for them to go hunting or fishing with Randall. I could do this because often when he had no partner to go with him, he would ask me if I knew anyone who could go. Many middle-class whites got to know Randall through me. This was my old foreman Mike's hope for a long time. Mike introduced me to a money-lender. His name was Jaspers and he was supposed to be a 'coon hunter like myself. Mike had told him about a good dog I had on my father's farm. I didn't like Jaspers right from the start. I just didn't like his expression. One Sunday morning, I caught the bus and went out to my father's place. Jaspers came to my house. When my wife told him where I was, he drove down. He had two young hound dogs with him and a police dog. He told me that he wanted to borrow my dog to train his dogs. He said he would leave the police dog with my father as security. He said he would come by and get me every time he went hunting, so that we could both train his dogs. My father was rather agreeable to the idea, I didn't care too much about the bargain, but I let him take the dog.

I didn't see Jaspers for three months. One day I saw him getting a haircut in the barber shop. I walked into the shop and Jaspers told me he had been trying to contact me for two months. He asked the barber to tell me what had happened to my dog. The barber asked Jaspers if he meant the dog that had the black plague and died. He had taken the dog to the city dump and burned it. Jaspers said the only bad part about it was that practically every dog in the neighborhood had died from the same disease they had caught from my dog. He told me the dog had died a couple of weeks after he came to town.

He had many ways to contact me if this story was true. He knew where I worked and where I lived. I went to the office and told P.L. the story. P.L told me he didn't believe the dog was dead. He said if I could find out where the dog was, he was sure I could get him back. He asked how I had met the money-lender and I told him through Mike. He told me to contact Mike and put pressure on him. I called Mike and told him that I had almost worked up a deal for him to go fishing with P.L. I told him I didn't know how P.L. would feel if he knew about the dog and how Jaspers had treated me. I told him I would never be satisfied until I heard the truth. He told me he would see what he could do. Mike called me one week later at the office and told me he knew where my dog was. It was sixty miles from Memphis and a wealthy dairy farmer by the name of Collins had him. P.L. said he knew this man. He had me describe the dog. He wanted me to tell of any special markings I would know the dog by. Then he called Collins long distance and told him he wanted to see him and asked when he could come to the office. P.L's prestige and influence was such that Collins said he could come right away if necessary. In one and a half hours he was there. Randall had me sit in another office across the way while he talked to him. Collins was a white farmer and Jaspers was also white. P.L. told him that he had decided to take up 'coon hunting; someone had told him that Collins had a very good dog. He asked him if he would go 'coon hunting with him. Collins was glad to go and told P.L. about the 'coon dogs he had. Randall asked him to describe the dogs. When he started to describe my dog, Randall asked him what name the dog answered to. Collins said, Rover, and that he had bought the dog from Jaspers. Randall buzzed me to come to his office at this point.

"The dog you bought from Jaspers is his dog and I will see that he gets it." When Collins objected, Randall said, "I don't want to prosecute you."

Collins asked me if it was really my dog and would I sell him? He had paid Jaspers fifty dollars for the dog and he would pay me seventy-five more. I refused his offer. Randall warned Collins that nothing must happen to the dog until he heard from Jaspers. Collins called Jaspers from the office and a few minutes later he was there.

P.L. asked Jaspers what had happened to the dog he borrowed from me. Jaspers said he was dead. Randall called him a liar, and said he knew where the dog was. Randall cursed Jaspers. I was shocked, a middle-class Negro could never curse a poor Negro like that.

Randall said, "Any time a white man is low enough to lie to a Negro to get something from him, he ought to be run out of town." He repeated this several times. He looked at his watch and told Jaspers he had two hours to go to Collins' farm and return with the dog. If he didn't do this he was to move out of town.

While Randall was cursing Jaspers in such a vicious tone saying that a white man who lies to a Negro should be run out of town, it came to me what he was saying. I said to myself, "My God, is this it? Is this the Southern system, white supremacy and the laws of the South?" They feel that a white man has no need to lie to a Negro or lie about him. I was not thinking of the dog then. I said, "No wonder, when a Negro is involved in an incident with whites, he is always guilty if the whites say he is. That's why in the courts when a Negro is in trouble, if he has twenty Negro witnesses testifying for him, and one white is against him, he is guilty on the one white's statement." I began to wonder if they really believed this way. I could see that Randall was serious with Jaspers when he made his statement. Then I could see that anything involving a Negro and the word of a white woman was even more true in their minds. I knew then they believed this way. But how could they? Why? This kept spinning in my mind. If Jaspers had taken my dog by force and said he wouldn't let me have it again, the lawyer would have gotten the dog back for me, but not cursed Jaspers at all. But a white man stooping low enough to lie to a Negro in the South was what made him mad. I watched this part about P.L. and the Randalls closely. P.L. himself did quite a bit of lying. But he never made one promise to me that he didn't fulfill. I feel sure that it was not because he was white. But he was wealthy and he could afford to keep the promises he made to me. I pondered about these two cases, the Negro and white fighting and what Randall had said and now, this one with Jaspers.

I wondered, "Did they really think that Negroes always lied in their testimony?"

Many times I'd tell lies for P.L. He'd know it, in fact, he would ask me to do it. Often his little son would tell lies. Randall would say, "Sandie is going to be a politician." It was different when Negroes lied.

Jaspers did what Randall told him. He was back in less than two hours. While Jaspers had gone to get the dog, P.L. had sent for my father. When Jaspers came in, P.L. told him to drive my father and the dog back to the farm. I was worried about my father being alone in the car with Jaspers. P.L. told me there was nothing to worry about, that my father would get home safe. P.L. was right. My father and the dog got home safe. Whenever Jaspers saw me after that he was very polite and always smiled. He never mentioned anything about the dog.

6.
WORK IN THE SOUTH II

WHEN I WASN'T busy for P.L. Randall I used to sit over at the Court House. I was always interested if it was a big case, and especially if it concerned a Negro. I knew the judges, police and clerks. I could go in on practically any case. A Negro was accused of killing a white woman and beating her sister unconscious. Every Negro in town talked about it. It was the most unreasonable case I ever heard in the Court House.

Two white sisters were doing nursing at the Orphans' Home on the outskirts of the city. One Saturday they got in their car and drove a mile from the Home to the woods. It was a thick wood with a gravel highway running into it. They went into the woods to pick some flowers. Sunday there was a large talk about one of the women being beaten to death and her sister was in the hospital expected to die. The afternoon paper said there had been a brutal murder attack on the two sisters. Tuesday, a reward for the person responsible came out for two hundred dollars. By the weekend, the reward had risen to one thousand dollars. No one had been arrested or picked up. The following week the reward was two thousand. By the end of the fourth week the police claimed they had found and captured the man who had killed the sister. A Negro, Jim Dalton, was caught in Chattanooga. He was brought back and locked in the county jail. Before they had his trial they put him in a nearby state penitentiary for fear he'd be lynched.

At this time the remaining sister was able to go out of the hospital. Many witnesses they scraped up gave very vague statements that the murderer was a little darker. Some witnesses said he was taller, some said he was heavier. At the trial there were at least twenty-five to thirty Negro witnesses for Jim Dalton. There were about seven or eight witnesses for the white woman. One was a bus driver who drove a city bus. The only thing the sister said, was that "he kinda resembled the Negro."

When they put her on the stand and asked if she would swear on the Bible that Dalton was the man, she said, "Frankly, no, I won't swear. But I swear he *looks* like the man."

That was enough, she was white and Dalton was a Negro.

She testified that she and her sister went to gather flowers. As the sun was going down they put the flowers in the back seat of the car. She was driving and her sister was sitting in the front seat next to her. She turned on the switch, started the motor and began to move the car. A Negro walked out of the bushes and said, "Hey, wait." She waited, he reached in the car, turned the switch off and told them to get out. They got out on the opposite side from him. He walked around the car holding a blunt instrument, grabbed her sister and began to beat her. When her sister was unconscious he pulled her off the fender where she had been waiting and beat her until she was unconscious. She was the only eyewitness to the scene.

Two witnesses were fourteen year old boys from the Orphans' Home. They said they had been picking flowers one-half mile away and heard a noise that sounded like someone was beating something in the bushes. As they came within eye-sight they saw the back of a Negro man running through the bushes. They said Dalton looked like the man they had seen.

The bus driver said a Negro caught his bus, at the end of the line, one-quarter mile from the crime. When he flagged the bus he was running, excited, and kept looking back over his shoulder. He rode downtown to the Square. He said Dalton was the Negro.

The only witness who really had something to say looked like she had been schooled thoroughly. She was a Negro woman who was supposed to be a fortune teller. She was the one who had Dalton arrested. She said that on the afternoon of the crime Dalton came to her house and said he was in serious trouble. He heard she could help people with her hoodooism. She told him to take a seat and tell her about his trouble. She said that he told her he had just killed two white women.

She said, "My God! If you killed two white women there is nothing I can do for you. I don't have anything that pertains to white women. I can't help you. Catch a train, get as far away as possible."

She testified that she gave him a pair of overalls and that her husband had walked him to the train.

When she finished her testimony Dalton took the stand. He stated that he was not at the scene of the crime on Saturday. He was on Beale Street from the time the woman said her sister had been killed until the following evening.

All over the South there are money-loaners who insist that Negroes borrow money. Twenty to thirty cents is collected on the dollar by the loaners. The loaners make themselves police, complete with pistols, and rough as the police force itself. Many police are money-loaners. These men beat or kill any Negro who doesn't pay.

The defendant claimed that he borrowed fifty dollars from a white money-loaner. He hadn't been working and couldn't meet his payments. He had gone to talk to the loaner and the man told him he was going to beat and kill him if he didn't pay. Saturday morning the loaner had been to Dalton's house telling everyone he was going to kill him. That was why Dalton stayed on Beale Street all evening. It was so thickly crowded on Saturdays that he could hide and get protection from other Negroes. The next morning friends told Dalton that the loaner came with five or six men and threatened to kill him. They testified to this in court. Dalton didn't know what to do. He went to see Mabel Jefferson and told her he was in trouble. She told him hoodoo could help him and that she would fix it so he could live peacefully with his family. He would have to go away until she could work it out. He was to send his address and she would write often and tell him when it was safe to return. Dalton went to Chattanooga and got a room in a flophouse. After he was there for awhile, wondering how the hoodoo was coming out, he wrote Mabel a letter giving his address. Several days after he wrote, two detectives walked into the flophouse and arrested him.

Dalton had, what seemed to be, a serious, earnest white lawyer from another city. After he made his testimony he began calling the Negro witnesses. They told with the firmest conviction, some with tears, that Dalton had been with them at the very time of the murder.

An elderly Negro had been coming down the road Sunday morning. As he approached the little road leading to the woods, there was a white woman standing without clothes shouting at him. He went to whipping his horse and rode a mile down the road to call the police. He had been the first person at the scene of the crime. He was never put on the stand. Two detectives arrived on the scene shortly after the man called the police. They testified they had found one woman lying dead and her sister unconscious and practically nude. The back seat of the car was pulled out of place on the floor. There were signs of scuffling, and a heavy instrument was on the seat. They said it was the instrument used for beating the women.

The Negro's lawyer intervened: "Where is this instrument?" They replied, "We threw it out in the bushes."

The sister testified that the man hadn't hit them one lick inside the car but the court accepted the testimony of the detectives. The bus driver testified that he had read about the case the morning after the murder, in the *Memphis Advertiser*. The *Advertiser* is printed at night and thrown in the morning. He couldn't have read it.

At a recess, I overheard one of the police telling one of the lawyers: "If that nigger did it he's the hardest nigger we ever had in jail. We put him through the worst things we could think of and he still says he's innocent. We took some pliers and pulled out every one of his fingernails and he still says he didn't do it. I doubt very much that he's guilty."

The testimony of the thirty Negroes was completely ignored. They kept the Negro hoodoo woman locked in a back room until adjournment. When she started down the aisle the packed courtroom of Negroes stood up, and shouted and roared, "Traitor. Liar," and every name they could think of.

Eight or ten police got around her, patted her shoulder and said, "We'll take care of you. Mabel, you did a good job."

Tower Roman, the state solicitor, who every Negro disliked, was the prosecutor. He got on the floor and began:

"This man is guilty without doubt. If these niggers are going to rape and beat, let them rape and beat their own women."

Until now rape hadn't been mentioned.

"Nothing I hate like a nigger laying his black body on a white woman. If this man is freed I'll take my wife and baby and move. This town won't be safe for white people. Without any doubt this man should get the electric chair."

His talk went along those lines.

The defense of Dalton's lawyer was:

"Brothers of the Jury, I hope there is one thing I can instill in you before you make up your minds. Life is sweet to everyone. It is just as sweet to this Negro as to you, me, the Governor or the

President. Every mother loves the life of her child. Consider these things very carefully before you make a decision."

He said for them to remember the case of a Negro in Mississippi. The man had said that he wouldn't die but would still be alive after all the twelve men of the jury had passed on. This was a true story, not told to excite them, not anything anyone could take for fun.

"I can prove this man did not die although he had been sentenced to death. He outlived the jury and the judge because he was not guilty. Look at the frame-up testimony of this case. I thought there was a law saying a child could not testify in court. Why would you take the testimony of these two children? Everyone of us knows how easy it is to bribe a child. They say they were one-half mile away. They heard something which sounded like beating in the bushes. No crying out, just something that sounded like beating in the bushes.

"The bus driver said he read of the case in the paper that morning. He knows, but not only the bus driver, myself, everyone in court knows that the murder story wasn't in the paper the next morning. The *Advertiser* is written at night and thrown in the morning. The first person to see the woman didn't see her until eight o'clock in the morning. The first detective didn't see her until eight-fifteen. This was after the paper had already been thrown."

He went on to ask how such a lie could be accepted so openly. "How can any of this man's testimony be believed after such a lie? The bus driver said that the man got on the bus and went to town. It is customary for a man to get away from, and not go toward, law enforcement if he has committed a crime."

"Take the testimony of the crystal gazer: When a serious crime is committed it is a slander and shame on the police force when they are unable to solve it. But when the police force must rely on crystal gazers to solve their crimes then we are in a bad situation. This crystal gazer should be tried along with this man if her testimony is true. She aided him, she gave him her husband's overalls, helped him escape, and gave him money for food. Let us look a little further into the testimony of this crystal gazer. She says Dalton came to her directly from the crime, yet she waited two weeks before notifying the police. Why did she wait two weeks? I'll give the answer. The first week the reward was only one hundred dollars. She waited until it got to two thousand dollars before she felt she could get some money out of her crystal gazing. She then sent her husband to the police with the address of this man who was in hiding from one of the cheap money-loaners who thrive by tormenting Negroes."

Dalton got life imprisonment. Many of us were sick. All of us had our heads down when he was sentenced. We wanted to burn Mabel Jefferson's house. Dalton's lawyer said he would work for an appeal to the end of time. I walked to the office. Miss Brian asked me what was wrong. I told her the jury had found Dalton guilty.

She grabbed her head with her hands and said, "My God, you don't mean it. One of the men on the jury is a friend of mine. If he went along with this conviction I'll break off with him."

She called me close and said she had a very important secret to tell me and I was never to mention it to anyone. It was something I couldn't do anything about. Secondly, it would get me and her in serious trouble. She said, "That man no more beat and killed that woman and her sister than I did. What is involved is that she and her sister have been having serious trouble over the same man. They have had arguments and fights before. I have no doubt she drove her sister out there to murder her and this beating of hers was a sham." She said if it was possible that Dalton's lawyer could question the woman in front of her boyfriend, she bet the woman would break down.

The following night I was driving the judge who presided at the trial. I asked if he felt that Dalton was guilty.

He said, "Damn right. Guilty as hell."

The next conversation was with Mr. Randall and I asked differently. I said, "P.L., if the boy is guilty he should get the chair. What do you think?"

P.L. said, "I think he should too. But if they can't find enough evidence to give him the chair, then he should be freed." After an appeal was granted for the third time Dalton received a ten year sentence.

Bill Will was a rugged Negro, six feet and a half tall and weighing two hundred and forty pounds. He was known to be one of the strongest men in Tennessee. He lived on the corner of Lowe and Johnson in the center of the Negro settlement. Will was picked up by the city police on suspicion. They locked him up downtown, beat him and released him the next day without charges. He was pretty mad about the police beating him and went to Colonel Root, the police commissioner, to complain. Colonel Root was a World War I veteran and about the lousiest white man that ever lived. After Colonel Root took Will's report he called in the two policemen.

"This nigger's been in here complaining about the slapping around you gave him. I told him I'd see you. After you get off duty you'd better go by his house and teach him a lesson. Better teach him not to report on white policemen."

My friend, an errand boy in the commissioner's office, overheard the police talking and got on his bike to come tell me. He said was there anything we could do because the Randalls had so much authority. Could we report Will as a relative and have Randall call Root to stop the police? But the Randalls were out of town and the best thing we could do was to go to Will's and warn him.

Will told us, "Thanks. When they come—I'll be here."

Will loaded his 38-40 Winchester rifle and stood waiting at the door. He didn't have to wait very long before the two police got off their motorcycles. One went to the back door.

The one in front knocked and called, "Is Will in?"

Will said, "Yes."

"Nigger—open this door!"

Will said he wasn't going to open the door.

"If you don't, I'll kick it down and come in to get you."

"You'll have to kick it down. I'm not going to open it."

At that, the door crashed in. Will was in a sitting position in front of the door. When the door crashed, Will fired. The bullet went in the policeman's throat and took part of his head off. Will rushed to the back door but that policeman was halfway down the block. Will fired a shot after him but missed.

Thirty minutes later every Negro on The Hill was around Will's house. All the police on the force were there. I was there but I couldn't get any closer than a block. The police were cursing, calling him "damn nigger with a bitch mammy." After a half hour of this, everyone was saying that Will had made his getaway.

I saw six Negro fellows around Will. Some were talking and pointing in the direction away from his home. As Will would try to go back in the house with his rifle they would talk to him and hide him with their bodies. Finally, he was persuaded to turn around and go. He walked across the street and down the alley.

Five years later he was captured in Los Angeles, California. He beat up two policemen in a bar. Other police rushed in and arrested him. After the fingerprinting they found he was wanted for murder. Many statements were made by people that the police wouldn't bring Will alive through Texas and Alabama. The police guaranteed that he would reach safely and have a trial. He arrived a week after his capture. I sat through his trial and listened to the testimony of the living policeman and the testimony of Will. I don't know how it happened but this time the state solicitor was defending Will. After listening to the testimony, the solicitor, Tower Roman, said:

"Gentlemen of the Jury, it hasn't been too long ago that we were in the midst of a war with the Kaiser in Germany. We sent niggers there to fight white folks. We taught them how to kill white folks. I'm not saying when a nigger kills a white man he is justified all the time. No, not at all. But when you look through this case you can see that this man was at home, the place he is supposed to be when he has no other place. A man that won't defend his home isn't a man in anybody's opinion. There was no place for him to run. There was no place for him to go. When we were in war with Germany we wanted men like Will. We wanted men who would not run. We wanted men who would shoot whites.

"This is what we taught him. I think if a nigger can shoot white people to defend his country he has the more reason to shoot one white man to defend his home. And it may not be very long before we will need Will, and many more like him, to defend our homes again."

The jury took one and a half hours to make a decision. Will received ten years in prison.

In 1940, Warren Peters ran for Governor again. His opposition was Adam Brown and John Exeter. The Negroes in the state liked Exeter better than the other two men because he was common. He'd go around visiting, take off his shoes, sit down on the farm and talk. Randall was again the leading campaigner for Brown. In the closing stages of the campaign, P.L. talked to Brown several times a day on the phone, and sent him many letters. Late one afternoon P.L. called Miss Brian to take a letter.

He looked out the door and asked if I was busy. I didn't say anything. Many times I was hesitant trying to figure out what he wanted me to do, or where he wanted me to go, before I would answer. He asked me to wait to take the letter to Brown's home.

When he gave me the envelope he said it was very, very important and that I was to put it in Brown's hand. When I got to the door I asked P.L. what to do if Brown wasn't home.

He said, "He'll be there."

I insisted, "What if he isn't there? What shall I do then?"

P.L. kept repeating, "He'll be there."

Now, I knew white folks very well. They'd say they'd be there but many times they would go somewhere else. I didn't want to get into trouble, so I asked again. "Shall I give it to his wife if he isn't there?"

He looked at me for a minute and then said, "If you just can't find him, leave it with the cook. She'll probably come to the door."

I drove out to Brown's house. I saw a real light-skinned boy who seemed to be twenty or so. I asked him if this was where Brown lived. He told me, yes, and I went around to the back door. A very stout colored woman came to the door.

"Is Mr. Brown in?"

She said, "Yes," and I handed her the letter.

The next morning I opened the office at nine o'clock. Miss Brian came in and when she saw me she began to laugh. I asked her what was wrong. She just laughed harder. She laid her hands at the side of her face and laughed until the tears came.

She said, "You like to have killed me, bringing a confession out of P.L. yesterday."

I didn't know what she meant.

She said, "When you asked about the letter to Brown—should you leave it with his wife? That s.o.b. never did have a wife. He lives in the house with a Negro woman and has five or six children by her."

I'd seen the light boy in front of the house but I had nothing on my mind about his being related to lawyer Brown. I asked Miss Brian what he would do with his family if he got elected. Would they live in the Governor's mansion with him? Miss Brian was sure they wouldn't live in the Governor's mansion but would live close by.

She said, "As far as I know that man has never in his life been in bed with a white woman."

Brown was elected in 1940. They had an even bigger parade than usual. There were many Negro soldiers in the parade and the Governor, as always, was riding in the front car. It was a new convertible Buick and I was driving that car for the Governor with P.L. sitting inside. After Brown spoke for one and a half hours we walked away. One Negro said what did we get out of Brown's speech.

Another man said, "It's the same old thing that every governor says. He didn't mention the Negroes once."

The closest he came, if you wanted to cover up for him, was to say he would do his best for *all* the people in Tennessee.

I later read in the Tennessee *Advertiser* that Truman had visited Brown in 1944. He was campaigning for the vice presidency. Brown and the state officials met him.

Brown asked, "Since you're running for vice president, what we want to know down here is where you stand on equality. Where do you stand on intermarriage between the races?"

Truman's reply was, my mother was a rebel, my grandmother was a rebel. My wife's mother was a rebel, her grandmother was a rebel. You should have no doubts as to where I stand on interracial marriage.

This always got me. How could Brown, and hundreds of other men in the South, live with a woman and have children and then discriminate against them.

I never felt the laws in the South meant anything. There wasn't one law in the interest of Negroes. I had no idea how the law was written or where. One day I went to the Capitol for P.L. All the Negroes working at the Capitol were prisoners. Some of them were trustees and could go home at night. Many were very brilliant men. A prisoner and I got to talking. He asked me if I knew where the laws of the state were written. He carried me into an office and showed me a list of names on a paper. On the list were the names of the most reactionary people that I had heard talking to P.L. These were the names put down as writing the law. We talked about the state and the government. The trustee said he always felt that the Negro people were the most hated of any people. But since the war he found some who were hated even more. The Negro soldier was hated worse. He said he heard talk at the Capitol and all over the city, every day, about white people hating the Negro soldier.

Before the war the bus drivers and those on city jobs didn't carry weapons. But as the Negro soldiers increased, the bus drivers had trouble getting them to say, "yes, sir" and "no, sir." In a short while all the bus drivers had a revolver sticking out of their pockets or up over their heads in the bus. Many drivers complained that nothing did any good. There were fights all the time with Negroes getting wounded or cutting up bus drivers.

One night I was walking toward Elder Avenue and I ran into a fellow I had worked with in the machine supply company. He asked me to stop with him at a friend's house to collect some money. He lived across from the Cavalcade Night Club. We were sitting at his window when we saw a crowd rush out of the Club. They walked around the corner and stood looking on. We went down to see what was happening. A Negro G.I. and a drunk Negro civilian had been fighting but by the time we got there it was all settled. There had been so much trouble, the army sent white M.P.'s with the Negro G.I.'s to protect them. The M.P.'s also rode with the city police to protect the soldiers from the police. The night of this fight there were three white M.P.'s standing by with two truckloads of soldiers. There was a Negro technical sergeant in a jeep. Everyone relaxed after the fight and started back into the Club. Two cars drove up with four police and four white M.P.'s. Each car asked what was the trouble. One man started to speak. A policeman walked up and struck him.

A colored woman said, "What in the hell did you hit that soldier for? He was only telling you what had happened."

The cop hit the woman in the face. The soldiers rushed up and said that maybe a civilian would take that kind of treatment but they sure wouldn't. They said they had been trained to fight and they would start right now. One Negro soldier hit a policeman with a beer bottle. The M.P. with the police caught him, hit him and put him in the police car. The three M.P.'s stationed with the Negro soldiers made no attempt to interfere. There was a ten minute fight with both Negro civilians and Negro soldiers fighting the police. It ended with the police putting three soldiers in their cars and driving away. The sergeant drove off and followed them to jail. In a few minutes he came back with his eye swollen and told us he had been hit by the desk sergeant. The soldiers were raging. The civilians were pretty mad too. They walked up to the white M.P.'s and cursed them.

"What in the hell are you here for?"

"We didn't do anything. We didn't hit you."

"Goddamn right you didn't do anything. Why didn't you protect us? Why didn't you say something to the police?" They gave a story about the four other M.P.'s with the police. The sergeant pulled off and asked five of the guys to talk to him. He told all of us to stay.

"We'll have it out once and for all with the city police of Memphis."

He went to the field where they were stationed and came back with revolvers for twenty Negro soldiers. They took the M.P.'s and cursed them and made them phone for the police. They made the M.P.'s say that another fight had broken out and to come back.

The soldiers said, "Our battleground will be right here."

We staked ourselves up and down the street. We waited for thirty minutes but no police showed up. The M.P.'s made another call and we waited again. Still no police. They drove up and down the streets firing one hundred rounds of ammunition into the air and into the sidewalk. The police never did show up. I never thought I'd see scared white cops. When one cop had pulled his gun his hand had been shaking so much he almost dropped the gun. I never saw that before. The M.P.'s hadn't been so scared. They were more aggressive than the cops.

Each year the Randalls went on vacation. The fourth year, they decided to go to New Orleans. On our way down P.L. decided to spend the weekend at Point View on Mobile Bay. This was a hotel built for millionaires and one of the swellest hotels I ever visited with P.L. The hotel sat on a point jutting out into the bay. As we headed down to the hotel, P.L. kidded me about how maybe a German submarine or a Jap would come up on the beach. When we got there I saw this huge hotel. It wasn't like anything I'd seen before. As we drove up a doorman walked out, checked where we were from, and the Randalls were ushered in. The doorman came back and I was ushered around to the back door.

There were several Negro maids and chauffeurs standing around. As we registered we called out the name of our boss.

When I got through registering I was shown the commissary for the servants. Anything your heart or mind could want was there. I was under the impression we'd have to pay the clerk. They showed us our sleeping quarters in a long low building, a hundred yards in back of the hotel. We'd drive the car into the garage and close the door. The steps led up from the car into each chauffer's room. The room was beautiful, equipped with shower, telephone and screened casement windows. After I got adjusted to my room I went out and introduced myself to the different people. They were from Philadelphia, Chicago, New York and all parts of the Southern states. The hotel employees told us we would have to go to the dining hall to get our eats. We also were told we could go to the commissary and eat and drink, or smoke anything we wanted. A chauffeur who had been there two weeks explained to us that we didn't pay for anything. Everything was charged on the boss's bill. It was explained in very careful detail. The boss didn't pay until he was ready to leave. The hotel didn't accept anyone without a big bank account. They expected them to spend a lot of money. The good part was that nobody knew exactly what the bill was going to be. The boss was handed a bill, not separated, what he bought, his wife, his chauffeur, but just added all together. The chauffeur with the experience told me that each night they got together and took up things for a party in the rooms. We began to arrange a party for the night. I was to get the whiskey, some would get the food, sandwiches, cigarettes, cigars, candy, whatever we needed. We had every kind of sea food, every kind of the best whiskey.

We had a continuous rotation. Every afternoon we'd organize ourselves for the party that night. It was the best time I ever had. We stayed for a few days.

When we were driving away, P.L.'s sister said, "Matthew, you have such good times, you'll never stop working for brother will you?"

P.L. told his wife that it was one of the finest places he'd ever gone. He said the expenses were not too bad. But he didn't think they'd used as much as was on the bill. I laughed to myself. I know I drank my part of the bill. I spent twenty-five bucks a night myself.

Miss Brian and I used to steal from P.L. every day. When I started my job some of the older men on the block told me I'd be tried for stealing. The whites would leave money on the desk, drop some out of their pockets, leave pens around. They said always pick the money up, even if it is only a quarter and give it to them. Do this for at least one year. If you can do it for a year and they get confidence in you then you can steal all you want. If they don't catch you and if you say you don't steal then they have confidence in you. The whites are very funny, they won't believe anything against their Negro worker if they haven't caught him themselves.

We had a stamp list. We bought ten or fifteen dollars worth of stamps every week. Sometimes we would order more than fifteen and when I was in a real hurry, I'd tear off a roll and put them on the letters on the way to the post office. One afternoon a white man came in to see Mr. Randall. I tore off a roll of stamps and stuffed them into my pocket. I didn't know he was watching. After I went out he asked Miss Brian how long I'd been working there. She said four or five years.

He said, "Have you ever caught him stealing? He just stole a roll of stamps."

Miss Brian said, "Go tell that to Mr. Randall." She knew what P.L. would say.

Mr. Randall called the man into the office and he began to tell on me. Mr. Randall thought he was talking about someone else. He asked Miss Brian who had been in the office.

Miss Brian said, "Matthew."

Mr. Randall turned to the man and said, "He's not stealing any stamps."

The man said, "Well, he sure acted like it."

Mr. Randall told him, "If you have business with me and are trying to frame Matthew by lying, then you can take your business somewhere else."

Every so often P.L. would throw out some old bills thinking he'd never collect them. After he threw them out a lot of people would pay their bills. Miss Brian took the money and put it away for a few weeks. It would sometimes be fifty or sixty dollars. After awhile we would half it.

Randall had a lot of Negroes renting some of his houses. He'd tell me, "Go down and put the fear of God into those people and you can have half of whatever you collect."

I wouldn't do it. I never collected a dime but he also owned blocks of white homes. I always collected from the white folks. What every Negro hated, and every white as well, was to see a rent sign on their house. The sign gave them so many days to pay or get out. Sometimes I was so rough collecting and putting on the sign, the white people would call P.L. to complain. He never did anything, just called me in and said to wait a few days.

One of Randall's houses was funny. Not funny either, but a prostitution house. They had a Negro maid and the woman who ran the house was very friendly. She had the maid fix me coffee and sometimes, eats, when I came to collect rent. She always complained about the roof leaking, or said that some painting should be done. I walked in one day and saw a young woman lying in bed with a man. I went back outside. The woman of the house called to me and told me to come on up. I went past the door and the couple were sitting on the edge of the bed, talking. I asked the maid what was going on in that place. She told me it was a whorehouse. She said she had needed the job and took this one as a maid.

I told her, "I'm afraid. One of these women could walk through naked and something might happen."

She said, "You're kidding. You're working for Randall, the biggest lawyer in town. And if anything did happen I'd help you. We'd tear this place apart." The four girls who were working in the house became very friendly. They'd walk around nude and sit around kidding and talking. I told Randall that I was nervous going to collect rent.

He said, "Don't worry, just get the money. If anything happens just call me up."

I collected there for three years. I was just as common as the maid; they continued whatever they were doing.

One day I had P.L. and the banker in the car. I wanted to get P.L. up at that house. I told him one of his places was leaking. When we got out and started up to the door, the girls said to P.L. and the banker: "Come on in honey. I'd like to take you in my bedroom."

The banker said, "What's going on here?"

Randall said, "I don't understand it myself."

I was standing and laughing.

The landlady came in and said, "This is the landlord—Mr. Randall."

The girls just disappeared. The doors closed like they were automatic. In the car I was laughing all the time and Randall had to cover it up as if he didn't know anything.

While I was working for P.L. I picked up extra money at a local hotel. I was a close friend of Bob, the chief bellhop. He was a big shot Negro and owned an apartment house, a beer garden and a mansion. When the Depression was on he had eighty-five thousand dollars in cash. His father had been a wealthy Methodist minister in Atlanta. He had a racket with the bellhops. A bellhop worked eight straight hours one day and a broken shift the next. The best tips came at night. The swing shift gave each man a chance. Every bellhop paid Bob, the chief bellhop, twenty-five cents out of his tips for each shift. Bob had charge of all the hiring of the help at the hotel. One day when we were coming in from hunting, Bob asked me if I had ever been in bed with a white woman. He said that every bellhop in the hotel was going to bed with white women. The women would call for service and the bellhop would end up in bed with her. They were single women, married women travelling alone, or prostitutes. A prostitute would come to town and ask the bellhop how business would be at the hotel. He would outline everything for her. Every client he'd send her he'd get a percentage. After a certain number of clients, the bellhop would collect. The question was usually asked whether he would like cash or trade it out in bed. Bob said that many times the bellhop would reject bed if she wasn't the type he preferred and she had to pay.

I asked Bob if it wasn't dangerous. He said that it was one of the safest places because they worked out a system. When the girl and the bellboy made an agreement he'd come out and tell a buddy the specific time. The buddy waited on the same floor. Only two people had keys to the rooms—the manager and the hotel detective. Because of discrimination, only whites used the front elevators. The buddy watched those elevators. If the detective came, the buddy walked by and shook the knob, or gave a knock at the door. The boy inside got up, closed his trousers, took his tray, shook the change around on it and walked out.

Two boys had a fight because one pulled a joke. One boy had a date on the seventh floor. His buddy was real devilish and liked to play. Each bellboy knew the hotel detective and the manager's knock. The boy with the date said he was going to have a good time for a change and pull off all his clothes and spend awhile in bed. His buddy waited until he thought everything should be over then he gave the door the hotel manager's knock. The boy with the woman came down sick and nervous. He said that when he had heard the knock he couldn't get his clothes on. He looked out the window, said, "Hell, too far to jump." He shook so that he dropped his clothes on the floor. The woman had to get out of bed to put his clothes on for him. He came out tipping but he didn't see anyone. He asked his buddy where was the manager. His buddy said he thought he'd seen him. The boy who'd been with the woman was so nervous and shocked he went home for the day. The next day his pal was laughing and all the boys were laughing. He told about the knock in an outburst of laughter. The other boy leaped on him and they had to part them. Since that day the boy hasn't ever pulled off his clothes with a woman and says he never will again.

Many whites came to the hotel for breakfast every morning. They liked the homemade biscuits and butter. One day, when I was there, a Negro waiter carried some biscuits to a white man at a table.

He felt them and said, "God damn you nigger. Send me hot biscuits, and the next time you bring them carry the pan on a towel and not in your hand."

The waiter took the tray back and told the cook. The cook and the waiter walked around the kitchen and spit all over the biscuits. They got them wet and put them in the oven. When they were hot the waiter carried them back to the man. The white man buttered one and bit into it.

"Now these are the kind of biscuits I want from now on. Bring me these every time and we won't have any more trouble."

About three weeks before I left P.L., and had planned my definite departure, I told him that many Negroes and whites my age were being drafted. I told him I was afraid I was going to be drafted and I felt the safest thing for me would be to go back to the farm. Work on the farm was supposed to be defense work. After a day or so of talk, he agreed that anything that anyone could do to stay out of the army they should do. He asked me to come to town each weekend and see him and the family and go on outings if I had the time. The Negroes around where I worked all knew I was leaving for Detroit, but only one white person knew,

Miss Brian. I knew I could trust her. Many of the whites in the bank building began to ask how often I would be coming back to see them after going back to the farm. I felt that P.L. would have some resentment of my coming to Detroit, and to keep our relationship as it was, I felt it best to use this. The last Friday that I worked, Miss Brian went out at lunch and bought me some very nice presents. P.L. gave me twenty dollars and said he hoped to see me soon. Miss Brian winked her eyes at the statement when P.L. turned his back. When we closed in the afternoon two Negro women that worked in the building and Miss Brian were standing around me.

Miss Brian said, "I'm sorry to see you leave, but I can't blame you. I wish I was leaving tonight, going someplace up North. I don't know how I'll make it without you, and don't feel I'll ever get along working with anyone as I have with you."

It seemed that tears were about to start in her eyes when she told me goodbye. It was about three weeks before I wrote her. The colored maid told me that when she received the letter she acted like a kid who received her first toy. She ran to the office where the maid was working.

"Look what I have. I got a letter from Matthew. I will read it and come back and tell you what he says."

After P.L. didn't hear from me in a month he drove down to my father's farm. My father told him I came home to farm but that I didn't agree with farming any more. He told him I had gone to Detroit to go into defense work. P.L. said that Matthew was sure trying to keep out of the army and that he didn't blame me.

"Tell him any time he wants to come back home and to his job, it will be there waiting for him. We are still the same as we were when he left."

7.
WORK IN THE NORTH

I CAME BACK to Detroit in April, 1943, and I was never so glad for anything in my life. Wide Modden, my roommate, was working at one of the newer plants. One morning, he said for me to come to the plant because they were hiring Negroes. He hoped I'd get into the department where he was working. They had recently had a stoppage because Negroes were put in that department.

I said, "How come? Isn't there a union now?" I had seen pictures of the union when I was still in the South.

Wide said, "The union doesn't mean everything to Negroes that some people think."

There were only three Negroes in Wide's department. I asked what the jobs paid. I had the feeling all the time that I'd like to get a higher paying job. Christine and little Matthew were down South and I had to send money to them. Wide said that his job paid a dollar nine cents an hour. I asked what the best job paid and he said the best job was riveting and that it paid a dollar sixteen cents an hour. I told him I would try to get riveting. Only a few Negroes were riveting. They had gone to the company riveting school. It took three months to complete the course and they earned only sixty cents an hour while they were learning.

The employment office was practically filled. I met up with a white fellow from Tennessee who had just come to Detroit. We got in a conversation. He asked me what I was going to ask for.

I told him riveting.

He said he didn't know the names of any jobs and would ask for the same thing. He'd never been North before or in a plant. He was in the line behind me.

When I reached the desk I asked the man for riveting. He told me that there weren't any riveting jobs. He asked if I had riveted before.

I said, yes, in Mobile, on bridges and in shipyards. I was lying to him but I wanted to get the job.

He said that was an altogether different kind of riveting and that my experience wouldn't apply. If I wanted to learn he could send me to the school and they would pay me sixty cents an hour. He said he had a laboring job open, it only paid eighty-seven cents an hour but it was in the department with Wide. The man promised I might get on another job in a day or two that paid more. I accepted on that basis.

We had to sit after we were hired, until twenty-five, or so, were ready and then a girl would carry us up to the foreman. I waited for the fellow from Tennessee. When he came up he asked if I got a riveting job.

I told him, no, because I had the wrong experience.

He said they had given him a job, riveting. "And I just come in from the fields."

I asked him if he had said that he had experience or if they mentioned going to school.

He said, no.

I got kinda mad and went back to the man at the desk. He said he was busy and that he had given me the last available job.

On the job the next day, I asked the foreman where the dope room was located. They gave me a job in the dope room with Wide Modden. It was a small room sealed up very tight. The air was pumped in to the workers and then pumped out again. We glued cloth on the airplane's aileron. After several coats of different kinds of glue the aileron would be as hard as any other part of the plane. The glue had a strong, peculiar odor. There were many men and women who didn't last an hour in the dope room. The odor of the glue made the average person sick. The fumes took away our appetite. We ate only because we were supposed to eat.

The foreman was a German named Hans. I could never remember his last name. I was about the fifth Negro hired into the dope room. After that, they came in regularly from three to five each week. When they hired about twenty men they began to bring in Negro women. In two or three months, they had sixty-five Negro women. As the men were drafted to the army they were replaced by older men. As the women came in they transferred the white men out and left only Negroes. After a few months there were only about ten percent of the whites left. Four or five white women came in to repair tears and snags in the cloth covering the aileron. They hung around outside in the sewing room. The sewing room was nice. It had fans and the women had stools to sit on and they wore clothes like the office workers.

Throughout the plant they worked in teams of two. One would drive a rivet, for example, and another would buck it. All the time I was griped. In the dope room Negro women could come and be put on a team as quick with a white man as with a Negro. But you never see a white woman being teamed up with a Negro man. Only one Negro worked with a white woman. He was an Uncle Tom type and always saying, yes, mam. When a white woman talked too long with a Negro, she was transferred or else the Negro would be transferred and nothing would be said. If one of the white women had a conversation with a colored man the foreman would call her away in a few minutes. The Negroes noticed this and got very sensitive. I asked the foreman why he did this. He said that it wasn't anything he was thinking of. I told him maybe he thought we were dumb but it sure was something he was thinking of.

Bill, from Arkansas, came in three weeks after I was hired. He was a cripple, one leg was shorter than the other. When he first came in, he told us horrible stories about the refinery company where he had worked. He had gotten into trouble with the boss. The boss shot him in the leg and that was why he was crippled. At first he was very shaky and quiet at work. After awhile he asked us if we could talk back when we got in an argument with the boss. He asked me if the whites could do anything to us. I told him, no. After that he talked all the time. We called him "loud mouth Bill." If he had anything on his mind, or knew anything we had on ours, he hollered it out.

In two months the Negro women complained about the dope room. They wanted out. They asked why they couldn't get work in the sewing room. The work was more relaxing and easier. They asked the foreman if they had a chance to get in there. I wasn't acquainted with anything about the principles or program of the union. One thing I had heard was that they didn't allow discrimination if the union had a contract with the company. I didn't think the union knew what was going on in our shop. I saw the steward with his button but I didn't think our discussing was carried to the union office.

I went to the steward to ask him if the Negro women, the first six especially, had any chance to get in the sewing room.

He said he didn't think so. All the women in the sewing room were old-timers at the plant and the union went by seniority.

I told this to the women and the men. Some of them felt the steward had told me a lie. The next day three of us went to the foreman and asked him. We made a mistake, we raised the question of what the chief steward had told us and he said the steward was right. The company was hiring every day.

One night the Negro matron who cleaned up after the sewing women, rode home on the same bus with me. I asked her how long all the women had been in the sewing room. She said they were hiring two and three new women a day.

I told the women the news and they got mad. We called the steward into the dope room. All of us stood around. He said he didn't know anything about it. If we wanted to make an issue we had to get the badge number of one of the new women. He knew when he told us, that no Negro man could do it.

I got one Negro woman to find out where the matron lived. The matron brought us in the names and we made two lists and handed one to the steward. At this time he stretched his eyes. He said if they had just hired these women then the Negro women had a chance.

We went to the foreman but he said it wasn't his affair and that his job was to see that everybody worked. He said for us to take it up with the steward. We didn't know anything about union procedure. But we decided if we didn't get the six oldest women out to the sewing room in a week, all of us would walk out. We thought it would be easy to get another job because the plants were crying for workers and we felt another shop would act differently. We said we wouldn't take this crap and told the foreman that we would leave.

He said he'd work it out and called the superintendent of the department. The superintendent said he would work it out and he was sure the women would go in if we waited for a week.

We had heard of strikes, but how they were formed, or carried out, we didn't dream. Not one of us knew the difference between an authorized strike and a wildcat strike. The week came around and we started arguing again. We had a vicious argument. We didn't get production out. We collected our pails of dope, brushes and scissors, walked over, and set them down.

The steward came running up and said, "What are you doing? Go back to work."

We told him, "We want the women in the sewing room. We're not going to work."

The steward called the foreman, the foreman said the company had to get transfer slips and it was the same old story they gave us the week before.

We said, "We're not going to work."

As we walked out of the dope room three Negro men and two women yelled, "Let's go!"

All the workers in the other departments saw us walking and stopped work. "Are you going home?" they began to holler.

Work stopped completely on that floor. The plant had a fence around it with three or four guards at the gates. The guards closed the gates to keep us in. They held up their hands and said we had to stay. Other workers began milling around.

Three men came out of the main office and asked, "What's wrong? We want to settle this the right way."

Someone came up and told us that this was the plant manager. Several men came running across the street from the union hall. They went to telling us to go back.

"Wait a minute. You can't do this, it isn't authorized. Go back to work."

We insisted that we would go out, even if we had to wait until they opened the gate at lunchtime.

The plant manager called two of the women, me and Bill into the office. The union officers introduced themselves as president, and vice president and two shop committeemen. We argued for two hours before we agreed to go back to work. We agreed on the basis of time. They would take not more than one week to get the transfers. We had the word of the plant manager, the union president and the vice president. They told us they hadn't known about the situation and would have done something had they known. We didn't know, we thought they were telling the truth. We talked awhile and finally went back in the department.

Shortly after we started work, the white chief steward gave up his button and quit his job. We had put him on the spot. He claimed he had heart trouble and couldn't take the commotion. They selected a white woman. She and the committeeman came in the dope room and pinned a button on me. We had a talk, they said that I had full privilege to talk to the foreman.

"If you can't settle something, call in the chief steward. If the foreman calls the superintendent, then call the chief steward. We always try to negotiate a grievance peacefully."

I asked her about the women and she said it was all taken care of in the office. She told me the union had just signed a no-strike pledge and that we had wildcatted.

"Wearing this button means you have an obligation to the union. You have to obey union procedure."

I told her that I, personally, had no grievance, except that the women in the dope room wanted to be in the sewing room. I told her I hadn't joined the union yet.

She whispered, "Don't tell anyone. You can go over this afternoon and join. Keep the button on."

When she left, one or two Negroes said she gave me the button to stop my pushing for the women. We all said we didn't care what she or the union or the plant said. If the union took sides with the company we'd go to another shop. We weren't thinking of the union or abiding by any procedure. We didn't know what procedure meant.

Monday came, no news. At noon we asked the foreman about the transfer slips. He said they'd be sent down. We said we wouldn't work unless they were sent now. He called the superintendent and the steward. Both of them told us that there were thousands of transfer slips and that ours had gotten mixed up. We said if they weren't unmixed by the next morning, we were leaving.

The steward said, "This is a wildcat."

We said, "We're not asking anybody to come. If they work, okay, if they don't work, okay. We'll leave and go to another plant."

We huddled ourselves together. The chief steward came but we were so mad we didn't listen. She ran out. The steward yelled that I would be fired because I was wearing a union button.

Bill laughed, "That's why they gave you the button, to keep you quiet. We're going out even if you don't go."

I pulled the button off and asked if that was why they'd given it to me. I thumped it up in the air as far as I could thump it. "I'm going out. God damn it. The women should be in the sewing room."

The plant manager and another official came when we were part way up the aisle. They talked for an hour. After a long plea and threats of blackmail we went in the office. They told us there was a war going on and that we had to work. We still said we were leaving. We told them they had gone back on their word. The superintendent said they would make out new slips and within three days the women would be transferred. We accepted, all the women signed and we felt we had won a victory.

A Negro committeeman came to see us the day before the women were supposed to go out of the dope room. We didn't know him but we felt glad when he said he was a committeeman. We thought everything would be solved fairly now, because he was a Negro. The white committeeman stayed but the Negro did all the talking. The white man backed him up. He talked for half an hour telling us the transfers would be ready the next morning. But, he said, the sewing room at the larger sister plant was a better place to work, the women could go there and they would get more money. The large plant would pay fifteen cents more per hour and we had to remember a war was going on. It wouldn't last very long and we would soon be without jobs again. Every worker wanted to make money.

"You decide. It's entirely up to you. The transfers are ready and they'll be here in the morning, but I'd like to know if you wouldn't rather work in the other plant and make more money?"

The women looked at me. He saw them and turned, "Wouldn't you like to make more money, Matthew?"

I answered him, "Well, yes."

He said, "Come on give me an answer. Why not make fifteen cents an hour more?"

None of us were familiar with union politics. We accepted and the transfers came in at once.

The women went to the new plant but they were put on machines. There was no sewing room. The women got mad and drove over at noon for three days in a row. It smelled bad to us. The women drove up another day and told us there had never been a sewing room at that plant. We immediately started a group to discuss what to do. We went to the Negro committeeman and the white committeeman and told them what the women had said. They told us to meet them in the union hall. They said we could ask for transfer back but it would take a month before it went through. A few days later the women came over and said they had gotten accustomed to the work and to the women they worked with and had decided to stay.

The sewing room in that plant is still lily white. It was moved to the main plant and then to smaller plant. But there are still no Negroes in the sewing room today. The Negro committeeman is now international representative of the union. Every one of us said he was the one who caused us to be sold out. He is the one responsible for the lily white department in the plant. All of us hated him; some guys said he ought to be killed.

A week later, we were still organized. The Negro committeeman came to see me. He said, "We noticed that you asked for riveting when you applied for a job."

I said I had, but that I wouldn't go to the riveting school when it meant that I had to work for sixty cents an hour.

He said the company and the union had discussed the situation and had changed their minds. They had found that many workers who had never had training were as good, or better, at riveting as the trained ones.

"If you want that job and ten cents more pay it can be arranged."

They transferred me to riveting and I had never held an airgun in my hand before. At that time I didn't know they changed me to break up the gang we had got together.

After the first wildcat, if you want to call it that, I was invited to the union hall. I met the local's educational director, Ray. We had a long conversation and he asked me where I had learned about organization. He said I could be a real union man if I'd support the interests of the union. The union was giving a social at the Eastwood Gardens Ballroom. He asked me to sell some tickets. I took fifty and told him I would like to know what the union was all about. I sold all but ten tickets the next day. One of the Negro women asked me if it was a dance where the Negroes would dance on one side and the whites on the other. The Negro women said they had heard white women saying that they'd be dancing separate from the Negroes. I went over to find out from the union. The Negroes had bought to help the union but also to help me. They told me at the union that if any whites didn't want to dance with Negroes, that was their business. But if some wanted to, then that was their business too. They said there wouldn't be any distinction. I told Ray I wouldn't play any tricks on these people because they had a strong confidence in what I said. The union called a special meeting and about one hundred workers attended. Ray spoke:

"If whites and Negroes want to dance together at the social they will dance. And my wife will dance with whomever she chooses. Those who don't want to see this don't have to come."

I thought, there was the man, the one we should have. I went to the social and he introduced me to his wife and said if we wanted to dance to go ahead. We danced one or two dances. Some mixed couples were dancing but the majority of whites danced to themselves.

A week after the social Ray sent for me again. He asked me what I thought of the position he had taken on the social. He invited me to go with him to an outside meeting. As soon as I got to the meeting I sensed it was radical. I hadn't been around much but I felt something in the talk with which I didn't agree. They were discussing the no-strike pledge.

I had read a sign in a streetcar. A worker drew it and put it up. There was a lion and a tiger. The picture showed them meeting in the jungle and fighting each other. One picture showed them talking instead of fighting. The lion told the tiger that both of them should have their claws filed and their teeth drawn out. Then they wouldn't hurt each other. The tiger had his teeth drawn and his claws filed, the lion didn't. The next time they met, the tiger got killed. The idea was, that's what would happen if we took the no-strike pledge.

I took that position. I could see clear that we had to fight for keeping the strike. It poured into me that if we gave up the strike then we would have no teeth or claws.

At the meeting with Ray they were for the no-strike pledge. Ray tried to argue with me and finally asked what political organization I had been around. That was the first I heard about a political organization. I had heard something about the Communist Party but I didn't hear of it as a political organization. I only knew they fought for the rights of Negroes during the Depression. They went around and fought the police and put furniture back in houses where people were thrown out. I felt I joined hands with them, in my emotions, during that time. But no one told me about it being a political organization. It came out during the evening that Ray was for the Communist Party, as well as for Reuther. They couldn't get me to agree on the no-strike pledge. They didn't want my company when they couldn't beat me down.

Two days later Ray tried to convince me to give up my position and support the no-strike pledge. The lion and the tiger stayed on my mind. I couldn't agree with him. Ray finally asked me if I would run on their slate. I ran for Wayne County CIO delegate to the Convention. I was elected and I didn't even know what it was all about. I was around at the Convention, I didn't know what the hell I was there for. They were sure I was some type of radical, or political, when I pulled that off with the women about the sewing room.

I attended union meetings regularly for a year. A beef went out among the foremen. They wanted to be organized. After two weeks of beefing, they walked out on a Monday morning. That was the best time of my life in the shop. We got out production and the inspector didn't knock down half so many jobs. The workers in the plant and in the UAW all over the city would do other workers' work. Some would go home at ten o'clock with all their work finished. Workers didn't come in at all other days. A man would punch his card, and his wife's card, and she would stay home. The next day or so she would work and punch for both of them.

We organized a regular routine on the line. One would do the work and punch for the others. We had time for ourselves and no one hanging over us. Some workers didn't come in but paid other workers to punch for them. Only one guy was caught, at Ford, he was punching for six workers and they caught him with the cards in his hands.

After the first week some of the foremen came scabbing. We cursed and booed when they came around. If they came near us we all sat down. The company had to keep them in the office. When the foremen came back to work we felt they only came because they were afraid the company would see we could work better without them and they would lose their jobs. They would have to work like we did then.

At one time, a Negro committeeman, Bowen, was a militant fighter for Negroes in Ford. This was during the time Thomas and Addes were in charge of the UAW. Bowen organized four hundred union members into a separate group to settle all specifically Negro questions. I was told that the group forced the Ford plant to hire Negro women. It was one of the first plants during the war to put them on. Bowen lined up with Reuther. When Reuther came in and got complete control of the UAW's top staff, they appointed Bowen to the Fair Employment Practices Committee of the union.

The Negro group was still organized and fighting for the rights of Negroes in the plant. I was told that Reuther told Bowen that the group had to dissolve. Reuther said there shouldn't be any organization but the union. Bowen called a meeting of the four hundred and said the group was against the rules of the union constitution.

He apologized for his past work saying, "During the time I led the group I didn't know I was violating the union principles. Our problem is not a separate problem from the white brothers. We have good leadership now and this group must be dissolved."

Bowen became co-chairman with Reuther. His attitude changed completely. All international representatives are call pork-choppers. Everyone called Bowen an Uncle Tom pork-chopper. He's the worst kind of Uncle Tom for Reuther. At a union meeting recently Bowen was on the platform with the other union leaders.

One of the Negro workers pointed to them and said, "Look. All whites."

Bowen never takes a progressive position unless he is forced to in order to save his face. He's a peculiar fellow. He takes blows like a trained prize-fighter. You can call him anything and he just laughs.

Reuther says Negroes shouldn't raise any problems about Negroes as Negroes in the union. He says they should raise the questions about workers in general. This has held back Negroes in the labor movement. Bowen is on the line with Reuther on this.

The union officials say if you raise the question of Negroes in an issue, that it is discrimination in reverse. Reuther was the first to say, and Bowen backed him up, that Negroes should be on the executive board of the union only for ability and not because they are Negroes. Bowen has never tried to get a Negro on the executive board of the union. His role itself is top Negro leader in the UAW. His position seems secure there as long as Reuther is in control and as long as he can hold down the rest of the Negroes.

Two years ago the companies were hiring all whites from the South. Southern white workers were signed down there. Some companies paid the fare for them to come North. We were sore. I talked to Bowen about this many times. Negroes who had lived in the North for years lined a hundred yards long and were refused jobs at the gates. A group of us met Bowen at an FEPC meeting. The pressure was put on him so strong that he said he would meet with the UAW officers to discuss the question. He told us that the union put money aside to fight things like this and he'd see what could be done.

He said, "We should be able to spend it on this matter because it would be justifiable." Then he gave a big laugh. "But I like my job. I'm going to keep my job and I intend to look out first for my job."

Every Negro in Detroit was talking about the discrimination in hiring. There was so much pressure, the NAACP and the FEPC called a meeting. They invited one or two representatives from all the organizations who claimed to fight for Negroes. The meeting was at a local Negro hotel. There were two members from the Mayor's inter-racial committee, one from the Jewish Community Council, two from the Women's Auxiliary Council and two from the Urban League. Bowen, and a woman member of the union, were there representing the union FEPC committee. A friend of mine was known as a responsible man in the NAACP and one who always fought for the rights of Negroes in the union. Jennings, the NAACP leader, invited him. He told him these were big shots with big titles and they might kick on his being there. Jennings said they probably would, but that he would say he had invited my friend.

The meeting was called to order, and the discussion on discrimination in hiring began. As each one spoke he gave his title. They asked my friend to stand and give his name. One raised the question—What was his title?

He said, "Plain factory worker."

This struck them with amazement. It was the biggest surprise they had.

Everyone in the meeting seemed well informed and knew the discrimination was true. They couldn't understand why management would act in this way. It seemed beyond their comprehension. Bowen got up and said that before we did anything we had to be sure there was discrimination. He had only *heard* something about it. He had heard also that he had been called a porkchopper. He wanted everyone to know that he had been up some mornings at six a.m. to go stand in line at different plant gates to investigate the question of discrimination. He said every plant was hiring some Negroes. He suggested that an investigating committee be set up to do the same thing he'd been doing. They could report at the next meeting. The committee was formed of Bowen, Jennings, and one or two others. Bowen was set up as chairman.

After Bowen, this friend of mine started to talk: "I am a worker in the plant different from Bowen. I am *forced* to get up *every* morning *all the time* to go to work at six. I see Negroes lined up every day who are not hired. I have experienced it myself. Maybe they hire one, or two, in fifty but that is the complaint. We've lived here all our lives and they send South for workers instead of using us. Everyone in the city is talking about the question and that is what has caused this meeting. I don't think we need a committee. Does the president of the FEPC have the same power in the union as I understand the President of the United States had when he signed executive order 8802? I feel positive that with a stroke of the pen from Governor Williams the situation could be changed overnight."

The chairman said the speech was forceful and that the points were well taken, but that he didn't think it was up to the Governor to settle the question with a stroke of the pen. At the conclusion of the meeting the chairman said it was the best meeting they had ever had but that no record was to be kept. They didn't care to have the meeting known. He said we would meet in a week or two to hear about Bowen's investigation. There was no investigation carried out and no meetings were called.

In those days I had friends who worked with Bowen on the NAACP board. There was a committee to fight against discrimination in restaurants. Bowen said he was opposed to the committee. He wasn't opposed to fighting to break down discrimination in restaurants but he was opposed to their methods of doing it. They were following the Diggs Civil Rights Law, a state law that makes it unlawful for any public place to discriminate against anyone because of race, color or origin. The committee could never get Bowen to take part, not one time. Every progressive measure I ever saw proposed for Negroes Bowen took a reactionary position.

During the time my friends were fighting restaurant discrimination Bowen was forced to take one fair position. A group of workers came in from Chrysler and Hudson. They started to break down the restaurants around their plant. They took a restaurant owner to the police station. He said he would sign a statement that he would serve Negroes if only they wouldn't take him to court. They called Bowen to be in on the signing. The owner served Negroes for one or two days and then stopped. He said the white workers were putting pressure on him to discriminate. Some of the discriminatory remarks had come from people in the union hall itself. The committee called Bowen and said he'd better come on out. Bowen met with the local officer and called a membership meeting. The local officer had to get on the floor and say that Negroes were going into that restaurant. That anyone could stay away if he didn't like it. And that Negroes had made a fight for the union in the early days of the CIO when many of those present hadn't even been around. Anyone caught saying anything against Negroes eating in the restaurants would be brought up before the union on charges. In two weeks they were able to break down every restaurant in that area. All are freely serving Negroes today.

Many Negroes raised the question to Bowen: Why is it since the FEPC came into birth because of the feeling of the Negroes and their March on Washington, that Bowen isn't the chairman and Reuther the co-chairman? Reuther always says he feels the same as Negroes. We don't accept it. And as bad as the positions are that Bowen takes, we still think he should be the chairman.

Another auto factory in Detroit never hired Negroes on production jobs before the war. Most of the Negroes were old-timers who did nothing but sweep and other low paying laboring jobs. In every other plant Negroes had somewhat better upgrading than at this plant. During the war they couldn't get enough workers. When the government took over the plant they upgraded old-timers and gave them the same jobs as whites. The Negroes had these jobs until the war was over. Then the factory had all the workers come back to the main plant. They sent the Negroes back to their old jobs of sweeping and laboring. The union didn't do anything.

George Harding was chief steward of the janitors department. He was a small man about five feet six inches tall, with a dark brown complexion. He was a quiet talking guy who talked forcefully. When a man was attacking him he looked like he was going along with him, just let him talk but when he said something you couldn't change him for anything. He understood what Bowen had done in the early part of the war. He started to organize the Negroes in the plant and ninety percent joined him. They called a strike. If George shut his department down the whole plant was closed down. After a second or third strike when they couldn't break George they began to upgrade Negroes. George's influence was throughout the whole plant, every Negro knew him. A union meeting was called to bargain directly with George about upgrading and the discrimination against Negroes in the shop. They won and older workers on production were gradually upgraded. George pulled strikes through the FEPC committee. It wasn't the committee it was through his department, an all Negro department, but George wanted it to be legal.

He used to laugh at the Communist Party during a strike. He'd call an FEPC meeting and anything he would say would be carried. The CP would pack the meetings. George would get up and laugh: "Go get your boys. Borrow some from another plant. You'll never wreck this meeting. We'll carry through what we came out to do."

There was more difficulty with the company and George called another strike. He wanted every Negro to be upgraded according to his seniority. Some of the union leaders were fighting him. But the whites went on strike too and the plant shut down. After that they were able to crack departments where Negroes had never worked before. The company was very bitter against George and they tried to fire him. They had him offered money to quit the plant but he said he wouldn't leave; this was his fight and he would see justice done to Negro workers. The union also made all kinds of offers to him of good jobs. Many times Bowen called on him and tried to make him accept appeasement. When George took issue with Bowen it was a riot. He let him open up and talk and talk. Then George quietly told Bowen exactly what he said and tore him apart. Bowen sure hates George. That plant today has better upgrading for Negroes than any other plant. The only department where there are no Negroes is in electronics. George told me that the only Negro who knew electronics could work there. He applied for a job and the company gave him the runaround. George got busy and the company agreed to hire the man but he didn't come back to take the job.

One of the company's other plants put on a new additon. They put all new workers, just up from the South, in the new section. As soon as George found out, he pressed the company to send Negroes into this department. Three went. The day they went in, the whites stopped working. The company sent the men back to its main plant. The next morning George organized his department. He had all the highlow drivers drive up to all the entrances of the plant and lock the cars together. The drivers walked around in the plant and wouldn't move the highlows. Within half an hour everybody stopped work. The plant manager called the steward and told him to get George on the phone.

George said, "Tell him I'm working. I haven't time to talk on the phone."

They called two times. The committeeman came and asked what was the trouble.

George said he didn't know, the men had just quit working.

They told George to come to the office.

"I have no reason to go to the office."

They sent again and told him that the president of the local was there. The manager asked what was wrong.

George told him he didn't know. "Why in hell did you send for me?"

The manager said, "Go tell the drivers to remove the highlows. Tell them we're thinking of sending the three men back to work over at the new section."

George said, "If you're just thinking of it then there's no use talking to me because the reason the workers won't work is because they're thinking of it too."

The union officer started to talk and George interrupted him. "You know what's involved. Those people over there are new from the South. If you'd get off your fannies and explain to the workers, these things wouldn't happen. We blame you as strongly as we blame the company. When those guys understand what union means they're better to work with than you who've been

North a long time."

The company said they would send the three men back and for George to tell the drivers to move the highlows.

George said, "I know one of the fellows involved. When he starts to work have him call and let me know and we'll start work here." George turned to the president of the local, "If any white won't work with Negroes *you* tell them they'll be paid off and won't have a job with this company again."

George said he'd go back to work and be there when the man called. In twenty minutes one of the men called and said the work was going well and that they would be there every morning. George told the highlow drivers to move and the plant started to roll again. That was just one he pulled. That was the best strike. George had to pull several similar ones in order to get Negroes from brooms to better jobs. That factory was broken down better than any other shop in the city.

When we were fighting restaurant discrimination we carried the second owner to court. George and I were sitting up facing the prosecutor. The whites had packed the court. There had only been three or four whites in the place the night we were refused service. We had only expected to see the owner and the waitress. The owner claimed that I had called him a God-damned crippled Greek. I didn't even know he was a cripple until he said it in court. The judge asked me if this was true and I said I had never been able to tell white people by their nationality. This was the first time I knew the man was a Greek. The owner went on to say that he had seen George looking in the restaurant window the day before we went in. He knew that George would be back to make trouble. The judge asked George if this was true.

George said, "This guy acts like the CP in the union. There were four or five people in the restaurant when we went in and now he has the place packed. He also says things that just aren't so—just like the CP. I am a union man and I can bring any number of workers to tell you where I was the night I was supposed to be looking into the window of the restaurant. The night I was refused service was the first time I had been on Woodward in two months."

The restaurant owner asked for a compromise and guaranteed us he would serve Negroes in the future. We compromised making it clear that we weren't taking him to court to pay a fine;

we only wanted service. We wanted every Negro who walked into his restaurant to be served as everyone else. He agreed to this and is serving Negroes freely in his restaurant today.

These were some of my experiences with George Harding and I don't believe that anything could move that man, the management, the union bureaucrats—nobody could move him.

When the union was organized I was in the South. We talked about it all the time and talked about John L. Lewis. We thought he was the greatest man and that the union was the most wonderful thing. Even a white foreman in Memphis said that Lewis' tactics were right—"just take over the plant," and that came from a foreman. I got to feeling what the union meant, or was, when they showed the sit-down strikes in the movies. They were showing these two or three nights a week and we could see what they were doing. That made practically every Negro worker in the South feel good for months. The rich whites were saying that Lewis wanted to be President of the United States and if he came South they would kill him. For the first time I felt then that the union and John L. were okay.

I was amazed at the change when I came back to the shop in 1943. It was altogether different than it had been in 1924. The whites now could be known to Negroes. Many whites were inviting Negroes to their homes for social outings. Some active unionists would invite us to their homes or come to ours. I never saw this in the early days. In fact, I remember only once or twice that the name, union, was called in the early days. One of my foremen in 1925 called it near the phone.

He said, "We should pray that the day will never come when we see the union. It means we will be out of work and if you come in the other workers will beat and kill you."

That scared me, I didn't want to beat and I didn't like even to hear about anyone being beaten.

A Negro worker, who had roomed with me, spoke to me about the sit-downs. This was when I first came back from the South. He explained what the union meant. And he told me how many whites he now knew personally since the sit-downs. Before that, in fifteen years, he hadn't had any friendly relations with whites. I understood what he was saying better after I got in the plant. I felt, for awhile, that the North was getting to understand us. I had some doubts of course.

In the dope room one white and I would discuss the Negro and white situation. He pointed out how he liked Negroes. He was glad of the union and glad that we worked together. He wanted me to tell him about the problems in the South. Finally we had a big discussion. There were Negroes moving into one section of a white area.

He said, "Matthew, I like Negroes as well as anybody but I think they should stay in their own backyard."

We'd be eating together and were very close. I said, "As long as we stay on Hastings Street it's all right with you. If we stay in dumps over there, on one side, you like us."

From that time he broke relations with me. He never had much to say from then on.

Many of the Southern white workers put on a job with Negroes will accept Negroes much better than the Northern workers. To the point that a Southern worker accepts, he says it, and to the point that he doesn't accept, he says that too. But Northerners and hillbillies who have been taught by old-timers here are what we fear the most. The Northerners talk frankly about certain things but we always hear them going behind instigating racial hate.

A white Southerner, if he gets over his racial hate, is more accepted by Negroes. You hear many Negroes, I've heard a hundred if I've heard one, say they like a white Southerner in the North. (In the South we say, "The only good white man is in there" and point to the cemetery.) Many will say, "Bilbo is my friend." He says this in a way that practically any Negro understands. We understand Bilbo, Bilbo understands us. We understand where he stands on all questions. There is no doubt. But where the Northern white stands—he doesn't stand where he says he stands.

A Negro friend of mine said to a Trotskyite politician, "I tell you frankly, I'd rather go in Bilbo's back door than come in your front door."

The Trotskyite was very upset and asked why the man said what he did.

I told him, "You've done something. You don't stand where you say you stand. You tell him come in the front and the man doesn't believe you. He feels you hate to see him come. He feels you don't accept him as anyone else coming in your front door.

Bilbo is ready for him to come in the back and accept him coming in the back door freely. Bilbo would say to him openly, 'I don't want you to come in my front door.'"

We see white workers come in from the South. They are prejudiced to the core. You can tell because they won't say anything. They'll walk away. If one wants to talk, then he'll talk on anything, the woman question, prejudice or anything. If he's purged, he's purged. No phony business. If he gets in a department with Northerners and they're loud in their prejudice he gets to operate like them. Even then sometimes he'll come back and tell you what these guys said.

I had an experience with two Southerners not long ago. Three white women were brought on the line. Two were from the South and hadn't been North very long. When I first went to tell them how to work they resented it and turned their shoulders. I left them, until the foreman added extra work on one woman. I told her she didn't have to do it, let the job go by. She said in a vague way, "All right." I went away.

The foreman came back and told her, "You let a job go by, do it."

She started to try and I went back and said, "Let it go by. Do what you *can* do."

The foreman started back and said she had to do every job. She called me back and said she couldn't work so fast. I told her not to do every job. The foreman came again and asked her if she could do it: She said she didn't know and he came to me and said, "I thought you said she *couldn't* do every job." She kept trying and finally got tired.

A Southern white fellow, from Tennessee, went to her and asked, "Why in the damn hell don't you do what the steward told you? You just don't want to because he's a Negro. If you holler about how you're tired, and he isn't able to get the things regulated for you, you'll say he's no good. And the foreman adding extra on you, he'll add extra on us. And we're damn sure not going to do it."

I didn't say anything more until noon. We all eat together. She asked me if she had done anything wrong. If she was wrong she was sorry. She didn't know about unionism. I told her I was trying to save her and that the company could put on someone else to do the extra work. But if she did it once they would figure that she could always do it and that would help the company. She asked me how to keep from doing every job. I said for her to work awhile and then call the foreman and tell him she couldn't keep up. She carried this out and the foreman came over to her. She called me and we forced the company to put on a helper. The next morning she came in very friendly. She had told her husband, also from the South, and he had cursed her. He told her to "Take the advice of the steward. He's right regardless of the foreman."

On my line we had been sitting separate when we ate. Some of the men and three new women sat off to one side. I ordered some extra benches and arranged them so that we'd all be around together. I asked one Negro worker to sit at one end where the women would sit. I sat in the middle of the same bench so that we would have to be sitting together. After we'd arranged everything they came in and began to eat. Now we sit and eat and talk just like one big family. No one notices anything. The women come to talk and whisper jokes in our ears in front of the white men. The Negroes do the same to both men and women. I felt if there was any feeling, especially with those from the South, that they were accepting us better than anyone had since I'd been in the plant. We all talk of our personal problems, or any other problems. We decide things together. It was discussed sincerely about white men and Negro women, and Negro men and white women. It was the only job I ever worked on that was so free.

When the women were laid off recently they got every telephone number on the line. One white woman came up and said, "I'm not sorry about being laid off but I'll miss everybody and the relations we built up in five months. I feel closer to everybody here than I have to anyone in my life before."

We teach the Southerners about the union and the problems of the union. Some will accept a Negro unionist much quicker than they will a white unionist. A white hillbilly—I don't like the expression, "hillbilly"—a white Southerner said he wouldn't join the union. The men and the chief steward said they would walk him out. The men were getting rough. They asked me to talk to him. They were all crowding around telling him they were going to walk him out.

I said, "Wait a minute." As soon as I spoke, the man looked at me and relaxed. I asked him his name and what was involved. Another worker said, "He's a Goddamn scab. Damn it, if he works here without joining."

I said, "Tell me the other side."

He began telling me, but the men wouldn't leave him alone.

I said, "Leave him alone for a minute, I want to talk to him." I went to explaining what the union meant to me and to the other men. I told him how it was before we had the union. I said you could be fired for nothing. You had to smile at the foreman. You had to give them part of your paycheck each week. You had to bring them something from the store. I said we didn't have to do that any more. "You don't want to protect your own interests, that's why the guys are sore."

He said if they had talked to him like I had he'd have joined sooner. He joined after work the same day.

Soon after Reuther gained control, a fight between a white worker and a Negro worker broke out. The Negro worker pushed bodies around in a department which was ninety percent Negro. There was a broken pane in the window above the worker and the wind was blowing in. The white worker, an inspector, could move any place, but the Negro had to go to the hot oven and push the bodies down the line. He would perspire and catch cold from the wind. He put a cardboard in the broken window. Every time he came back the cardboard was gone. The white inspector had taken it out.

The Negro worker said, "I'd like to leave the cardboard in the window because I'm catching cold."

The inspector said, "That's too bad because I'm catching fresh air."

They began to argue: the white man called the Negro a son of a bitch and the Negro hit him and broke his glasses. The Negro worker was paid off. The white man was off the next day getting his glasses repaired. The Negroes swore that if he came back, and the Negro didn't come, but was still fired, they would walk out. When the inspector returned to work the Negroes shut the plant down.

A department meeting was called. They had the Negro and the white man sitting on the platform with the union officer and a Negro chief steward. Every Negro was boiling mad. They had the fired Negro speak first. He said that he had gotten too mad. He was sorry and felt it could have been avoided. He shouldn't have fought the inspector and if he could meet him tomorrow he would shake hands. He said he would wait until the union could get him back.

The union had told him to say he'd wait so that the workers would go back to their jobs. Many times the union tells the fired man that he will get back right away if he gets the workers to go back and stay on the job. Many times he doesn't get back to work at all. After two or three weeks the issue is not hot and the workers are not so mad. They'd come out every day though, if the union didn't promise that the worker would come back to work. But if the fired man says it's okay, the men stay on the job.

After the Negro worker spoke, the inspector got up. He amazed me, he said he would shake hands if everyone would go back and not shut the plant down. If they didn't go back he wouldn't beg the Negro's pardon and he wouldn't shake his hand.

A very angry worker got up to speak. He ripped into the union officer and the Negro steward, "They'd sell their own mothers down the river for their own individual selves. In the beginning, we felt the company was instigating the strike. We weren't sure, but on the day both men were off, everyone was saying if they brought one back, and not the other, we'd walk. We said we would fight for *either* man. But since the white man has said we should start rolling for the company, before he will shake hands, then we see the company is in on it, and therefore, the union is in on it too. I never thought I'd see the day that a union brother would tell us to support the company before he would shake hands with a union brother or worried about his getting fired. We're not striking against you. We're striking against the company for firing one and not the other, when both were guilty. We won't make you any promise to get you to shake a brother's hand."

The president of the local, in a mild tone, told the white brother that he was wrong. He shouldn't have said he wouldn't shake hands with the Negro brother. The white brother retracted his statement and said that he would shake hands. He said he wished the men would go back to work and give the union a chance to get the brother back to work. The men went back to work swearing that if the brother didn't get his job, they would walk again. He isn't back today. Every time the workers start agitating about it the committeeman runs in to say that the man will be back in a week.

8.
DETROIT RIOTS 1943

THE DETROIT RIOT broke out in June 1943, on a Sunday afternoon. The riot actually broke out two weeks before, in the Eastwood Amusement Park on Gratiot and Eight Mile Road. Both Negroes and whites attended the park but Negroes were not admitted to the swimming pool. Some jitterbug kids had been drafted and were going into the army in a week. At the park, they were talking among themselves:

"Why can't we swim in the pool with whites if we're going to fight a war and die with them?"

They pulled off their clothes and got in the pool. The manager and some other whites, rushed out and a big fight started. The police force came and closed off the area. They turned the streetcars back and sent away all the cars of people. The fight was quelled.

The following Sunday I was visiting Mrs. Gordon. One of her grandsons was telling about the fight. He said they were going to go swimming at Eastwood and that they would swim in any pool. They had to go to the war and they were going to accept their equality before going, and not after, when they might all be dead. He told me that there was going to be a big race riot in the city soon. The tension was for it and it wouldn't be long in coming.

I talked to Mrs. Gordon until about eleven o'clock, and then went on home. I lived on Harper Street and as I was going to bed I heard two women raising hell across the street; they were very loud. I looked out the window. There seemed to be some men holding them apart. I listened for three minutes to see what was involved but I couldn't hear anything except cursing, and, "turn me loose." I went to sleep with them still shouting. About three o'clock in the morning I heard a lot of shooting, cars running fast and glass breaking. First thing I said, in my mind, was that those two women had started all those men out there to fighting. I tried to sleep but I kept hearing the shots, the horns blowing and loud talking.

I shared a room with Wide Modden, a very religious man. He was a deacon. Just as I dozed back to sleep he ran in, jerked the covers off, "Get up. Get up at once. Get in the streets, there's a big race riot going on. Some white man just threw a Negro woman and her baby off the Belle Isle Bridge into the river." He said several Negroes and many whites had been shot and killed. "They just killed one white down on the corner."

All the time he was talking he was getting his shotgun out of the closet and putting in shells. I was pretty frightened. All I asked was if anyone had saved the woman and baby.

He said he didn't know, he didn't think they had been found yet. "Get up, man. What in hell you waiting for?"

He spoke in a vicious tone, put the shotgun on his arm and headed for the door. I got to the door and heard some more shots; there were bullets whistling. I didn't have a gun. I thought I'd make a target for someone to shoot, so I turned around and went back to bed.

The next morning I was up early and went out on the front porch. An old man, who lived in the house, was sitting by the steps breaking up bricks.

I asked him what he was doing.

He said he was going to use the bricks in the riot.

I kinda smiled and told him they wouldn't be much good in a riot.

He said, "Never mind, David killed Goliath with a rock. These bricks will come in handy."

The street was so crowded with Negroes that you couldn't see the sidewalk. Everyone was quiet, but every store that was white-owned, in that block, was completely smashed. Many things were in the street, groceries, druggist equipment, dry goods, everything. Nobody was touching the stuff.

With everything so quiet I thought the riot was all over. I went to one man and asked him about going to work.

He said, "You can go if you want to, I'm going to stay here. The Oakland streetcar isn't running but you could catch the Russell bus."

I caught the Russell bus to the crosstown and went to the plant. Many Negroes were missing. It looked as if all the white workers were there. There was no tension in the plant between Negroes and whites. Mainly, the Negroes got in groups themselves and talked about the riot. About eleven o'clock the company began to put up notices in the department telling the workers which route to take home and which streetcars were running.

On the streetcar that evening, there were very few Negroes. When the car got to Mount Elliott and Forest it was supposed to turn left, but instead, it went out Mount Elliott.

I yelled at the conductor asking him where he was going. He said he was going to the West side and asked where I wanted to go.

"You won't get there on this car. There is a race riot going on and we can't cross Hastings at all."

He rang the emergency bell and stopped the car. He said he didn't know how I would get home but he gave me a transfer to the Gratiot car. When I got off at Hastings there seemed to be more Negroes on the street than in the morning. I spoke to one or two people, saying that I thought the riot was about over.

"Hell, no, man, we're just beginning."

They told me about someone they knew who was shot and killed. They told about this white, or that one, who killed some Negro. One told about a friend of his who was an ex-prize fighter. The police were beating his sister and he rushed up, knocked one of the police down, took away his revolver and killed two policemen. Two other policemen came up and shot the fighter in the head. The blood was very fresh on the sidewalk.

Another man told how the city wouldn't send a wagon out for three or four hours to pick up the dead Negroes. They just let them lie in the street.

I walked up Vernor Highway and saw one of my company trucks coming through. The Negroes blocked the street and in only a minute the windows were torn out and the driver beaten up. After the riot the driver laughed about how lucky he had been that he was only beaten. He said he never would have come through there, but he hadn't heard about the riot.

Halfway home I was talking with some other workers in front of a store. The store hadn't been harmed. About eight young Negroes came up, walking very close together. They looked at the store and one began to curse all the others as if he was the leader.

"How in hell did you miss this store? Who put that mark on it?"

One seemed to be the second leader and he tried to make some friendly excuse. He said the mark was accidental.

I was looking as hard as I could to see the mark but I couldn't see anything.

The boys grabbed the protection bars on the window and started rocking back and forth. Two white police were only ten or fifteen feet away but they only watched and didn't move or say anything. In less than three minutes the bars were down. In less than one half minute every piece of glass was smashed in front of the door. The boys went inside and began to throw things into the street.

Two Negro police appeared from somewhere and jumped in behind the boys. We could hear the police yell at the boys to quit. They began to fire shots inside the store. Almost at once, five hundred Negroes were in front of the store. The two white police were still standing about fifteen feet away.

I said to a worker beside me: "Man, isn't it a damn shame these white police are not saying anything and the Negro police are in the store shooting the Negroes?"

After at least fifteen shots, the police and the young Negroes walked out of the store. No one had been shot. The two leaders seemed to be arguing with the police. I was as much surprised as I ever was in my life.

I said to the worker, "What is this? What's really going on?"

When they got to the sidewalk one Negro policeman said, "You know we weren't trying to shoot you. I wouldn't shoot one of you for nothing in this world, unless you should try to overpower me and take my gun. But I sure hate to have you wreck this store. We were assigned to this block and it would have been nice for our record if you hadn't smashed the store."

All the Negroes and the young leaders shouted and they picked up the police on their shoulders like some football players who had just won a game. They were glad that they said they wouldn't shoot. The two white policemen walked into the center of the street, and with the loud noise of appreciation for the Negro police it was hard to hear anything. One cop made a shot into the crowd and stuck his gun back in his pocket real quick. They turned around and went back to where they had been standing. I saw a Negro man walk away from the crowd and go toward the alley.

I said to the man next to me, "Those must be blanks they're shooting."

"Blanks, hell, man, look around their belts and you can see those bullets are lead."

"That's lead in their belts but those must have been blanks in their guns because one of them shot into the crowd and nobody fell or hollered. How could he have missed when he was only ten feet away?"

As we walked down the block a woman rushed out to us and said, "Come help. A man just got shot, he's lying on my steps asking for water."

We ran to her house. The man asked me to open his shirt. He was shot in his navel and asked for water. The man with me went back and told the young Negro boys. In less than two minutes the majority of the crowd was around the shot Negro.

Several Negroes began telling the police: "You sons of bitches. I thought you wouldn't do it. I thought you were on our side."

The police shouted, "Please let us talk, we didn't do it. We didn't do it."

I recognized the man who had been shot. He was the one who had walked away toward the alley after the white police fired into the crowd. I yelled as loud as I could: "They didn't do it."

The two white police had come up and were standing ten feet away. I pointed out the policemen to the young Negroes. By the time I left my hand down they had the police on the ground. A riot squad came that very moment. Fifteen police were on top of the wagon with sawed off shotguns. They pointed them at us and began to fire. I didn't see how I could keep from being hit. In a few seconds I was out. I thought I was killed. I began to move like I was trying to wake up from a very bad dream. I seemed like I had been lying on the ground for hours. I opened my eyes and got on my hands and knees. My eyes filled with water and my nose was burning like fire. There were Negroes lying all around me trying to get up. The police were still there with their guns pointed at us.

"Get up and get home. Every one of you sons of bitches—before we shoot you with bullets."

Then I said to myself, they shot us with tear gas. As we moved away, I was staggering. I started home. A block down the street some bricks came from an upstairs window and landed on a scout car, hitting one policeman on the head. The other jumped out and threw a tear gas bomb through the window.

At Hastings and Forest, two white women came through in a car. The Negroes had a way of letting cars in and closing up both ends of the street. They couldn't pass and they couldn't go back. They let the women in and stopped the car. They pulled them out like police, real rough, and pulled their dresses straight up over their heads, and whipped them for five minutes.

They shouted, "They whip our women—we'll whip theirs."

The women screamed something awful. I'm positive that they didn't know there was a race riot.

As I went toward home I saw two kids sitting in a park. A white man came through the park and they got up and walked towards him. One of the boys seemed to know him and the other boy didn't. One boy tried to tell his buddy to let the man go. His buddy knocked the man down and beat him in the face. The white man pulled a gun and killed the boy who was trying to protect him. His buddy tried to help his friend and the white man ran away. A man across the street fired, and followed him around the next block. Ten Negroes came back, walking slow, and said they had killed the white man. The pal of the dead boy just sat by his body. He sat on the stone with the body until the wagon came to pick it up. After the wagon took the boy's body his pal continued to sit on the stone and didn't move.

We got news that Woodward was blocked off. The people said when night fell they were going over and wipe out all the whites and wreck the stores in the white neighborhood. State troopers had begun to arrive that day. The first thing they did was to pass a curfew law. Everyone had to be off the streets at eight o'clock. The troopers were as bad as the police. They were beating and cursing and killing Negroes.

The landlady where I lived lost her keys out on Hastings. She asked me to go with her for them. We got across the park, on Hastings, and saw a carload of state troopers. They got out and pointed their guns at our heads.

"God damn, it's two minutes after eight. Why aren't you in the house?"

We explained that we couldn't get into the house without the keys we had lost.

"Get in your house, we don't care what is lost."

The boy whose pal had been killed was still sitting on the stone. The troopers asked him, "Don't you know that it is after eight?"

"I don't care what time it is."

The boy didn't look at them when he answered and he didn't move. A trooper placed a gun at his head. He still didn't move or look around. One trooper snatched him up.

The boy began to curse, "God dammit, go ahead, shoot. No one is scaring me."

Three or four troopers rushed up. One took his feet and the others his head and dragged him to the house.

The fighting continued the next day. It was said that a leading Negro detective had shot and killed several police for shooting into a crowd of Negro women. Wires and messages from Negroes in Chicago were received saying that Detroit Negroes didn't know how to fight a race riot. They said they would be over that night to show us. Two or three truckloads of Negro G.I.'s stationed at Battle Creek, Michigan, broke away with a truck of guns and ammunition and headed for Detroit. They were stopped by the police who blocked the road, ten or fifteen miles before the entrance of the city.

It was organized among us that in the community, half of us would work one day, and part stay home, during the riot. Three carloads of workers came by my home and said they were going to work. I got in the car and one of the men asked if I had a pistol. I said mine was left down South.

He said, "Man, you're sure going to need it now."

Some whites on Mount Elliot had got after one of the men the night before. He said he wouldn't be driving as fast today, as yesterday. His father, and some other men, were coming to the plant during the day to slip some weapons into the car for us to have on the way home that evening. We had the guns that night. When we reached Hastings we saw machine guns sitting on every truck. The army troopers had come in. It was said there were two or three army tanks downtown. The Negroes said that all the white troopers were hillbillies.

"Why weren't there some Negro soldiers?" was the question everybody asked. "Why aren't these guys overseas fighting Hitler?"

We felt we'd have a better chance with Negro soldiers. They

wouldn't shoot us as quick as white soldiers would. The armed trucks were parading all around our houses. If we just broke a stick these guys would jump with their guns.

I went down to the Y.M.C.A. with a worker from my department. One of his friends was walking in the door of the building and the troopers cursed a Negro. He looked around, stuck up his hand and said, "Heil Hitler." They shot him through the back as he went in the door.

At Brush and Vernor Highway a Negro killed a policeman. A riot car came with machine guns and set them up across from the building where he was hiding. They machine gunned the building from one end to the other. The building housed one hundred and fifty Negroes.

The afternoon after the hotel was shot up, the man I worked with told me to go to a certain real estate dealer. Someone had told him I could shoot a gun very well. He said they were trying to get as many guns and bullets as they could into the hands of good marksmen. Wednesday, I went down and got one of the guns.

The city officials thought the riot would be over in a couple of days. They Negroes said when the troopers left they would start the riot again. There wasn't a store from Hastings to Grand Boulevard that wasn't completely smashed. Most of them were set afire. Many of the white business places on Oakland, north of the Boulevard, were wrecked too. From Russell to John R. Negroes took charge. The whites who lived in the Negro neighborhood weren't bothered at all. They sat in front of their houses and watched what was going on. A friend of mine, from Alabama, had his mother-in-law visiting. She was a mulatto and very white. She was mistaken for white and killed. She hadn't lived in the neighborhood long enough for them to know her. There was an albino Negro living above me. He started out one morning and the police rushed to him thinking he was white. They asked him where he was going.

When he told them they said, "Hell, you can't go there. Where do you live?"

They asked him what he was doing living in a Negro neighborhood. "If you know what's good for you you'll go in the house. The niggers will kill you sure as they see you."

"I'm a Negro myself. I'm not worried, everybody knows me."

The police were so amazed they stood and looked at him for

five minutes. Then they drove away hurriedly, without saying anything. Nothing happened to the albino Negro. He lives in the neighborhood now.

The Negroes were kinda sympathetic to the Jewish businesses. They didn't want to kill the Jews. They just wanted to wreck their stores because they were robbing Negroes. Jews weren't active in oppressing Negroes. (The Negro people in the South put the Jewish people in a different category because they were not part of the lynch mobs and were not part of the police force. If a difference arose between a Negro and a Jewish person to the point of a fight we were not expecting a lynch mob to come to our home or for a Jewish man to act in the same way as the rest of the whites.) During the riots some people would say, "I don't give a darn if I beat the hell out of a Jew, but I don't want to kill them. They're not in on everything. There aren't very many on the police force. But they deserve a beating because they've been robbing us too."

All during the riot the story went around about the woman and the baby that were thrown in the river. My chief steward, a hillbilly, asked me what I thought about the riot. He asked me if it was the fascists that caused it. Did the Germans plant people to start the riot?

I said, "Hell, no. Some of them Goddamned hillbillies from down South started the whole thing."

He looked real sad about my statement, "I don't know, I'm from down South."

He felt pretty bad. At first I was sorry for speaking so sharp, I had forgotten he was a hillbilly. But I thought, hell, he knows how they treat us down there.

Everyone, everywhere I went, was asking who and what had started the riot. No one seemed to know. The riot seemed to spring up everywhere at once. The riots seemed like a dream to me. I was wondering if this was the way death felt. All the time I felt like I was tipping on thin ice and any minute I would fall through. I saw all the police passing and I'd see a group breaking up a store and the police would leave them alone. A little further on, another group would do the same and the police would shoot into the crowd and go away laughing. I was wondering if this was like the war. What struck me was how grim all the Negroes were. I've known my people all my life and when anyone would die they would moan and cry. The expression everybody carried on their face was forceful, solid and firm. All during the riots there wasn't one tear—except for one time.

I'd say, "It's a riot, it's true. Why is it nobody seems to be bothered about it? How is it they're not nervous, or crying, when they tell about their brother or mother getting shot up?"

One time I got to a crowd and some people were crying. Two policemen had just killed a little kid and his body was still lying in the store. An older woman had told the child to go in and throw some stuff out of the store. The police came and the kid ran and hid behind the icebox. He lay down, scared, on his face. The police shot him through the back as he lay there. That kinda got me too. If I had had my gun I would have shot every police I could see. After the crowd told me the story, and I could see the little kid lying there, I really got mad. I got a pistol that night. I was with them then.

There were mounted police everywhere. Everyone had to walk in the middle of the street because the pavement was so crowded. There were threats from the whites that they would burn us out. We decided we wouldn't wait for them to burn our families and our neighborhood. Every one of us went down and laid on John R.

We said, "We won't wait. We'll make the battle-line at Woodward." Half an hour after that, the state troopers came and went to shooting in on us and we went home.

Some of the white businessmen tried to go back to their stores when the riot was over and many were killed. There was a drugstore on the corner of Hastings and Henrie Streets. When they opened up they lasted one week and were killed. The store was closed up and later sold to a Negro. Places where Negroes could never get jobs opened up with Negroes running them. The owners didn't ever come around.

9.
THE LEFT WING CAUCUS OF THE UAW

AT THE LAST election held in our shop, I was working with a Negro group. I helped to write some of the platform. In it we said we must do something about the discrimination against old men, Negro women and Negro men. I was at the union hall passing out the slate to get support for our group. One of the union representatives was there, Bob Simone. He used to say he understood Negroes. He was a Frenchman and he said he opposed discrimination.

"I'm French, and you know the French are against discrimination." He said this in the early days but he turned out to be just another opportunist. While I was passing out the slate, he and a Negro Reutherite, and a couple of other guys came over.

The Negro said, "Matthew, this is going to hurt you."

"Yes? You mean the word, Negro?"

"Yes, it should always be left off."

"From what I know about Negro history, that word has been hurting us for three hundred years in this country. I wasn't the first to write the word. Since I can remember, it has been hurting me. But as long as nobody is willing to say anything about it, it will go on hurting Negroes. Bob Simone told you to oppose the word. That's why you're doing it and I'd like to hear *your* answer."

Eight or ten Negroes standing around said, "That's the truth. That's what they need to be told, Matthew." Several of the Negroes standing with Simone ducked their heads and disappeared into the crowd.

Simone told me half a dozen times, "If you work with us you'll be the leading Negro of the Reuther caucus in this local."

In the Reuther caucus I learned how the trade union leaders operate with Negroes. In the caucus, there were seven or eight active Negroes. But the union would have only three posts open for Negroes out of a possible fifteen. These three positions were the lowest: guide, trustee and one shop committeeman. The shop committeeman is a higher post than the first two. These three posts *had to be filled* by Negroes. The union had to show the Negroes and everybody else that there was no discrimination. In eight years of the UAW in my local, only one Negro had ever gotten to be shop committeeman.

Before the election slate would be formulated, and the names would come out, the leaders would have meetings to decide what Negroes they would put up. The nominating committee of the caucus prepared the slate to the broad caucus. There were one or two Negroes on the nominating committee but the whites settled who were going to run and which Negroes would be put up. The Negro members never knew until the names were put out at the meeting who was to run even though they were supposed to help decide.

Before a meeting the union bureaucrats would take three Negroes into a corner and tell them the three positions were for them. Another leading white would do the same with three other Negroes. In every corner of the hall, there would be this type of group. All the Negroes in the caucus would be told, "We're pushing for you for these positions. If only some of those fellows don't try to cut you out. If those Negroes wouldn't be out for themselves and would vote for you, you would win."

This would start a hostility among the Negroes before the slate even came out. The Negroes wouldn't support each other, they voted for the Negro running on the opposing slate. The whites often don't vote for Negroes or else vote very lightly. There is also open discrimination. A white leader will go up and say, "This is so and so, this is so and so, this is a *colored* guy so and so."

I met Albert Jeffers and Sherman Deeds and several other Negroes in the left wing caucus. I had heard their names called many times as leading Negroes in the opposition caucus at the plant, but I hadn't met them. We discussed union politics on an every day basis until the election rolled around. The Communists were going to put up Albert and two other Negroes. Another white was going to put up three Negroes for the other caucus. I got the floor and made a rough speech about what was going on. Jeffers and Deeds were pleased and said that I should have been in the left wing caucus long ago.

Deeds and Jeffers, and every leading Negro in the caucus got together for a meeting. We were disturbed about what was happening in the left wing caucus. It was going the same way as the Reuther caucus. During the meeting I pointed out how they had us cornered. I told them I noticed very carefully that the Negro members of the nominating committee didn't know who the Negro was to be and that the whites always knew. I felt if we were working in a caucus, and if they wanted us, we should know who was to run. I suggested that we decide among ourselves who we wanted.

I said, "Let's ask, why *these* posts and no others? Let's tell them who we want and which posts. We're liable to see a big reaction from the whites."

We agreed who was to run. If the committee wouldn't accept our proposal then we wouldn't accept any of the posts they had to fill.

When we presented our names to the nominating committee, it was a hell of a thing. They had picked Deeds to run for guide.

I said, "We think Deeds should be shop committeeman."

Deeds said, "Yeah."

You should have seen the look on their faces: "We were thinking of someone else."

The caucuses always pick the weakest negro they can. They put everything in his mouth and he carries it out. Our proposal caused a row, but they had to go along or we wouldn't have supported the slate.

The Communists got very mad with us. When the slate was proposed to the board caucus and they accepted it, the Commies called a meeting in the plant after work. They threatened to pull out of the caucus if the union leaders didn't support the people they had planned to run. The morning after their meeting the chairman of the bargaining committee, a Reutherite, asked me if I thought our names would appear on the slate. I said they would. He bet me five dollars that the names we had chosen would be removed. I put up five, but he wouldn't take the bet.

He said, "I don't want to steal your money. The Commie boys had a meeting last night. They called the leader of the caucus and had the slate changed."

I got sore and phoned the leader of the caucus and asked why I hadn't been called to the meeting.

He said it had all happened too quick to call me. (The meeting had been held fifty feet from where I had been working.) He said there would be another meeting on Sunday.

Some of us got together and we agreed that all of us were pledged to abide by caucus discipline, if the decisions were democratic. Nothing could have been more democratic than the last meeting. Now we had to have a special meeting. We knew that the CP would pack the caucus and change the slate. We decided we wouldn't accept the change. If they insisted we would walk out of the caucus. At the meeting the Commies had put so much pressure on the leaders of the caucus that some of the bureaucrats got up and let it out that they wanted the slate changed. If it was not changed they said they *couldn't* go along with the slate.

Deeds got the floor. He told them, "We'll abide by any decision that is democratic but when certain cliques maneuver to change the decision of the caucus then we will walk out."

This put the house in an uproar. The Communists had packed the meeting with Commie members. Another meeting had to be held.

At the third meeting, twenty percent were Negroes. We declined every position. We nominated Deeds for vice president of the local. It was the first time a Negro was put up for that post in the local. Many rank-and-file whites were disturbed at the action of the CP in the caucus and voted with us. Deeds lost by only five votes to a white man who had helped to organize the caucus in the early days. I was nominated for bargaining committee and Albert for recording secretary. We got beat by a close margin. It was so close, it scared the caucus leaders to bits.

We told them we were declining all positions they offered and were walking out for many reasons. But that the main reason was that we were going to see a Negro elected to the bargaining committee. We said we would support a Reutherite Negro and if we walked out they couldn't put any Negro up for the left wing caucus. The caucus was torn to pieces.

We met and discussed with the Negro on Reuther's slate. He was elected. We haven't worked for either of the caucuses since that time. The left wing caucus since then, hasn't been able to get a Negro with enough support to defeat the man on the Reuther caucus. We exposed all the union tactics, both right and left, on the question of Negroes.

10.
JED CARTER, THE FOREMAN

EIGHTEEN OR TWENTY of us worked on operation number sixty-eight, a job in building autos. We worked with one foreman we'd broken in. We ran the job just as we saw fit and worked forty or forty-five minutes each hour. We'd get production ahead and then sit down to talk or rest or kid around. We never worked more than forty-five minutes out of an hour, and sometimes, only thirty-five. One of the women in our group went with the foreman on the fourth floor, Jed Carter. He would sit and eat with her and come to our floor during the day. He could see how we were working. Our foreman stayed away and never said anything to us but Jed couldn't stand the way we took time off. We didn't know until later how much he had it in for us.

They moved us to the fourth flooor and Jed became our foreman. Under him were about fifteen white workers and one Negro worker before we moved up there. He used the Negro as a brown-noser to tell him things. In his department I was made lead-off man. I worked at the head of the line and my operation fed the others. We worked for two days before Jed got rough with us.

He called me into his office and said, "You're to work as I say. Remember you're not working for Fred anymore. You work on the hour, and don't stop until I say so. Go on out and tell the boys." He handed me the union rule book.

I said, "I've been in the plant for six years. There is nothing in the rule book which says a worker has to tell another worker what to do. If you want them to know something you tell them yourself. I'm not telling them anything."

This made him mad. He just stared at me.

The men on my line asked me what he had said. I told them and the brown-noser told us that Jed had been a guard over Negro prisoners in Ohio. This offended us and we told the brown-noser to tell Jed he was not working prisoners. We were human beings and we would teach him pretty soon. There were eight

Negroes and about twelve whites and we all felt the same resentment.

Jed started in on some of the others but he wanted to get me because I was lead-off man. We got in a bad argument in a few days but the boys came around to pitch in for me and it cooled off.

One morning I was going up the steps to the restroom when the whistle blew. Jed and his woman friend, May, were walking up the steps. I was one and a half minutes late.

He asked, "Why aren't you working?"

I said that I punched down on the third floor at six fifty-nine and if I *had* been in my place when the whistle blew, I wouldn't be working because the stock man hadn't brought my stock.

Jed said for me to get my own stock and to go to work. He wanted to see me working one minute after the whistle blew.

I told him I wouldn't get stock because I was supposed to have stock by my machine. After I said this, the chairman of the shop committee walked by. I could see madness on his face but when I asked him if I had to get my own stock he said, no, not if they usually had a stock man.

The stock man brought the stock but Jed went to the office and gave me a warning slip. Three warning slips and you are fired if the company wishes it. I refused to sign the warning slip. That started the argument again.

The chief steward called the bargaining committeeman back again and they got the slip from Jed. They went to the superintendent's office and got it torn up. They settled on the terms that I was to go for stock if the stock wasn't there. I could knock off the time in my work. This was no good; it left me only five minutes out of the hour instead of fifteen or twenty.

Shortly after this fight, the company wanted overtime of one hour. Everyone of us was mad and we felt this was our chance to get at Jed. We went home at the end of eight hours. The contract says we must work eight hours a day and forty hours a week. There is nothing in the contract to force us to work longer than that. We went home for three days and Jed was getting mad and sick.

After three days the plant couldn't work overtime. One department can stop the plant. We had a little production ahead but when it ran out no one in the plant could work. Other big corporations were calling for parts. This focused all the blame on Jed because he couldn't make us work overtime.

One Negro in our group wouldn't go home with us the first day. The second afternoon we had a talk with him. We said that if we stuck together then what Jed pulled on one he pulled on all. We said that if he scabbed on us we wouldn't do anything to help him. He went with us that night. The next morning Jed told him to go to work and not to talk to us. The fellow said he would go to work when he was ready. Jed told him to come to the office of the superintendent. The fellow started to go with Jed because he didn't know anything about union procedure.

I called out, "Where are you going?"

"To the office with Jed."

"You sure aren't going to the office without union representation?"

Jed said, "What the hell do you have to do with it?"

"I have plenty to do with it when you're trying to fire a union brother without representation."

The young Negro turned and said, "I don't have to go?"

"Hell, no, not unless the steward or the committeeman is with you."

Jed got furious and said, "I'll fire him anyway."

He got the superintendent and the assistant superintendent and a pay-off slip. Some of the boys went down the line and told the men to stop working and to come up and see what was going on. I went to a white line steward and asked him if he would help a brother from being fired. He said he would come down. The chief steward went to find the bargaining committee but he didn't come back. I went to the next department and told the men to come get a drink of water at our place and mill around and point at the worker. When the superintendent saw all the workers, he came over and asked me what was wrong.

I told him I didn't know, that I was still working. I said, maybe you can tell all these workers milling around what is wrong.

He asked me why I wasn't working overtime.

I told him that we didn't feel like it and that we wouldn't work overtime for the foreman we had. (Jed had been telling the white workers that they were afraid to work overtime because the Negroes had said they would beat their asses if they did. He told the Negro workers that they were following the Communist white workers out who wouldn't work overtime. We told the whites and they told us. They got madder than we did.)

The superintendent said that if we would say we would work overtime he would tear up the pay-off slip of the Negro worker.

We told him: "We don't want to make you do anything. And if the worker goes out we go with him."

The superintendent said, "We only want to know what the trouble is. We don't know what is wrong."

I asked him why he came out with a pay-off slip then, if he didn't know.

He took me aside and asked me to tell him what it was all about.

I said I would, if he let all the men listen. I asked the white men, "What did Jed tell you?" I asked the Negroes, "What did Jed tell you?"

The workers told and all hell broke loose. The men shouted they didn't want to work with Jed any more. They'd better move him out.

At another plant we had heard that the workers wanted to throw some Communists out of the windows. Many times we had discussed this. We thought there might be something to it, the workers might have been Communists. But we had decided that the workers probably had a foreman like Jed who started the lies. We told the superintendent what we thought and that Jed had started all the trouble. He was ready to lie to the point of bloodshed. Some workers in our shop might have gotten angry enough to throw other workers out the window. The workers were cursing Jed and calling him a fascist foreman.

They said, "If anyone goes out the window it will be Jed."

The superintendent begged us to talk low so the other departments wouldn't hear. He called Jed over. We lit into Jed like he wasn't a human being. We said he had been showing off to his woman friend how he could boss us around. We said that we had put out production while he made love in a corner. Jed accused me of threatening to phone his wife and tell her about his affair with May.

I said, "I thought she *was* your wife. This is the first time I know you aren't married to her. I thought a woman wouldn't go with anyone like you unless she was married to you."

The superintendent said this was the worst situation they had ever had in the plant.

All the workers were screaming, "Move Jed."

The superintendent said, "We tore up the pay-off slip. Let Jed stay a day or two longer." He asked to talk to me alone. He said, you know what it means to move a foreman. He said he wouldn't mind it, but if they moved Jed because all of us in our department said to move him they wouldn't be able to run production. "Every worker will want to move his foreman."

I said production would be better if we could *remove* all foremen.

He looked at me. Finally, he said he would make an agreement. Jed would work with his mouth sealed like a tomb. He wouldn't say one word to the workers unless they asked him a question. If he said anything the workers could come into the office and they would move him.

I told him I didn't know what the other workers would say. They would be the ones to decide.

The superintendent told Jed, in front of everyone, that he wasn't to say one word, or he would be moved.

Jed dropped his head and said, "Matthew is the one who made up these things and they aren't true."

A worker yelled, "They are true, be quiet, we're the boss now."

Jed's eyes were full of water just ready to burst out. His friend, May, hid in a corner and wasn't looking around. We went back to work laughing. We'd had a lot of fun. All the other foremen came around singing "Nature Boy" at Jed because we had exposed his love affair. Jed cried, and with tears running down his face, begged one foreman not to sing it any more. He went home four straight days without punching out. He was that nearly insane.

The victory was told to the bargaining committee the next day. We ran the job just like we wanted to. We played games and did the work and had a good time for two weeks. Jed didn't open his mouth.

In two weeks a man from the bargaining committee came to tell me they had discussed me at union headquarters and said I wasn't on the committee. I had no right to take up any grievance or go into the office. If anything happened I was to call the committeeman. If I was caught going into the office again I'd be fired by the union. I had had a fight a few days before this meeting with the committeeman, with the union. The company laid off a man and a woman for horseplay and said it was a three day suspension. The company brought the man back and fired the woman. We had a Negro group going and talked to the woman to see what we could do to help her get her job. A Negro stooge carried the news back to the union that I was carrying the lead and the union was mad with me any way for talking against Reuther in the shop.

Jed heard what the union said to me. It was the happiest news he had. He began giving us a hard time. We gave him a hard time, all day we were calling for the bargaining committee and calling names. Jed gave me another warning slip. I called the committee man. He laughed and said this was something good. He said I'd been walking all over the shop talking against the Reuther slate and they wanted me pinned to the job. He said they had me now.

I asked him what the consequences would be and if I could go into the office with them.

He said, no. The committee took Jed into the office with them. They tore up the slip but they agreed I had to stay beside Jed the whole eight hours except for the half hour at lunch. Anytime I was going anywhere, I was to tell Jed and get his permission. If I had to go to the toilet I had to ask his permission first. This made all the workers mad. The three women were as mad as anything. They asked me what I was going to do and I said I didn't know yet. One white woman asked me if it was true that I had to ask permission to go to the men's room. She said it was the damndest thing she had even heard. No one ever had to ask if they could go to the lavatory unless they were handcuffed.

For two days I asked Jed when I had to go to the men's room. The third day he was showing a new white woman an operation and didn't answer me. I got some distance away and he yelled, "Where do you think you are going?"

I shouted, "To take a piss!"

He stared at me, just looking. When I came back he said I knew better than to talk that way when he was standing by a woman. I told him he had asked me deliberately and that I thought I was doing what I was supposed to do.

A week later a worker from another floor came up to see me. He said he saw Jed in the front office talking and having a time with the foreman. It would be safe for me to go to the men's room. I walked toward the office figuring this was the way I could get behind in production and fix Jed. I sat behind some piled up stock watching Jed through the office glass. A foreman started out so I got up and walked in. I'd been off work for a half hour.

I said, "Jed, what are you doing? I've been looking for you all over. I had to go, and I sure got to go now."

Jed asked me why I came to the office.

I told him that I had a family to support and that the company had told me to stay with him. I wasn't going to take a chance on getting fired.

One of the foremen asked what it was all about.

I told Jed I hadn't got out any production for an hour looking for him.

At this the superintendent jumped up from his desk and said, "What? No production for an hour!"

"Not a piece. I've been looking for Jed. I can't go to the toilet unless I tell him first. I wish you'd tell him to come out and tell me I can go. I'll have to hold myself together until I can get in the restroom."

Jed told me to go ahead and from then on not to look for him.

All the workers were looking for me. They thought Jed had carried me to the office and paid me off without their knowledge. Two workers were in the door as I started out. They said they'd been looking for me for an hour. They couldn't work without my operation. The three of us stayed in the lavatory ten minutes. That left twenty minutes of the hour. We got out one-half of production. The superintendent came out of his office as mad as hell. I told him I was only doing what the union had said, and if they wanted to give me a written statement, that I could go to the men's room without asking the foreman I would accept it.

They wrote it out but they tried to pass it off in the letter that they had only been teasing when they had sent the ruling to me by the shop committeeman.

A couple of weeks later the model of production changed. The company tried to set the speed higher than before. On the line we started riding the jobs past. One worker would follow his job and push the next worker out and the next would do the same all down the line. We had a new white Southerner working with us. He was the only one to stay in his spot.

I bumped him and whispered, "Ride it."
He said, "What do you mean?"
I told him.
Jed rushed over and said, "I've got you now, Matthew. What did he say to you?"
The worker said, "He didn't say anything to me. I said something to him."
Jed asked him what he had said.
The fellow said, "I asked him what this other worker would say if I kept standing on his feet."
Jed asked, "What did Matthew say to you?"
The worker said, "Matthew told me he didn't know, but if it was him, he'd knock me off."
Jed rushed to the office and got all the superintendents and all the foremen to stand around to watch all afternoon. When they left he tried to make me do two jobs. I said I wasn't going to do it. The super came and asked me if I had told Jed I wouldn't do the job. I started to tell him about the jobs and he said that was all detail and he wasn't interested in detail. He only wanted to know if I had said that I *wouldn't* do the job. I told him that I hadn't said it.

He said, "It's a good thing, because it would be your last chance. You know union procedure, you can't refuse to work."

Although I had the most seniority, Jed transferred me to the hardest job on the line. I put in a grievance and kept the committeeman busy until they put me back. Jed was so mad that I was back, that he kept me around all afternoon and wouldn't put me to work. He finally figured out a job for me. It was too much for two men to do.

I called the committeman and told him I couldn't do the job, and if he could get any one who could do it, I'd like to see it.

The fight took place in the super's office. The super wanted to transfer me to another department.

I said that I liked my job, but that Jed hated me and that he hated all Negroes. The superintendent, Jed, and the chief steward were there.

Jed told me, yes, he hated Negroes, "What are you going to do about it?"

I asked the chief steward if he had heard what Jed had said.
He said, yes, in a troubled voice.

After work that night I called a Negro committeeman, Morton. He was the only Negro committeeman at that time. I told him Jed had been speaking to me but that he said he hated all Negroes. I told him that the reason I had called him, was because he was a Negro too and I knew the white bargaining committeeman would cover it up. We had charges against Jed because the steward had heard him too.

Morton came on the job the next morning with another white committeeman, a member of the Association of Catholic Trade Unionists. Morton hadn't told the white man what was involved. They called the chief steward and the bargaining committeeman and asked what remark Jed had made the day before.

The steward said he didn't remember clearly and to ask Matthew.

I said I had told Morton already and that he was trying to check the story to see if it was true.

The steward said, "I think Jed said that he hates Negroes."

Morton said, "What did you say and do at that time? You know what the union stands for and doesn't stand for."

The steward said he had been so intent on saving my job that he hadn't wanted to press it.

The white committeeman with Morton said, "Morton, I thought we came up to fight a speed-up on this line. That's the most serious problem, that we are faced with today."

I said, "It is a serious problem, this problem of Jed hating Negroes. It isn't serious for two whites. But it's as important to us as any other problem in the shop."

They called Jed over and asked him what he had said about hating Negroes. He said he didn't remember anything. He asked the steward, sort of surprised, "Did I say that?"

The steward dropped his head, and said, sadly, "Yes, Jed."

Jed burst out, "If I said it, Matthew made me say it. He's worried me nearly crazy. I can't think when I go home about anything but him. He posed the question so that he forced me to say it."

I said, "Jed, for a long time I thought our fight was a question of production but now I know that it is personal. What gate do you go out? We'll settle this personal question right now. Instead of bringing you up on charges we'll settle it between us."

Jed said, "It isn't personal, it isn't personal" and rushed away.

The Reutherite Negro didn't think we could bring a foreman up on charges. He would tell me in a day or two. He said he felt the foreman would say that I had asked the question—do you hate Negroes?—and Jed would claim that he hadn't understood the question. I reported the incident to several Negro leaders who got mad. When I raised the question of an all-out fight they were so tied to the Reuther machine they said they'd better not. They covered themselves saying that the foreman would maneuver out of the situation.

From that day until we transferred out of his department Jed and I got along the way we should. He tells workers now, that I nearly drove him crazy. He says that his health has not been so good from the time he started fooling with me.

Everyone hated May, Jed's woman friend. Lincoln, a Negro worker got drunk and said he was going to annoy her. He went to her and in a very superior way, as if he were very important, asked her to go out for a turkey dinner with him. She ran to Jed and Jed sent Lincoln home and said he would be fired. The workers, both white and Negro, were mad. They said, "That whore, why didn't she say, no, thank you, or come to us instead of running to the foreman." She heard the talk and drew up like a mouse and stayed quiet after that.

One day she asked me what I thought about white and Negroes mixing. She said she was opposed to it.

I told her it wasn't a question of being for it or against it, that it was an international question. I told her the Pittsburgh *Courier* was packed with pictures of European Negro babies. I said, "They teach us the English are superior people. They're supposed to be blue-bloods. England is full of babies from mixed couples. You say, where do I stand and that you oppose it. That won't stop it."

Another time she asked me where I stood on attacks.

I didn't know what she meant. I said, "I'm opposed to any attacks if they're not justified."

She just looked at me, "I mean these attacks such as Negroes attacking white women. Like catching them at night and attacking them."

I said, "Well, if you're talking about rapists, I'm opposed to raping. Anyone would oppose it. But what you want me to say is that I oppose Negro men attacking white women. I'm opposed to any man attacking any woman. In your mind every Negro will attack a white woman. You don't see George Washington Carver in science, you don't see Roland Hayes in singing, you don't see Joe Louis in boxing, you don't see Jesse Owens in running, or Satchel Paige in baseball, to you they are just black men who want to attack white women.

"If a white man attacks a white woman the papers say a certain individual, but if it is a Negro they throw a cover and make out that this is what every Negro does, or wants to do."

She took a deep breath, "What do you think about what Lincoln said to me?"

"If you didn't want to go to dinner with him, all you had to do was to say, no."

She said, "You were mad at me."

"Didn't you notice that every white worker was mad with you too?"

"I thought you were mad and had made the other workers say they were mad."

"Now you're making out your race to be ignorant."

That ended our conversation. Now she smiles real broad when she sees me and walks up to start a conversation. When she first came into the shop she wouldn't talk to any of us.

11.
SOUTH WITH MY SON

FOUR YEARS AGO, in 1948, I bought little Matthew Jr., my son, an air rifle. He always wanted to copy me. He practiced shooting in the backyard for a year and could shoot very well. I promised to take him to the South with me for two weeks hunting, and in 1949 I bought him a shot-gun.

We left Detroit a couple of nights before Christmas. Many people were going South and the train was full. We were late in leaving and ran very slow to Toledo. The conductor was trying to pacify everyone because we were so late. We were afraid we would miss our connecting trains. By the time we reached Ohio the people were cursing, and almost threatening. The conductor said he would call ahead and have the trains held up. About one hundred Negroes got off in Cincinnati to take the train to the deep South—Nashville, Birmingham and Mobile. We ran into the station but the red cap told us that our train had just pulled out. Everyone cursed. Many people hadn't enough money to stay over until the next day. The crowd got so loud the red cap said that if a group of us went to the station master they could run a special for us. There were many whites in the group also. The red cap whispered low to me and two others. I called the crowd and all of us went together. The station master fixed up a special train in fifteen minutes.

The train was full with the Negroes in the segregated coaches. There were two coaches for Negroes and eight for whites. There were twice as many Negroes as whites. When we got on, the Negro porter called the conditions to the attention of the conductor. He said we needed at least three extra coaches.

The conductor said there was not time to get them and he'd wait until Nashville.

The porter said that they might have trouble because it was Christmas and there would be some drinking.

We had to sit in the baggage car, on the floor, and on our bags or stand in the aisle. I took Matthew as far to the back as I could so that we'd have a little free standing room. Several young Negro fellows from Ohio came back with us. They were going to the deep South, Birmingham, Alabama.

I asked one of the young Ohio fellows to come with me for a sandwich. My purpose was to look at the white coaches. They were practically empty. There were men with their feet stretched out on empty seats, women with two seats and a child lying on the extra seat. I pointed it out to the fellow with me. I said it was a damn shame that we were packed like calves in a truck. We couldn't even squeeze by to go to the restroom. It took the porter thirty minutes to walk through the coach. The Ohio boys were sore. There was a fellow from Birmingham ready to do anything. I suggested that we sit on our luggage, and on the floor, and fill up the aisle. We were adjoining a white coach and the conductor would want to get through our car to take care of the whites. In ten minutes the porter came and asked to be let through. We said we couldn't move and that we wouldn't move. There was nowhere for us to go. Women and babies were sitting on the floor and we sure weren't going to take a chance of stepping on them. It was their fault, they had crowded us up like cattle.

The porter reported the conditions to the conductor. When the porter came back he said, "Let me through."

We yelled, "How are you going to get through? Nobody better step on me. If you'd put the car on we wouldn't be causing all this trouble."

The conductor came in and said that he had to go through to the white coaches to call the stations and take tickets.

We said, "You'll have to get a helicopter or jump out of the train to the next car. Damn it, if we move for anyone."

The Negro cook came to the door at one end and wanted to call for dinner. We told him he couldn't come through, we wouldn't move but that one of us would call for him in the Negro coach. I suggested to one of the young fellows that he go through the Negro coaches saying that since it was Christmas they were serving a free dinner in the diner. All the Negro passengers got up and came to our coach. I pointed out to the conductor how much money the railroad was losing. All these people wanted to spend their money in the diner and they were unable to get through our car.

He said, "But what can I do?"

I told him that the other cars were half-full and why couldn't we sit in them.

He said, "I don't own this train or make the rules. You know the law."

Several whites who could hear what was going on were nodding their heads and appeared to be saying that we should have seats. Of course, there were some people with resentful faces.

The conductor was so sore he cursed the man from Birmingham.

The man answered back, "No cursing and no killing. If you want to fight you're sure looking for it."

The conductor turned on him quickly.

My young son said, "We've got two guns in the rack overhead."

The man from Birmingham said, "Get them."

Young Matthew jumped to get them. I stopped him and said we were not to that point yet. We pressed for the Negro women and babies to sit in the white coach. One of the Ohio Negroes was calling names and saying that we didn't mind trouble if we had to ride like animals. The conductor closed and locked the door into the white coaches. He soon came back and opened the door. He called the young Negro from Ohio and me, and took us into the next coach which was empty.

He said, "Since you're the ones making so much trouble, I found a coach for you, and since you're the ringleaders I want to be sure that you get seats."

I said that the women and babies should have the seats. He walked to the other end and said they could sit in the next coach. He had emptied two coaches.

The Ohio boy said, "They finally picked up two coaches for us on the fly."

We sent the news through the coaches. Every Negro had a seat within two hours out of Louisville.

12.
IN THE PLANT

EVERY TIME THE COMPANY changes the production model they have to change everything in the plant. They change the line, the guns—both quantity and type—and try to get out production with less men. They always fail. The workers at my plant never get out the production they could get out.

The job I do sits on a jig. The operation had always been turned toward us. We used four guns, sometimes five, on our line. We were running a hundred and twenty-five jobs an hour, with eight men doing the work. The foreman, the superintendent, and the engineer came around with blueprints and changed the model. They put the operation bottom side up, put different clamps on, and set it up for two hundred and thirty-five jobs an hour with eighteen men. They put on twelve guns and the engineer came to show each man how to use his gun in a particular way on the new model. We tried the engineer's way of using the guns for two days and the best we could get was fifty jobs an hour. We were fed up, each of us decided to do the job his own way. We started figuring it out for each other.

"You try your gun there."

"This is what your gun should weld. You try your gun over here."

"What about trying it this way?"

We found that only two of the guns were sitting correctly in order to weld the job as the engineer had shown us. After we found the best way to work, the superintendent and the engineer came back down. The superintendent could only ask questions—he didn't know anything. The engineer didn't say anything. They decided to let us work as we wanted.

The superintendent and the foreman began to yell every day. "You'll have to get the jobs up. We're set for two hundred thirty-five an hour."

I was the line steward and we all said he was talking crazy. How could we ever run two hundred and thirty-five?

One worker told the foreman, "The way you completely messed up this line and the job, we're lucky to do it at all."

After a week of continuous arguing and fighting they gave us two more men and we ran one hundred and fifty jobs an hour. We were yelling for a time study. The company has been so beaten by us that they won't send a time study man at the beginning of a new job. The union doesn't do anything about this. The company sends a time study after we work the job for a month or so. If they'd time it at the start then in a month we'd be used to the work and able to do the job in twenty to twenty-five minutes. The company would lose forty minutes. They try to threaten us by turning the line up by degrees.

The superintendent kept trying to get us up to two hundred and thirty-five. We held to one hundred fifty and one hundred seventy-five. The superintendent called us into his office for a talk. We knew if the time study man came now the job would be timed two thirty-five. We said if he would agree to settle for two hundred, and if they wouldn't have the time study later, we would try to do two hundred. We also told the superintendent that if he fired the two new men we would go back to one-fifty. He agreed. We called the union rep and tried to get it in writing but we couldn't. The next day we ran two hundred with the same number of men. The day after, we ran the job so we could have fifteen minutes off every hour.

Before the job changed we completed the operation and put it in a box for shipping. Now the way the engineer had it fixed, the back piece had to be put in separately, and the operation went to another line to another group of workers. It takes all these extra men to complete the one operation we did before.

Every time there is a new job they have to hire men, even though they are always trying to cut down. The more they make the machine able to do the work without the men, the more men they have to put on to get out production. The time for repairing our guns has also increased. On the old job there were only five or six guns and the repairman could keep them in condition. With so many new guns they had to hire an extra repairman. As long as we are mad at the set-up one of us can keep one gun out of order all the time. The pressure in the shop is so great that we would rather work very fast and then get a little time off to rest or sit and talk. But if they make us work without any time off then we wreck a gun and take a few minutes while it is being repaired. This happens all through the shop. Many times the guns could be easily repaired. A worker sees his gun going bad. He has no interest in saving it so he'll let it go completely wrong and burn clear up before calling the repairman. Many times we know what is wrong and if we feel good we repair it ourselves. The workers puts things in their guns or break them on purpose. A white worker was fired for this not long ago. Every time he got mad he would take his knife and cut the rubber hose. He would put something on it to make it look as if it had burst. This happened twice every day. The company got the foreman to hide and watch what was happening. He saw the worker cutting the hose and paid him off.

Everytime a repairman comes he has to ask us what's wrong. If the worker won't tell him he has to spend twenty minutes just finding out what is wrong. If the worker feels all right, and sees the repairman coming, he gives him a sign. He spits like water pouring from his mouth, that means the hose is broken. Or he holds two fingers together and that means the welding points are burned out. The signs save the repairman from going over and then having to go back to get what is needed for repairs. If the workers are real mad they will jam up the line by putting something in it or jimmying some part. The repairmen won't be able to find out what is wrong. After a rest, one of us will fix it and the line rolls again.

Every worker cheats on the company whatever the production that is set. The last half hour before quitting we can run a job two-thirds as fast as usual. The company never gets full production. Each month the foreman has to report if and why his department didn't get out production. If the sheet turned in shows a clear record then the job is counted out. Every foreman in the shop is supposed to have some set standard production. They catch hell on jobs that are short. No one can check where the job went or what happened. The foreman is afraid sometimes to make the worker mad with him. He may pick on a new worker but he's afraid of the group. We'll screw him up in production and he'll get it in the neck from management if he bothers us too much.

Our group is very friendly on the line. Usually three or four are close buddies. If a guy gets transferred, even to the end of the floor, it's like a family moving to another town. He comes around for a week but slowly stops coming. He finds another buddy on his job and it is like you never knew each other.

Two white workers and myself are very close, we eat together every day. Another group of two white men and one Negro eat on the bench across from us. Negroes never sit just to themselves. On our line we're all mixed up unless a hot issue involving Negroes comes up. It has to be something very serious if we're not all eating together. Then we eat with our buddy but we may go in a corner to speak alone. If there is a large percentage of Negroes in a department you see Negroes eating together because there aren't any whites. On the grinding line where there are only five percent whites there is a little separation.

We have one or two segregated departments at this plant. Maintainers, and tool and die, and crane operators are all white. The company has one hundred and one reasons for keeping Negroes out. The union, too, has one hundred and one reasons. There is one Negro in the carpentry shop and one Negro truck driver. The truck driver is a mulatto. When he was hired the company thought he was white. He kept his mouth shut until he got seniority of one and a half years. Then he told. The truck drivers had a stoppage but the union was on the spot. They blamed the strike on workers throwing cardboard boxes at the truck drivers in order to cover up. One official said it would wreck the union if the man lost his job. He said he'd looked it up and the man had a good job record.

13.
CHRISTINE IN THE PLANT

Christine also got work in a factory in Detroit. Her experiences are similar to mine. Here is her own story of her work.

I HAD BEEN working in Detroit three weeks when I went to work at Chevrolet. It was during the war and they were hiring women. When the employment man asked if I could run a machine I said, yes. I was thinking of a sewing machine. They put me in to work on a drill press. Then man who taught me the operation became a foreman the week after I got there. I worked so easy, he would carry me to whatever department he was transferred. My next job was with Dale, sure enough. He was foreman of my department. Milling became my regular job, grinding and running the screw mill. I got a dollar twenty-one an hour. I stayed there two years, until VJ day.

I worked with five white men. They were real friends, all but one who worked the drill press. You couldn't make him cut down on production, he always ran over. He made me work real hard. He'd run so fast he couldn't agree with anybody. I couldn't keep up. We'd all get together and try to stop him. The other men would try to make him slow down.

I'd tell him, "You're not getting any more than anybody else."

He was from Tennessee. He wanted me to look up to him and do what he said. He didn't like Negroes and no one liked him.

One man from St. Louis was real nice to us. He'd do anything we asked. If I asked for a relief man he'd come help until the relief man would get there. He wouldn't try to boss us around.

One day the man from Tennessee told me, "Go over and run me a small pinion."

I said that it wasn't my job.

He said he'd tell Dale, the foreman. Dale said I didn't have to do a job that wasn't mine.

Then the man told Dale I didn't cut right and Dale put a new cutter on my machine just to keep him quiet. He acted like that just because he was an old Southerner. There wasn't anything wrong with my cutting.

A colored girl was grinding with this man on one side of the machine with her. They had some trouble and the foreman asked what was wrong.

Eve said she was doing what she always did.

The man from Tennessee said, "These old colored girls want to do what they are told."

Eve got a piece of iron and was going to hit him. She was going to whip him and I sure wanted to see her do it because he was so mean. They moved him the next day. He wanted to be a foreman anyhow but he didn't get to be.

I always ate with a woman named Frances. I taught her how to work a drill press. They moved her to the back but we always met for lunch. We're friends today. Another woman from Montgomery, Daisy, ate with us too. All the white women sat with the white men. They were always mixed with the men and didn't eat with us. The white women had the light work. In the plant there were only a few colored people. Chevrolet was just prejudiced, no colored worked at Fisher Bodies until 1942. Chevrolet was the only plant that laid off the women, all the women, white and colored, on VJ day.

After getting laid off from Chevrolet I looked for another job. One time I went to Chrysler in a freezing day. They had a man sitting at the door of the employment office. I asked him if they needed help.

He said, "We don't need any." They he looked at me again and said, "Not for *you*."

The white women were just going in. The next time I saw an ad in the paper I didn't go to the Jefferson plant, I went to Highland Park. At Highland Park there were half men and half women in the line. The women were closer to the door. They must have gotten up earlier and gone out. They told all the women to come in the basement. They asked if any of us had worked there before. Three colored women raised their hands. The men looked and then said they didn't need any women. He was going to hire the white women but with the colored there, and experienced, he had to say there were no jobs. Three women backed off in a corner and stayed after we left. They were white. They came to the bus stop with application blanks. The next day they brought ten white women into the section where my friend was working.

Matthew's cousin went for a job at Matthew's plant. They gave everyone an application blank but they told her she would have to get hers at another of the company's plants. They did it to discourage her. She went out to the other plant, a long distance from her home, just to spite them. She wanted to see if they would hire her or what they would say when she came back.

I told her, "Girl, they just don't want us. There ain't no sense in going."

A month later, the company came out saying that the reason they didn't hire colored women was because colored women didn't apply for work.

I hopped on a bus right away and went out there.

They said, no, I couldn't have an application blank.

A white woman could go out there today and get hired, but not me. I'd like to be back in the plant because I get lonesome staying home by myself. I could be out there talking and working and everything.

I like it up North and I wouldn't go home to stay. But I don't like the Northerners. The white people that come from the South get better than the people up here. A Southerner, if he changes will sit back and talk to you about anything and he won't say, nigger, any more. They really change, they treat us better. You never see a Northerner going with a colored woman. Northerners are two-faced. They don't want to think anything good of a Negro. Colored women don't get mad if a Negro man and a white woman marry or go together. But a white man gets mad, especially a Northerner. I don't believe any colored woman gets mad at a Negro man, but a Negro man gets mad when a white man goes with a Negro woman. It's the men who get mad. A Negro man won't care as much if she still will go with a Negro, he'll say, "See? She still likes colored best."

One day a friend of mine was on her way to the employment office. A white man in a car drove up and asked her to ride with him.

She told him, no.

He asked her if she was afraid he would do something to her. She still said, no.

He said, "Look, I'll give you this car if you'll come with me. My wife has a Pontiac and you can have this Plymouth."

My friend just had to ask him where he was born.
He told her in Lansing, Michigan.
She was sure surprised. "You mean to tell me you're not a Southerner?"
He wanted to know why she was asking.
She said she never heard of a Northerner asking a colored woman to go with him.
He said, "I just like you. I've been noticing you for quite awhile."
She told him, "Men up North just don't talk to colored women the way that you talk."

14.
UAW

TODAY WAS THE fifth time this year that the Council meeting had to be called off because they didn't get a quorum of fifty-five people. This is the General Council of our local union, UAW, a union of seventeen thousand members with nine hundred members in the Council. I've been on the Council four consecutive years. We have adjourned more meetings this year than in all the previous years put together. Two months ago the union leaders blamed the poor attendance on the bus strike. Fifty percent of the members have cars and this is the second meeting to be adjourned since the end of the bus strike. Every chief steward is a member of the Council. The steward on my line hasn't attended a meeting in two years.

There was a big change in the union from 1943, when I first went in, to the present day. We used to hold our meetings in the auditorium of Cass Tech, a big high school. We had to hurry to get there. There were as many workers standing outside trying to get in as were inside at the meeting. There was a free and democratic setup. Any member could bring a grievance to the membership as a whole. Now, if any worker, white or Negro, tries to bring up a grievance at a membership meeting, the union officers tell him, "There are four of us at the union hall all the time. Come down and discuss it with us."

If we go down to see the union officers, as they tell us to, they either put us off or give us the business.

In the early days there was rarely a meeting that didn't mention something about our Negro brothers and sisters. There was a discussion around this at every meeting. Many Negro women were working in the plants then. Many of today's union leaders would discuss shop problems and issues that face our Negro brothers with the membership as a whole taking part. We used to go to listen to the other guys. We would always come away with something from these meetings. Now, there is no such thing as our union leader bringing a problem facing our Negro brothers and sisters before the members as a whole to be discussed.

I'm not saying this change was made the same day or the same year Reuther got control of the UAW. The powerful machine was not organized the same day or year. But since Reuther came in, if there is an issue raised by Negroes, as Negroes, we are told by the union leaders that this is the most damaging thing we can do to ourselves. They say don't raise the question of Negroes. The first two years a Negro woman, Alice Phillips, was on the Reuther staff her picture appeared in the Negro press every month at least, but it has not appeared this year.

During the UAW convention held in Cleveland, Ohio, a Negro delegate told me that many Negroes were assigned to leading white hotels. In some cases, a white worker put in for the room. But when his roommate, a Negro worker, would come in, the hotel clerks would stop him. They would ask the Negroes to leave. The UAW had a housing committee and they would send a Negro international representative to talk to the Negroes about a place to stay. The international rep would take them to his room.

He would say, "We're going to straighten this thing out. Have a drink?"

He would keep pushing the whiskey at them until they were drunk. When they were drunk, the rep would say that they had found rooms for them in a Negro hotel.

He'd say, "You see, we're good to you. We always do our best. If you will just stay at this place tonight, then tomorrow we'll really fight this thing out."

The next day the Negroes would ask for a meeting with the housing committee. The committee would be tied up all day. The day after they would be told the same thing. The committee was always busy. This would go on until the end of the convention when it didn't matter any longer. Every time a Negro brought up an issue along the lines of discrimination he would be sent to the Negro international rep. The rep would calm him with whiskey. All the reps had eight to ten quarts of liquor in their room at every convention. They also had women for the men. All of this is at the expense of the dues paid by the workers. Some delegates did not go to more than one session during the whole convention.

In Dodge, during a strike, union functionaries gave the Negro workers the run around about where to go for picket duties. At lunch time they sent Negroes upstairs to eat and left the downstairs for the white unionists.

A white worker asked a union official: "What if the Negroes make trouble at having to eat upstairs?"

The official pulled a black jack out of his pocket and said, "If they give any trouble I got something to handle them with."

A friend of mine worked in the kitchen. She told me than when Negroes came to be served she was told, "Watch those pork chops with the niggers when they come in. Just give them one chop. Let them come back if they want any more. You can give two chops to the white guys."

George Addes, ex-secretary-treasurer of the UAW opened a beer garden over on Gratiot. The Negro unionists say that Negroes can't go in to be served.

I was told by one of the ex-officers of our local that at the local's anniversary party the union hired Negroes to serve. They had the most Uncle Tom kind of Negro they could get. It was just like the South. The whites danced and talked to themselves. There was no mixed dancing.

Three years ago the lunch wagon owned by an outside chain company, brought food into the plants to sell to the workers at lunch time. They raised the price of their food after a few weeks. The workers felt this was too much to pay and put up a holler so the union decided to boycott all the lunch wagons. The stewards were to see to it that no one bought anything. The first day no one came near the wagon. The second day five Negroes went to the wagon and began getting food.

The white chief steward yelled and said, "Put down that damn stuff."

The Negroes looked around, very angry, and continued to pick up food.

The steward rushed to me and said, "What I say about your people is true, they won't cooperate. Go over and see if you can stop them."

I went over and before I could speak one said, "Matthew, we want to cooperate but yesterday we went outside and the restaurant where we can eat was packed. There was a long line waiting and half of us didn't get anything to eat. We were so hungry in the afternoon we had to check out early. We just couldn't make the day without eating. All the whites ate because they can go in any restaurant. We can't bring lunch because we don't have wives to fix them."

All the restaurants around the plant are jim crowed, there are only three places where Negroes can eat, and there are about three thousand Negroes working on my shift. I went to the white chief steward and told him the story.

I said, "If you can get some white workers tomorrow, I will get some Negro workers and we can go out and break these restaurants discriminating around the plant. We will see that the restaurants serve all of our union members. I will stand guard every day after that and guarantee that no one will buy off of this wagon."

This stunned him. He said he couldn't do it. He would have to take it up with our union officers and that would take some time. The Negro fellows continued to eat from the wagon and pretty soon all the workers came back to eat there too. The lunch wagon kept selling at a high price which hurt both Negro and white workers.

The Negro weekly newspapers in Detroit, carried an article on the 1949 UAW convention held in Milwaukee, Wisconsin. The articles said that a Negro delegate from St. Louis, Missouri, got the floor and called Reuther's attention to the discrimination that was being carried out in his plant, Local 25. He pointed out an agreement between the union and the company that Negroes would receive less wages for doing the same work as whites. Reuther replied that this agreement was negotiated by the former left wing leadership.

The Negro delegate said, "But after four years of right wing leadership this still exists and you did not answer my question."

A week or two after the article appeared, a friend of mine was visiting here from St. Louis. He works in the same plant as the man who spoke to Reuther. He told me that it is a General Motors plant. Reuther has been the top negotiator for General Motors for years. He also felt very sure that this was the home local of Livingstone, one of the UAW vice presidents. He told me the company would hire a Negro as quickly as a white; there were no complaints about discrimination in hiring. When the company wanted to speed-up, they put pressure on the whites first and said, "If you don't want to do it, we can get Negroes to do it for fifteen cents less an hour."

He felt sure this kept hostility between Negroes and whites. This hurt the white workers as much as the Negroes.

Sure, Reuther is always mentioning the Negroes in his big speeches. I heard him speak at an NAACP meeting this year, attacking America about the way Negroes are treated here. He said, "In America we can talk about our atomic bomb that can split this earth asunder—we can talk about the Iron Curtain here of Stalin, but we will never be the America we could be until we drop the iron curtain here, and let fifteen million Negroes have their full freedom as any other American citizen." After Reuther finished his talk, a Negro international rep asked me what I thought of the talk.

"Good," I said, "He always gives a good talk, but he has not as yet raised the Curtain on the International Executive Board high enough to appoint one Negro on it."

Reuther's line in the union is that there is no Negro problem. The bureaucrats say if you bring it up on the floor as a Negro problem it will hurt you. The Polish and Jewish and Italian don't do it, so why should Negroes?

When I was first elected to the Council it had been set up to discuss the problems of the workers in production. But it has turned into a machine of the union leaders. Whatever comes up on the floor, if the leaders want it passed—that's it. Any time one of the rank and file workers gets up and says anything particular about our work in the shop or asks about a specific incident in his department, he gets squashed down. Workers say there is no use going to meetings. They say what they want to bring up won't hit the floor. If a question does get on the floor, the Reuther bureaucracy calls the previous question. That means stop the debate and vote on the discussion. One worker may speak sharp and ten or fifteen hands go up. The labor bureaucrat knows his stooges and he recognizes one of them. Sometimes workers jump all over the hall trying to talk. The president gets up and gives his line, the chairman says, "We have to proceed along democratic lines. We are not going to let you have special privileges. Now we will vote on it," and the issue is killed.

When the bureaucrats want to put over an issue they have a way of taking their cars to pick up supporters. They haul out everyone they know, even some who haven't been in the plant or the union for three years. It is always on a political issue, city officials or something to do with the state elections. Two years ago the workers came out in a group to try to force discussion. They were so whipped and crushed down that now they say, "The hell with the union."

I point out the difference between the union and the union leadership to the men on my line. I say what the union means to me and to us. When I first joined the union in 1943, the words brother and sister—I didn't grasp their full meaning. But after getting active in the union and understanding what the workers did and went through in organizing the UAW-CIO, I could see that this was the first real emancipation for the white worker and the second emancipation for the Negroes. Then brother and sister meant something to me. Since then I felt that our relations as union members should exist as close as possible, next to the immediate family relations.

When we talk on the line, after a meeting, the men say, "Yes, what you say about the union, that's all true. But this is the union, the way it is today, and not what we want, so what the hell. The hell with the union."

But a question can come out about the company, or somebody trying to break the union and you'll have all the workers out the next day. If it is the usual meeting the workers won't attend.

When Ford Local 600, UAW-CIO, held its tenth anniversary celebration last year and announced John L. Lewis as their principal speaker, I felt that I could not miss it. I had always wanted to see and hear John L. Lewis, ever since I saw those pictures of the sit-down strikes while I was living in the South. At the celebration there were some eighty thousand workers from all over the city packed into an open field joining the union hall. I saw several busses loaded with workers from the coal fields. When Lewis appeared, the applause was so great, it felt to me the earth was trembling. When he started to speak, I felt I had known him personally for years. No one who had ever seen his pictures in the paper could mistake him. He was identically the same, not resembling anyone. He had strange features, it seemed to me his look was strange. He had a very deep heavy voice which roared through the audience. The more I tried to gather up in my mind some features of someone I had seen before, the stranger he seemed. Then I remembered one time I had seen a cartoon in the paper; it showed Winston Churchill with the features of a bulldog. I said to myself, "Yes, John L. Lewis has the features of a lion." His voice is like that of a lion, his face and his head, all of his looks seemed to go with his fight in helping to build the CIO.

Lewis said, "I am here with you to celebrate the tenth anniversary of you local union. I have heard there is a saying among many of you that I am also here to celebrate as the founder and organizer of the UAW-CIO. I do not agree with those who say that I am the founder and organizer. The UAW-CIO was founded and organized by many of you who are here today, and many like you who are not here. But if you want to bestow some honor upon men, I will accept that I did as much to help organize the UAW-CIO as anyone else.

"Don't pay attention to those labor leaders and intellectuals running around the place with a new briefcase and one piece of paper in it, getting up telling you what to do. Many of them don't know as much what to do as you do yourselves. They should be in the plant with you."

Somewhere in his talk he asked, "Who is responsible for the UAW-CIO?"

Someone in the audience yelled out, "You."

He said, "No, it was you, all organizing yourselves together, understanding the situation that was involved, that brought General Motors to sit down and bargain collectively."

He said, "This huge gathering here today is power, it is force, the working force of production that America and the world exist upon. It is the force and power that can bring any corporation to recognize you when you are organized together."

This is what I was thinking. This working force that everything hinges on; this was the answer. Lewis stated it. How much he meant it, I don't know. I was glad to be a part of this force that Lewis was speaking of and I knew there was no other place for me to go. Before Lewis finished speaking, I made my way through the crowd into the hall. I felt I wanted to touch him. He came down the aisle, pausing every step, shaking workers' hands. I reached out mine. He shook it, smiled and said, "Good luck." He walked outside and got in a large convertible and shook hands with workers for five or ten minutes. Motorcycle cops all around the car opened their sirens and the car pulled off.

The way that Lewis spoke; that's not how the bureaucrats act. I had a worker tell me today, swearing, that the union represents nothing but the company.

"Nobody can tell me these guys aren't paid by the company. The only guys who have fun in the shop are those who shoot crap all day or the guys who write the numbers."

Numbers are collected openly in my shop. A guy works numbers on my line. On Thursday he goes to the bank and draws out two thousand dollars. When the workers come on Friday to pay for the numbers they played during the week, he cashes their checks. There are always ten or fifteen workers standing around. The big shots walk up and down. They never say anything. Some workers think the numbers men pay off the union and the union makes it right with the company. Once in awhile the company will fire a small guy, but it's just like the racket outside, they never fire a leading numbers man. Numbers playing goes on all over the shop in every department and in every plant in the city. In a predominantly Negro department there is one fellow, who, the Negroes think, must be doing it for the company. He has a job but he doesn't do any work. The numbers man on my line brings a pistol to work on Friday. Many of us wonder why he doesn't get fired. He hangs his coat up with the gun showing but the company never says a word to him. If a worker hasn't any money left after paying, he stays and borrows from the same guy, paying him twenty-five cents on the dollar interest. He walks around all week and lends workers money. This is no different than what I saw in the South.

A Negro drove up to the union hall today with one of the biggest Chryslers made. He was so dressed up that we thought he was one of the international representatives. We were standing around talking and we all said, "Porkchopper."

He came out with the vice president of the local and they stood talking at the car. The vice president kept his hand on the Negro's shoulder and he was smiling all over his face. One of the men with us was so worried, not knowing this man, that he went to ask. After the guy drove off, the vice president said that he was a line steward in the plant.

He told us this and everyone said, "Oh, he's a numbers guy or else a loan guy."

Nobody would have taken him for a worker. He was dressed up and wearing a diamond ring and the car was a special Chrysler. The vice president was never so warm to any Negro before.

It makes me sick. There is a guy on my line taking numbers. I asked him one day how he had the heart to take the workers' money. I know one man whose wife came and begged the manager to make her husband stop playing. They had five children and he never brought home any money. When I asked the numbers fellow he said he was making money, had just bought a new car and was building a house soon. He didn't give a damn for workers or their problems. One Negro I know worked with me during the war. He started writing numbers and in four years he made twenty-eight thousand dollars cash.

Many workers won't come in to work on Friday. They get their check in the front office and when they see the numbers guy on Monday they say they are broke. Some wildcats are pulled on a Friday. These numbers men practically go insane if a strike is pulled before lunch on Friday. Sometimes a man will ask the foreman if he can go home at noon to avoid the numbers man. The foreman says, no, but the guy will leave anyway. The man will sometimes get fired for going home when the foreman said no.

Two years ago, with the model changeover, they tried to speed up production on the job. The bargaining committee said we wouldn't have to run one piece more than before. They said it was the same job. We had been running one hundred jobs an hour. The time study man turned in a report that we should do one hundred thirty-five jobs an hour and the company tried to beat us into speeding up. With stationary jobs, there is an agreement that a worker gets six minutes out of the hour, if he does not make production. If he makes production ahead of the hour, then he gets whatever time is left for himself. The workers were so mad about the speed up, that they gave up their fifteen minutes and took the six that were due them every hour. They said they'd be damned if they'd make one thirty-five an hour. The bargaining committee told us that as long as we worked fifty-four minutes we didn't have to make production. They were thinking that in a week or so the workers would give in so they would get fifteen minutes rest like the other workers.

After two weeks they still couldn't make the men do one hundred thirty-five jobs. They were still doing one hundred. The company called the bargaining committee into the office and the committee agreed that the workers should do one hundred twenty-five. The company always sets the figure higher than they expect so they can eventually get what they want. The union tried to get the workers to agree to one twenty-five. They wouldn't do it for three days. The bargaining committee said they had to do it, that the time-study watch showed one thirty-five and that "figures don't lie." They told us if we didn't do it we'd be in the street.

The workers hollered and yelled and said, "What kind of an agreement is this? We were told on the job changeover that we would do as we had before, and now you tell us that figures don't lie."

The committee said, "You have to do it."

The workers had to give in. In this speed up the union worked hand in glove with the company.

When Reuther came out against wildcat strikes it just meant the company would clamp down. All of us knew it. The union leaders said the wildcat was caused by the Commies, and at the same time, they said the workers were lazy and didn't want to work. One worker, Samuels, an old guy who had been in the shop for twenty-five years was looking out the window one morning. He saw some workers going out and cursed them; he said they didn't want to work. I told him he was talking like the company and the union. I tried to tell him what strikes meant. This was something I knew he didn't accept. His line was that we voted for these union leaders and we should follow them. Older workers are usually more conservative.

In the speed up from one hundred to one twenty-five the company put a special foreman over this old guy. They figured if they broke him the others would follow. The company was putting pressure on him and the workers were putting pressure on department. A bargaining committeeman will never tell the truth quit working eight minutes before the hour instead of six. The foreman rushed into the office and gave him a warning slip. Samuels got so mad he started talking about what we should do to the company.

He said, "We need a strike."

I carried a group over to him and told him, "You remember

what I said the other day? You remember what you said about wildcats?"

He said he had been wrong. "You told me it was always the fault of the company. God damn it, it's true. I thought the days were wiped out when they could put a man to stand over you."

The bargaining committee said the company could have a foreman anywhere they wanted as long as he didn't drive a worker. The old guy didn't have proof that the foreman was driving him. But he was driving.

We have benches to sit on to eat lunch. The foreman finally got so mad because we wouldn't do one hundred twenty-five jobs, that he broke up one of the benches. We got the chief steward in a position where he said if the bargaining committee didn't support him he'd pull off his button and go back to work on the line; it was too much to let the company get away with. He asked me if I would accept the job of chief steward. Before this time he had been afraid I might get his job because of the workers who liked me. I told him I didn't want the job and that it would be a mistake for him to take off his button. It was a fight the company was pulling off and he should see that all the workers supported him and not call the bargaining committee at all. I promised to help him and he felt pretty good. He got us a new bench. He would have been pretty well wrecked if he had stood for breaking up our bench. It would have been open to the workers that he hadn't supported them.

One morning I heard that the workers in another department were being sent home because of a shortage of material. I went to Samuels, the old guy, and told him that we all got so mad at what the company did to him, that we were wildcatting in the afternoon. He was so happy, he said he would be the first to walk out. To this day he thinks the workers left because of him. Now he's the first one to get the workers to walk out and always defends them. He's the most militant worker we have in the shop today.

If one worker gets in a sharp argument with a foreman, every worker who can get away from his job will come to find out what's up. Fifty will be around in no time at all. The crowd will be so thick you won't be able to see the two who were arguing. The union and the company try to keep a disagreement within its own department. A bargaining committeeman will never tell the truth about a dispute. He'll give the workers some story. None of us will ever believe him. They keep a grievance quiet because they know workers will support workers.

The company fired twenty-five men on the night shift and the union was stalling about getting them back. We didn't know for two days, that the night shift had gone out twice. On a Saturday the union held a department meeting of the night and day shifts. The workers got so mad they cursed the local officer. They told him if nothing was done by Monday morning they would put up a picket line of their own on Tuesday to keep the day shift out. This shook the union leaders because they knew it would spread around. Every worker would know the men were having trouble. The union had the bargaining committeemen go into every department of the plant and tell the chief stewards to instruct the workers that they were to ignore the picket line. The chief steward came to me first and told me to tell the thirty guys on my line. The bargaining committeeman stood off to the side, listening. I asked the steward to repeat what he had said.

Then I told him: "Do you know who you are talking to? I won't tell a worker on my line a damn thing. You know who I am. These workers know who I am. I stand on principles. I'm surprised at you telling me to go through a picket line. What's going on in this union? We used to fight and kill scabs. Now you're telling me to tell these workers to scab. You're trying to make me a scab. That's something I'll never be."

The committeeman stepped up and said the strike was not authorized by the union.

I told him, "That's why we are having a strike. The company knows that the union will try to whip us down on anything they want to put over on us. They make us walk out. I'm positive, and I'm sure every worker will say, that the company had forced these workers to call the strike. I'm sure the company knows we're not supposed to strike until we get an okay from the union. They'll drive the workers to do anything they want them to do. If the workers don't strike, then by the time the union gives its okay the men will be forced to do what the company wanted. If a worker does the work for one day then the company will put out that they should do it all the time because they are able to do it."

I pointed out the strike of the plant guards. The union made us support the guards, and they're nothing but cops for the company. They're not even members of our union. The union gave us the line that some day the guards might want to join our union. None of us wants these cops in our union. I told him that the union tried to poison us saying that the workers don't want to work. I said if a worker didn't want to work he wouldn't have to come to the plant in the first place. But the company knows we're not supposed to strike, and it knows the position of the union. They know that's the way to defeat the workers with the only weapon they have, the strike.

"You can tell the committee man that I work every day but if a picket line of my brothers is up, then I won't be in the shop."

The chief steward said he hadn't thought about it like that. He said, "It's the truth. I won't tell any of the workers in my department what to do. If they come in on their own, if they don't come in, that's up to them. If there's a line I won't be in to work either."

The union got the same resentment throughout the shop. At three o'clock every committeman and chief steward was in front of the gate handing out leaflets. The leaflets told the workers not to support the strike. It was a very well printed leaflet.

A worker said, "I'm sure the company is working hand in hand with the union. It's impossible that the union could run out seventeen thousand leaflets between two-thirty and three o'clock."

One worker said, "We should have shotguns and shoot every committeeman first. Those bastards are trying to push us through the line."

The workers feel they'll never be able to beat the union bureaucracy in an election.

"They'll stuff the ballot boxes, and if they get beat there'd be blood around the ballot box."

The next morning there was no picket line. The union got eighteen men back that afternoon and promised to have the rest back the next day. But the union had a sound truck out, in case the picket line was up. They weren't sure, and there was a line they'd yell for the workers to go through.

A worker friend walking in with me said, "A stool pigeon and a scab used to hide and cover his face. Now, the union is the biggest stool pigeon and scab and is trying to get the workers to be scabs."

At another plant the union had the flying squadron ready to take the scabs through the picket line.

One white worker said, that if a member of the flying squadron hit him he'd walk with a shot gun the rest of his life to kill those sons of bitches. He said that the flying squadron was paid from our money, and set up to help us fight the police. But now they talk about beating us back into the plant for the company.

All this is why they can't get the workers to a Council meeting. Last month we finally got a quorum for a General Council meeting. I reached the hall while the president was reporting on the wildcat strikes. Twenty-three workers had been fired. The union promised the strikers that they would get the men their jobs if they wouldn't wildcat. They got all back to work except nine. So the workers went out again. On the second night, the workers sat down in the plant for two hours.

The president of the local was speaking more viciously than I had even seen him. He was talking about stopping the wildcats. He said the men would be brought up on charges and expelled. They had been listening to cheap left wing politicians. They were cheap and yellow and without guts enough to come out in the open and speak against the local officers. They would be behind the union's back and get the workers to wildcat. They always managed to evade getting fired themselves. He also said that the workers in one plant were the biggest liars he'd ever heard. They'd said the union hadn't done anything about the fired men, but only seventeen of them came to the meeting to discuss with the union.

The floor was opened for discussion. A Negro was the first to speak. He said he was opposed to accepting the president's report. The general attitude of the president was vicious, low type politics. He said the president said left wing politicians caused the wildcat, but he wasn't left wing. He didn't care a damn about politics in the union. This was what the union always used when the workers faced them with any problem, this was used to evade the issue. When the president called the workers liars he had plenty to say in answer. At the last election the president of the local spent one hundred dollars or more of union money for stickers and advertisements saying that he opposed the dues increase. The Ford workers were fighting the dues increase too at the convention. He had suggested that our local unite with the

Ford workers. He spoke to the recording secretary of the union about it and the secretary said they weren't opposed to the dues increase. "We are for it."

The fellow asked the president, "If that phony work with stickers and advertisements isn't being a liar, then what is?"

He went head on in a fight with the president. He did one of the best jobs I've witnessed.

A Trotskyist spoke. He said he had been away organizing. He said he was disturbed. This was the third Council meeting this year and workers didn't turn out. Why, when the present administration controlled seventy-five percent of the members of the Council didn't they attend meetings? He was disturbed about executive board meetings too. They couldn't get a quorum of seventeen members out of a board of one hundred. This was a board with ninety-five percent control by Reuther. He said the meetings should be advertised well and the workers should be told there would be free discussion in meetings. He was disappointed with this in the union.

An old timer spoke next. He said he didn't know what was wrong with the union. The members should get an intellectual with clear understanding to help us in our union. That's what we needed.

A bargaining committeeman spoke next. He said, "I do everything I can for the workers. I can't seem to satisfy them. I wish someone would tell me what is wrong with the workers. We get three raises and insurance benefits for the workers. But when they were on strike they cursed the committeemen. During the wildcat strike, a worker pulled a knife, put it against me and said if I ever came back in the department he'd kill me. I surely wish someone could tell me what is wrong with the workers."

I got the floor. This is what I said:

"I noticed quite a few ovations when they said the workers didn't attend meetings and that the workers were not following the officers of the local and that they should and that that was what the trouble is. We're missing the boat and missing it far. I don't see it as you say, that you got the insurance benefit for the workers. The workers got it by putting on the pressure. When the present administration came in the first proposition Reuther made was that we could live peacefully with management. From that alone, management understood as well as anyone else that if we were not going to strike, but would live peacefully, then they could speed up the line and beat the workers at the point of production to make more profits than they did before they gave us ten cents and the benefits. The proof is that every year the president of the International gets up and tells that the corporation is doubling its profits and that we need to get more of what we produce. How can this be when the company has the right to control production by speed up?

"I don't agree with the old time union leaders of the local trying to say that a worker must be born in one department of the plant before he understands anything about the union, that we need an intellectual. That's saying we're dumb. The bargaining man thinks because he's a bargaining committeeman he's teaching the workers and getting a few things for them. This is it and they should go with him. Workers don't have to be in the union twenty-five years before they know what's what. The average worker comes into the plant, and according to the contract, the foreman is supposed to spend three days showing him his operation. The average worker has the foreman with him for only three hours. It's not that long before he can do his operation. In three days he is able to do the operation as well as anyone who has been in the plant twenty-five or thirty years. Many workers who have been in for thirty years, if sent over to the new worker could be shown by him. And as easy as a worker can learn an operation he can learn and knows unionism just that well in less than three months.

"One thing I notice that we are doing now in all these issues, the workers are faced with the idea that it is cheap left wing politicians making them do everything. That says the worker is dumb. The company is oppressing him and he isn't supposed to have sense enough to fight back. The union hasn't mentioned one time the role the company plays in relation to a worker at the point of production. But Harry Bennett has to write a book *We Never Called Him Henry* to let these union leaders know that this is the role the company plays. He only mentioned Ford, but all workers know that this is the role that all leading industries play.

"The brother that mentioned an intellectual. You should understand this—that the worker knows and understands better than the teacher, the President, or the intellectual, the role he has to play in relation to the company. He knows better than any plan that could be thought out for him. I think if we take the side of the worker and if the union leader becomes a part of the struggle he's carrying on, then we'll see and not be so confused. I heard a hundred workers if I heard one, make the statement that our president was at one time a good union man. He led many wildcat strikes. But, they ask, what has happened to him, today? I tell them, 'That's the sixty-four dollar question. But you won't get sixty-four dollars if you find the answer. You'll probably get thrown out of the union.' "

The discussion was closed and the president came back with his rebuttal. He said very little about the other speakers. He started in on me.

He said, "That's what I meant. These politicians know how to operate. They don't go far enough, they don't cross the line so that they can be brought up on charges. That brother just did one of the damndest chop jobs on us that was ever done in the union but he didn't go far enough to where he'd have to prove what he says and could be tried."

This tickled me. The president thought every worker around him is so dumb that he had to tell them what I said.

The president went on. "Many workers, he said, tell him we were good fellows six or seven years ago. What's happened to us now? The brother tells the workers that if they find the answer to the sixty-four dollar question they'll get thrown out of the union. He's accusing us openly, and frankly, before this Council meeting of being company stooges. But he won't go across the line. He just comes up to it and stops and leaves it hanging. I want everybody to know what he is saying. He knows if he says that we are stooges he'll have to prove it before a trial committee and will probably get kicked out of the union."

After the meeting the president came to me and said he wanted to have a talk about my accusation. I said that I hadn't made an accusation.

I said, "You made an accusation that you are company stooges. I didn't say that, but if you want to say it before all these workers you can say it and I'll accept what you say."

15.
THE COMMUNIST PARTY

WHEN I TALK to Negro Stalinists, I know and feel that it is the party first, second and always. With this the question of Russia is always tied in. But it is never the Negroes first, no matter what they say. A close friend of mine went into the Communist Party. He asked me to attend a meeting for Howard Fast, the man who wrote *Freedom Road*. My friend told me that the average Negro who came to a CP meeting was welcome; they'd be all over him. I told him I was afraid to attend the meeting because I might get into trouble. But after persuasion by my friend I agreed to go in order to show him how they would act if you didn't agree with them.

The meeting opened. When Fast came on the platform the audience jumped and hollered like people in church. The Negroes acted like Moses had come to lead us, now we'll get across the river and all will be clear. Fast talked about the time he spent in the Federal prison. He said the ordinary white worker was for the Southern Koreans but that every Negro was opposed. He said the Negroes were in support of the Northern Koreans and were following them all the way. He discussed the Negro question in the United States. He said the Negroes, if the Communists had their way, would have a section in the center of the United States all for themselves. He said that Dr. DuBois had just become a man in the last four or five years. He said Paul Robeson had just become a man, a real man, ten years ago. If the Negroes got their emancipation Paul Robeson would be the Negro who had led them to it.

Two things were hitting me. According to Fast, Dr. DuBois didn't become a man until he was eighty-five years old. The other was what would happen to fifteen million Negroes if Robeson should pass on. All our hopes for our rights would be done. Fast said some more about self-determination for Negroes and the rest of his talk was on the Soviet Union. After he finished speaking I saw the same hollering, the same excitement of conversion by these leading Negroes.

Several questions were asked in one hundred percent agreement with Fast.

After five or six questions, I asked: "Why didn't Paul Robeson support the March on Washington which was a mass struggle for Negro rights, and out of which came the 8802 order?"

"What is the relationship of the Russian workers to prodduction?"

Fast said he didn't know why Robeson didn't support the March on Washington movement. As to the second question: he would deal with the Russian miners first. He said the miners in Russia earned one hundred and fifty dollars a week. They all had their own beautiful homes, they had automobiles, and if the 1952 plan wasn't disrupted by war, there would be socialized bread, free bread. Then he sat down.

There were more questions asked by obvious CP members. Nearing the end, I raised my hand again.

I said, "You didn't answer my questions as I was thinking them. I'd like to know: Why didn't one of the leading Communists or why didn't the CP as a whole support the March on Washington Negro mass movement? Also, how much control do Russian workers have of production?"

Fast said he didn't know why the Communist Party, or Robeson, didn't support the March on Washington. The production in Russia was controlled by factory committees. He sat down again.

I got up again, "Who controls the factory committees? Are they like the UAW today where the national staff controls from the top down through the shop committees and the chief stewards? Does this control come from the workers on the line or from the Kremlin on down?"

"Another thing. This self-determination as you speak about it. I don't think Negroes want segregation into one area as you propose it. You mean Negroes controlling Negroes, in a section of the country by themselves—would you clarify that some too?"

At this time all the Negroes' and a few whites' eyes were real sharp like a bed of snakes, just tense. The Negro who brought me was shaky and nervous.

Fast jumped up, real vicious. "I don't know who you are or where you are from. But the Communist Party, like any other organization may make mistakes. But unlike any other organization we're only too damn glad to admit them."

One Negro jumped up and said in a vicious tone, "If you're after disrupting this meeting, I want you to know I supported the March on Washington movement."

I was very nervous, and my friend and I were looking for an attack. Fast came down and asked someone near me who I was. I told my friend we'd better get out. After we left my friend said he was really surprised at the way they acted. When he first went to the CP meetings they always tried to explain everything to him. He said he'd never go to another meeting.

16.
THE TROTSKYIST PARTY

SOME MONTHS BEFORE the war ended the company was laying off and transferring some of the workers into different plants of the company and into different classifications. I, along with some other workers, was transferred to one of the larger plants. I was put on a job where the majority of workers were Negroes. We had a Southern white chief steward. Many of the workers who had already been working this job were complaining that he wasn't much good. I worked there two weeks when one morning I noticed a new chief steward over us. I asked how he got to be chief steward and when? These workers began to tell me he was the regular chief steward, and what a militant fighter he was. He was a big man, weighing two hundred pounds or more and of some kind of foreign origin.

One of the Negro workers who was transferred with me said, "He looks big and rough enough to be a good union fighter."

Two or three days after this steward came in, our foreman fired one worker. We felt we would see the steward in action, but he didn't say much. A day or so after that another worker was fired, and again he didn't say much. Several of us began to raise hell with him, asking him why he didn't defend the workers and stop the action of the company.

I told him I heard this was the most militant plant in the U.A.W., but that it didn't seem to be as militant as the plant I had come from.

He explained that he had just got back to work. He had been fired three or four weeks before, along with twenty others for leading a strike against the company and how he and the rest had to be careful and quiet not to get fired again.

I asked him why in the hell he didn't give his button to someone that could fight and not be in such a position and come on back to work with us.

Many workers were saying the same thing, and the arguments between us and the chief steward were raging. A white woman spoke; she said that I was correct. That was new to me. I felt for the first time in my life a white woman had openly defended me against a white man. As she walked away I noticed she had on a chief steward button.

A few days later she came back, and the chief steward and I were in another argument. Again she said I was correct and began to tell me she was fired along with the others, but she wasn't keeping quiet on a grievance for fear she'd be fired again. I asked her her name. She told me Helen. She also told me where she worked. It was a short distance from where I was working. She asked me had I done much reading because she had a paper she wanted me to read. It was *The Militant,* the Trotskyist paper. I read *The Militant* and some of it I agreed with but I didn't understand most of it.

The chief steward asked me if I knew Helen. He said she was one of the best union women but very dangerous.

I asked him if she would get me fired.

He said it wasn't anything like that. She had radical ideas.

I said I wanted to be a good unionist and as far as the part he was telling me to be afraid of, I would judge for myself.

The next time I saw Helen was at a union meeting. She took the floor. She gave me more to think about than I had ever had before. However there was still one doubt in my mind. She worked in a lily white department. When I asked her why, she said that the company used it as a skilled classification to keep Negro women out, but she had got one Negro woman who knew that type of work hired in her department. The woman quit because she felt strong resentment from the white women who worked there. But Helen said she was still looking for some Negro woman to work in there, and if I knew any who would accept she would be very glad to fight for them because that was one aim she wanted to achieve in that department. I went into the department several times to talk to her. I could feel resentment from the whites but she didn't seem to worry the least bit. She would always invite me back to talk with her.

A few weeks passed and Helen carried me to a social. We talked most of the night. After the party I was invited to a meeting the following Sunday. I felt comfortable at the meeting and thought that some day I might agree with these people and their way of thinking. At the meeting the Trotskyites told me they planned to eliminate segregation and discrimination. This was new to me seeing such a small group of people believing this. It was hard for me to see such a small group planning to do so much for the Negroes, and for the workers as a whole. I felt I had to tell their ideas to every worker and make every worker a member. I felt there had to be a majority before the things they spoke about could be accomplished. I went to meetings regularly for a month and then asked to join. I was very active. I went right from work to the office and sold papers. I'd sell six or seven dollars worth in the evening.

I was puzzled that Negroes didn't accept the ideas as I saw them. I thought the average Negro should want to join. When they held out I wondered what else was involved. This didn't change my thinking of building the organization. In two weeks I had a relative in. We sold pamphlets and papers together. We sold them even to Negro police. They would sometimes buy, or sometimes just laugh. We organized socials and held one every Saturday night. In a month we brought in ten Negro members. But I felt that I should have recruited one hundred. Many of the new members were active unionists and I thought we were on our way. Two men in my union and Helen were the people who were closest to me. We were carrying on a fight against the leaders of the union. In six months we had seventy-five or eighty Negroes attending meetings regularly and going out selling papers. I felt good to see this. I hadn't done any studying along political lines before. But I felt if these ideas could be told to every worker they couldn't hold out.

A few months went by and I began to wonder why the party had no resolution on the Negro question. They had one on Trade Unions, on the American question, on Europe and many other subjects. It was always in my mind that it wasn't necessary to them. The leadership never mentioned that any Negroes had ever done anything progressive. The only Negro they talked about was Frederick Douglass. It seemed to me that a Negro had to be in the party or else be a Frederick Douglass. There weren't any other Negroes, no singers, actors, leaders, nothing. Often I tried to compare the Negro Trotskyist leader, Rollings, with many Negroes I know. He couldn't compete. Rollings' role itself was top Negro in the party. It kept striking me that he played the same part in the Trotskyist party that Bowen did in the UAW. He was the type of Negro who felt that it was always he that was important. Only he understood anything. This was a constant agitation in my mind.

Rollings gave an educational about Frederick Douglass that showed how much we disagreed. During the question period I told him he hadn't mentioned the independent slave revolt of Negroes in the South during slavery. That it was due to their pressure and support that Douglass had been able to do what he did. The disagreement was sharp.

Rollings said, "The revolt meant nothing, if the North hadn't gone in the Negroes would be slaves today."

Another time he gave a class on Garvey and said, "Garvey was a man who hated white people," and that Garvey was nationalistic because he was a West Indian Negro. That was his main contribution about the Garvey Movement.

I got in an argument with him when I told him that the leader of the party, Leon Trotsky, didn't look at the Garvey Movement the way he was putting it forward.

Rollings said he didn't give a damn what Trotsky said, he guessed he knew what a nationalist was when a Negro formed his own organization and wouldn't let whites in it. "Negroes can't get *any* place without white help."

That was too much for me. Rollings gave nothing to the Negroes in an educational way. He told a friend of mine that I was nationalistic about Negroes and that it was his job to get me in line.

After the Garvey class a white comrade said he didn't think Rollings and I had such sharp differences to have such a big fight in the branch.

He told me, "Rollings is what all Negroes are going to have to come to in the final analysis. He looks at things not as a Negro but as a Marxist. The Negroes will have to forget they are Negroes and be Marxists."

I said, "That is the difference. If a Negro can forget he is a Negro, that is as big a difference as I want."

I began to see resentment on the faces of each leader every time a Negro took a different point of view. I started to feel much closer with the sixty workers on my line, in truth. They were three

Polish, two Italian, two Russian workers and the rest hillbilly and Negroes. It would seem that this was where I should have had trouble because there were six white women also on our line. We talked and played and whispered together and there was not the least bit of resentment from the white men. You wouldn't believe your eyes. When we first started to work it seemed like we were among strange animals, but I talked to these women and men and felt freer than with some of the women in the party. I was a little afraid to talk freely in the party.

A few months passed and my cousin and I asked out two white women who were Trotskyites. They had known us for some time and accepted. We had a good time together. The next time we had a date after a meeting. There were two or three white men still at the hall and I could see that the women were trying to wait until everyone left. Finally all of us went out together. The white men walked with the women. My cousin and I walked behind. One of the women whispered that they would walk along with the whites and meet us later. This got me to thinking. Was this what they stood for all the time? My cousin and I talked it over.

He said, "Something is wrong if the women have to slip."

We met the women and they acted nervous. They were not nervous about being with us in general but were nervous about being seen by white men of the organization.

I asked them to explain why.

They said, "Well, you don't let everybody know your affairs."

But many times I'd seen white men and women who weren't married leaving a meeting. No one slipped or ducked or worried. I began to feel that Negro and white relations were a touchy situation in the party for all their talk.

Many Negroes began bringing complaints to Rollings and myself about remarks some white made to them that they resented. Rollings would always try to show these Negroes what the whites meant, trying to apologize for them, by saying, they didn't really understand whites. He said, "These are minor things and we always have to keep our minds on the overall objective."

On one occasion a young Negro who had recently joined was riding home with a white man who had been in the party five years and made this remark to him: "The Negroes are raising hell in the party about their equality. But under socialism, the whites will stay where they are and the Negroes will have to keep in their same place."

When I heard this I got very mad. I went to Rollings and tried to get him to bring the white man before the executive board or to bring it before the branch meeting because what the white guy said was not party policy, and it was making Negroes in the branch very angry. Nothing was done or said about it and the Negro involved, and his brother, left the organization. Many Negroes began to drop out.

Some said, "These people don't mean what they say. Take the question of white women. The women are afraid to let the men know if they go out with a Negro."

The men would tell us that it hurt the party, that we should be careful. Some came right out and said they were opposed to white women going out with Negroes at all.

One member of the party was a Negro doctor. He was treated differently from the worker members. He had a car and I and some other rank-and-filers felt that he made large contributions. Some of us felt that they made special privileges for him. He could take out a woman and it was like a white man. The leaders would even say that a woman wanted to see him. We asked him about it and he said they wanted to be examined, and since he was a doctor the leaders asked his help.

The Negro doctor told me he went to Buffalo to give an educational. He and the organizer of the branch walked home in the snow. Out of a blue sky the organizer asked the doctor where he stood on interracial marriage. They stood ankle deep in the snow and argued for an hour and a half. The organizer said he was opposed to *any* relations between Negroes and white women in the party. The doctor jumped about a foot.

The doctor left the party. I felt something was very wrong politically, but I just couldn't put my finger on it. I didn't quit but I attended fewer meetings. The doctor had given many educationals and I felt he knew politics and was serious. I felt bad over his leaving. Some Negro told me he left because the convention in Chicago was held in a hotel which wouldn't admit Negro members with the whites. The Negroes wanted to picket the hotel but the whites said it was more important to continue the convention. They explained that they were too busy and didn't have the time to fight on the issue of discrimination just then.

I talked to the doctor after he left. He said that the political education he got in the party meant much more to him than the education he got in college. He told me that many trade union leaders today got their political education through the Trotskyist and Communist Party. He said that he had also been around the Communist Party at one time. He had no use for them or for their maneuvering, or their politics, but on the question of Negro and white relations they stood way over the Trotskyist organization.

There were many other incidents too numerous to mention. I tried to keep it all inside me. There were only three Negroes left in the party out of a hundred. When I asked why, they told me we were in a period of reaction and that people got tired. I asked the leaders about the doctor. They told me he was middle-class. They said he'd rather be going about with his own circle of middle-class friends.

I still went to meetings once a month. I slept through every educational. I never learned anything. I began to feel that the meetings were a complete waste of time and that I could do something else more worthwhile.

I felt I should still be part for certain things they would say, not for what they were doing. Something was telling me not to say I was done. I'd get lonesome for meetings. But it didn't get better. A leader's wife would pass me on the stairs without speaking. She would turn her head away just like a Southerner. Yet, I found myself going back. I didn't know where else to go. After the Negroes dropped away, Christine wouldn't go any more. I could still feel warm toward them in the fraction meetings at the plant. In the fraction meetings I would promise to come around but it got harder every time.

Before the party's 1948 convention in New York I had a firm conviction that they felt it was the party first and last and always. This was just like the Communist Party. Negroes and workers never come first with them whatever they say in their writings.

At the 1948 convention in New York, all the Negroes were upset and meeting together.

When the session opened and the leader, James P. Cannon, came in, I saw the same thing that I'd seen at the Communist meeting with Howard Fast. Rollings acted like someone going into convulsions. It made me feel funny. He was worse than anyone else. He jumped up and hollered like the people do in church when they're getting converted. I clapped as much as the rest but Rollings' behavior seemed like an act.

I heard that another leader was going to speak on a Negro Resolution which he had written to be presented at the convention. When he got up to speak, I was never so shocked and surprised and happy in all my life. I never had heard about his ability, just that he was a good speaker. I was looking for a smoothing over like Rollings always gave in Detroit. When I listened to this leader's general presentation, I felt I was floating some place. What really got me was when he said that no Negro, especially Negroes below the Mason and Dixon line, ever believed that their problems would be solved by writing or telegraphing congress.

He went on to say that, "the Negroes' independent struggle had a vitality and validity of its own." He said the workers as a whole are the ones we must rely upon. But that this didn't mean that the Negroes must not do anything until the labor movement actually came forward. The Negro struggle would help bring the workers forward. That was complete for me. I couldn't see how I would ever think of leaving after hearing him. I was tied and wedged into the party. I had wanted to speak but after hearing this leader, I never dreamed of speaking. I tore up my notes. I didn't think there was anything I needed to do. The convention accepted the Negro Resolution. I felt good. Now we had something, something to go by. I thought we wouldn't be bothered any more. We could go out and work. I thought the party would go overboard in carrying out these ideas.

When I got back to Detroit I heard that Rollings was giving me hell about something or other, but I felt so good I couldn't be bothered with this stuff. I wanted to do something. I recruited three Negroes in a month. I talked to Rollings about a group of friends I had around me. I said I would try to get them going around the Resolution. I thought we could use the Resolution for educationals and form a solid independent group around us. I spoke about the Resolution and all said they were ready to go. Another Negro brought four Negroes from Ford. A Negro preacher gave us a basement to meet in. We were on our way at last.

In a month though, I began to feel the same thing I had felt before the convention. The party had accepted the resolution on the Negro but I could see them pushing any idea of independent struggle to the rear. I experienced it with Rollings.

At every meeting of the Negro group he would say, "Let's try to get the union in it before we organize to do anything."

And after, he would want some of the white leaders in it, to give the line, write the programs, and connect it immediately to the union.

I would oppose this. I felt the group should plan for itself what action it wanted to take. These were our main differences. They sharpened day by day.

I spoke to the leader of the party in Detroit about the tension, and the attitudes in the meetings and executive meetings. He said it was only that everyone was busy. There wasn't time for friendly relations. Talk started again about Negroes and white women but I tried to ignore it and build my little group. The group was gaining members. Suddenly without previous discussion the party called me in and told me that the group had to be directed into the National Association for the Advancement of Colored People—the NAACP. They said this had to be done or the group had to be destroyed. Those were the words they used. They sent Rollings into the group to speak. He knew nothing about them but told them they should go join the NAACP. Most of them were already members but were sick of the do-nothing politics of the NAACP. I tried to hold the party to the Negro Resolution.

But they said, "Damn the Resolution. We're talking about this group going into the NAACP. Will you obey discipline or not?"

This hit me hard. Without the Resolution I didn't want the party.

The NAACP

I'd been working in the NAACP for two years. The membership fell from 23,000 to 3,000. If they took a leading role they could have jumped the membership several thousand overnight. But on the question involving Negroes they wouldn't oppose anything advanced by the UAW. It was like a company town relation with the UAW as the company. They were completely guided by the UAW bureaucrats. The UAW gave big donations. It gave jobs and a social life to certain Negroes. This was used as a club over the organization. They were afraid to take any independent position, especially if the rank and file was involved because it might get out of their hands and they couldn't control it. They were, and are, a thousand cases submitted every day of Negro mistreatment. They are completely ignored. The NAACP grew before the 1943 race riot. After the riot, the leadership was scared. They tried to divert all action into legal channels.

Many Negro G.I.'s were hostile to the NAACP when they returned from the army. They had written many letters to them from the army about grievances. The NAACP didn't do anything about it.

The soldiers said, "They tried to teach us how to live in a Jim Crow army."

For several months a Negro disc jockey attacked the NAACP viciously. He said he, his wife and friends would not join the branch here. He wrote a letter to the Negro press attacking the NAACP. I didn't see why. A friend told me the reason. The reverend of the church my friend attended had told the congregation the story behind it.

A few Negro leaders and a large rank-and-file support had been carrying on a vigorous campaign to break down a housing project on discrimination. This group had the support of a noted minister and a disc jockey. The pastor of my friend's church and the disc jockey went to the NAACP for support. The NAACP told them it would cooperate if this minister would withdraw from the organization. The disc jockey didn't feel this was necessary. After one week of debate within this organization, they felt they could get this minister to withdraw if this would help Negroes get into the housing project. The disc jockey and the clergyman met with this minister and he agreed to withdraw, but he said he had no confidence in the support of the NAACP. He had already gotten commitments from city officials for the organization. After he withdrew from the organization, the NAACP would not come in and gave no support. The housing project still remains segregated. This was the reason the disc jockey was attacking the NAACP so bitterly.

There was the Gordy case. Gordy's son bought a new Cadillac. He was stopped and put in jail two or three times a week when he drove it but there never were charges placed against him. He was in jail one Saturday night and Gordy went to get him out. Sunday morning two policemen went to Gordy's home to take the boy back to jail. They said they wanted to question him in connection with a robbery case.

Gordy said his son was in bed, "Where is your warrant?"

The police told Gordy, "We don't need a warrant."

They wouldn't let Gordy's son dress but put handcuffs on and began kicking him and slapping him as they walked toward the door. It was more than Gordy could stand. He got his rifle, went to the window, sighted the police. He fired twice killing one cop and wounding the other. The police came and shot up the house so bad you could see holes through it from front to back and then they used tear gas that they use in the war. They didn't give the women and children a chance to get out but just started shooting up the place. I was hurt not so much about Gordy and the police but the complete disregard the police force had for the women and children that were in the apartment.

During the Gordy shooting, the NAACP leaders were called out by some workers. The national office was informed and the director flew in from New York. There were seven thousand Negroes on the streets, and many times that day, they asked what the NAACP was going to do. At last there was something big they could handle. That was the general opinion. The NAACP director from the national office together with the local NAACP president talked with the Gordy family. They told them not to have anything to do with the Civil Rights Congress. If they did, Gordy would be sunk. The Civil Rights Congress, they said, was a Communist front organization.

When support for Gordy was raised at the board meeting of the NAACP a big shot got up and said, "Be careful what you put in the letter. We don't want to go overboard."

All the militancy was drawn out of the letter.

After the meeting that big shot told a friend of mine: "We have to be careful. The police are mad as hell."

My friend said, "The Negroes are mad as hell."

The big-shot answered only, "Well, yes."

It was raised in the NAACP board several times that the NAACP should go on record to support Gordy. They said it was a community case, and that the community should support it. As individuals we could support it.

A prominent lawyer got up and said, "We're raising hell like this is a racial case. We must be careful and remember that it is not."

Everybody knew it was a question of police brutality that was at issue. The fight went to the floor with every rank and file member fighting to help the Gordys. The vote was carried through the ranks for the NAACP to give support. It was carried on paper. I haven't heard of any support they gave.

Many Negroes, including myself, said, when Gordy got sentenced for life: "What does this mean? The leader of the NAACP said for Gordy to keep away from other groups because it would hurt him and when he follows their advice, he gets the longest term of prison possible under this state law."

These were a few of my experiences with the NAACP. When the Trotskyists told me to send this group into it, I felt bad because I'd seen it before. Sell the group out to the party. I had to be careful or I would lose my contacts and my friends in the union and I did lose some. I felt the party as a whole didn't mean what it had said at the convention. At no time did they follow the Resolution or encourage any kind of action by the Negroes.

Talk went around that I had broken the discipline of the Party in attending meetings of the group and that I should be tried. I held long discussions with leading comrades but had no direct answers. I was again floating around trying to put myself on the ground. I felt a sharp antagonism from the leaders, especially from Rollings.

The Party gave a New Year's social. This time there were sixty-five percent Negroes. I could see a big change since I'd been around. The white women seldom danced with the Negro men. If they were asked they made some excuse. I asked the wife of one of the leaders for a dance. She said no, she had a stomach ache. Soon she danced with a white man. The whites crowded around on one side of the hall and talked among themselves like at the union dances.

A Negro was expelled from the party for attending a meeting of the Negro group.

After the expulsion a white comrade told me, "That son of a bitch needs to be shot."

I couldn't agree with this statement that a Negro should be

shot for not obeying discipline. I wouldn't want a Negro to say that to me. In the South the whites always say, so and so should be killed.

When the whites got up and said these things about Negroes I could only see my father telling me not to let any white man frighten me. It was the party leaders from the highest to the lowest, but never the rank-and-file. Most of them were always friendly and sympathetic to me. The leaders brought me up before the board for arranging a meeting with the group after they had said it must be sent into the NAACP. There were nine specific charges. They were too foolish to repeat here.

Rollings turned to a white fellow and said, "Take off on him, Jack." I felt like some son of a bitch was getting ready to get me. It was cooking me to death. I just felt sick. They knew my temper. They tried to get me to blow up so they could expel me. I just sat there with my eyes closed and listened.

I kept thinking: "Here these people say they are for a new freedom."

I kept thinking about Richard Wright's story of a trial in the Communist Party.

I thought, "If they try to jump me, or if anyone tries to keep me from leaving, I'll kill the son of a bitch."

Once before I had wanted to take something with me to the meeting to protect myself. I wanted to tell them what they stood for, and what they're good for and then walk out. I was sure that if I told them about their politics they would have tried to beat me. I never was ordered so sharply in the South as in the party. Even P.L. and the other lawyers never talked to me the way these people did. On jobs in the South I could quit or get fired. But I had to sit and listen and take whatever the party said. It was like the white men and the Negro women in the South. I couldn't get away.

These were political questions with me. I went into the NAACP not because the party said to go in. I went to fight restaurant discrimination, not because I wanted to sit side of some white person. I did these things because I see them as a struggle for the rights of Negroes in this country. Any Negro who takes part in this struggle is part of me and any white person who takes part in this struggle is part of me.

I felt worse about the party than I felt in the South. The party got me to believe them. In the South nobody ever made me believe they'd accept me. But these people I took in my corner and I felt a sharp pain. I felt the way the average human being feels when a friend double crosses him. You expect it from an enemy, then it's not surprising. But they stood like a shining star over these questions and when I saw them fall I felt bad. I got to the place where I couldn't see any comparison between them and a workers' party. That was the end of my life with those people. It was the beginning too because I was never happier at any time in my life than when I left the Trotskyist Party.

FOR THE FUTURE

For the future I can't make any blueprints but I know where I feel best. That's in the plant with my friends on the line when we're fighting the company and fighting the union on an issue. I have a feeling this story of mine isn't nearly finished but I want to stop now for the time being. One last thing I want to say:

I am just like any one of you. I didn't have anything whatsoever to do with where I was born. I didn't have anything to do with whether I would be male or female. I didn't have anything to do with whether I would be black or white. But if you can absorb this story, it may enable you to understand who you are. I have never lived one day outside the United States.

All of these things and many others, I have felt, seen and experienced here in the United States.

Some workers have read the draft of this book and have asked me: "Well, we know all this, so what?"

I don't think everybody knows all this. I have never seen all this in print anywhere and that is why I have written it and had it printed.

And some others have asked me, "Yes, it is good that people should know this but what is the answer?"

This means that I am supposed to give a big program about the world revolution and freedom for this or that and so on.

I have had enough of those arguments. Any reader of this book knows what I want and I will fight for it however I can and wherever I can.

PART II.

17.
VISITING MONTGOMERY

I DECIDED TO go back to the South when so many new developments were taking place among the Blacks following the 1954 Supreme Court decision outlawing school segregation and the 1955 murder of the Black youth Emmet Till in Mississippi.

A lot of tension was building up, and nobody knew where or when it would break. And on December 5, 1955, there wasn't a soul who thought that when a working woman, a seamstress named Rosa Parks, refused to give up her seat to a white man on a bus in Montgomery, Alabama, that the break had come. Each concrete act took everyone by complete surprise, from the refusal by Mrs. Parks to give up her seat to a white man, to the response to her arrest and court appearance, to the mass demonstrations led by the then unknown Rev. Martin Luther King Jr., to the Black community running their own transportation system. It became Revolution, a word none of us ever used referring to an action defying the segregated conditions of life in the South. That mass action of revolt was the Montgomery Bus Boycott.

During the boycott, I talked with Rev. King, and he told me very firmly what had happened. In fact, I asked him how he had been able to organize the people around the boycott, because there had been so many times before that a lot worse things had happened than what Mrs. Parks went through—like Blacks being viciously beaten, and even shot and killed for refusing to move out of their seats for whites. I'd had the same kind of trouble myself.

Rev. King traced the events, and said, "You know—I can't tell you to save my life why Mrs. Parks didn't move back when they told her to. She says she was tired. And I believe that; but I also know that she was active in the NAACP, never successfully. This time after they arrested her, all hell burst loose."

He went on to say that there had been a few Black college youth on the bus from State Teacher's College, and they found out that Mrs. Parks was going to be tried on a certain day—I think it was Wednesday.

"The students came here to the church," Rev. King said, "because we have a mimeograph machine, and they wanted to run off some leaflets. And to tell the truth, what I believe caused the Montgomery Bus Boycott was the *Montgomery Advertiser,* the white daily paper."

He went on to explain that the youth had run off a couple hundred leaflets and passed them out in the Black community. Somehow the *Montgomery Advertiser* got a leaflet, and reprinted it just as it had been written, so that everybody, and especially the whites, could read it that Sunday morning. They also editorialized about it, saying what the hell do these damn niggers want? What the hell are they planning? And that's what really set the whole thing off, the talking about staying off the buses for one day to protest Mrs. Park's arrest.

That Sunday, in practically every Black church in the city, the members were talking about the leaflet calling for Blacks not to ride the bus on the day of Mrs. Park's trial, and to be at the courthouse to support her.

"And that," Rev. King told me, "was the first I knew about it. All church members were asking their pastors what they should do, and practically every one of the pastors said they should stay off. I said the same thing to my members."

He said about 80 percent stayed off and walked that day. After that, the youth came back. The momentum had picked up, and they had something going. They wanted to use the mimeograph machine some more, and Rev. King helped them to punctuate and write the leaflets. He kept on talking to them, and they said, "Reverend, why don't you come on and help us." And Rev. King said that was his first direct involvement in it.

He didn't know how far it was going, and he was telling me he didn't know how involved he was in it. But he kept on helping them, and then it was him and them...running around all over the place.

Anyway, that 80 percent who boycotted the buses that day was more than anyone could believe. Rev. King thought, like everyone else in Montgomery, that it was just going to be a one-day demonstration for Mrs. Parks. But after the Blacks boycotted the buses that Wednesday, and then went back to the bus stops on Thursday, something else happened. All the bus drivers—and they were all white then—would pull up to a stop and, where there were all Blacks standing there, went on by without picking up a single one of them.

The reaction of the Blacks was, "What the hell! We walked yesterday... we can walk today." And that, Rev. King said, was the beginning of the Montgomery Bus Boycott. And they kept on walking from that day on—for over nine months—until they won.

I've talked with Mrs. Parks many times, and she has told me she didn't even know that plans for a bus boycott were going on, and that when she got out of jail, she actually felt she might have a a bad name and be thought of as a jailbird.

At that time, she was teaching a sewing class of about five or six young girls. She said when she got home from jail, it was the night for the girls to come to take their sewing lessons. She had set everything up as usual and was waiting for the girls.

Pretty soon, one of the girls came in, and Mrs. Parks said, "O.K., we'll start with the lesson, and maybe the others will come later."

But the young girl looked at Mrs. Parks and said, "Oh, I didn't come to take any sewing lesson." And Mrs. Parks was just waiting to hear her say, "because you've been in jail," or something related to that.

Mrs. Parks asked her why she had come then, and the girl told her she just wanted to drop in to say hello and see how she was, but that she was going on to the mass meeting. Mrs. Parks asked her what kind of mass meeting, and the girl looked kind of surprised and said it was the same meeting Mrs. Parks' other sewing students were going to; and then said, "Don't you know? It's about you. About them putting you in jail." That was the first time that Mrs. Parks learned that a bus boycott had been carried out because she had been jailed. She went to the meeting with her student, and became an active member in the boycott until it ended in victory.

Rev. King said that in the early stages of the boycott, there were several people in the leadership. There was no formalized leadership then as there was later, when Rev. King emerged as the leader.

After about a week of the Blacks staying off the buses, the

white bus drivers would stop and urge Blacks to get on and ride. But the Blacks were either walking or using a transportation system they had set up themselves. They were also meeting regularly, as often as two or three times a week, to make and carry out their plans to continue the boycott. At this point, no demands were made for Black bus drivers. That came in later as a part of the struggle.

During the early stages of the Montgomery Bus Boycott, almost all the so-called leaders opposed it, including Black Detroit Congressman Charles Diggs. I heard him speak on the radio after the boycott began, and he said that since it had already started, that he supposed it was all right, but he was opposed to this method as being the way to any solution.

Many labor leaders also opposed it; and it was only later, when they could see the Black people were winning, and after the Supreme Court knocked down segregated busing, that they got on the civil rights bandwagon. I know that when John F. Kennedy was running against Vice President Nixon for the presidency of the U.S., he was going around with Rev. King for nearly a year, saying how much he supported Black civil rights. Nixon was also playing the same game, and would show up at some of the mass meetings. But King was smart enough that he never once came out for Nixon, and said anything that would indicate support for him.

Walter Reuther opposed the boycott when it first started, saying it was detrimental to our way of life, to the free enterprise system. He would always find a way to twist it, to make it sound like he was for civil rights. He'd say that it was wrong what the whites were doing in Montgomery, but this was no way to solve the problems. The same pattern applied to all of them: they were all opposed until the mass movement showed it was not going to give in and was going to win.

The NAACP and the middle class Negro leaders also seemed afraid of, or were actually opposed to, the Montgomery Bus Boycott. It was only after nearly four months of continous struggle, during which the national NAACP was absolutely silent, that they finally came out in support of the boycott. This organization, which proclaimed itself to be the sole leader and reppresentative of the fight for Black rights, dared to hint that the reason for their long silence was that at first they weren't sure that the bus boycott was against segregation.

The unions, especially the CIO with its many Negro staff members who also sounded their notes to the world about their stand on civil rights, had deaf ears when it came to hearing the message of the colored people of Montgomery and giving them support.

Congressman Adam Clayton Powell, the Black Congressman from Harlem, N.Y., was another who waited for months before coming out openly for the boycott.

Actually, the idea of a boycott had been around Montgomery for a long time. People waiting at the bus stops were often passed by with the buses half empty in front and crowded in the rear. If Blacks could get on, they'd be shoved to the back and had to stand a lot more often then they could sit. As far back as 1947-1948, one Black bought a couple of old buses and tried to organize a service to carry Blacks to and from ball games. When Blacks would get together, they'd often talk about getting their own bus system so they wouldn't have to put up with their treatment.

After the end of World War II, groups of Blacks all over the city began to organize their own social clubs. Before they took their own actions, the only bars they could get into were miserable dives. So the boycott was a result of a lot of things that had come together in Montgomery where Blacks had a history of doing things for themselves.

Organizing social clubs for themselves was one thing, but boycotting buses owned by white interests was something else. The city pulled out all stops to try to break the boycott. Rev. King's home was bombed, as was the home of E.D. Nixon a pullman porter active in the boycott. No one was arrested for the bombings, but both King and Nixon were arrested, along with 90 other Montgomery Blacks active in the boycott. The Alabama law used against them had been passed in 1921 to break a miners' strike. During the strike, in addition to this vicious anti-labor law, Birmingham mine operators had tried to lure Negroes from the farms to work as scabs. Blacks who went and came back to the farms said, "Sure, you can go up and the white man will give you a job, but this is one time when you don't want to be on two sides. You gotta declare where you stand...and you better be with the strikers."

Scab laws like this were now being dusted off to use against Montgomery's Blacks. Despite these attacks and obvious violations of their rights, not a leading Black or labor leader took a stand for them. In fact, when some 90 white steelworkers in Birmingham, Alabama, sent a letter to AFL-CIO President Meany in 1956 telling him that if the union was for integration they would withdraw from it, Meany is reported to have simply turned the letter over to United Steel Worker President David McDonald without comment. By this time, practically everybody in the U.S. had taken loud and clear positions either for or against the bus boycott, but there was still not so much as a whisper from the labor leaders.

The labor unions stood exposed, because every single one of them had given loud and long lip service about organizing the South. On just what basis did they propose to organize the South, the workers were asking, when they couldn't openly come out in favor of something so clear and fundamental as what was going on in Montgomery? With the labor leaders so afraid to even speak out in support of the Montgomery boycotters, it's little wonder that the southern white supremacist leaders were not concerned about the organizing rhetoric of the unions. In fact, the unions openly admitted their own membership in the viciously racist White Citizen's Councils which were established to combat the Black freedom movement.

Here was a situation where theory could immediately be put into practice—and it revealed that the labor leaders, and many leading Blacks as well, were bankrupt on both counts. At the height of the Montgomery struggle in 1956, Reuther was making a trip to India. It was Reuther who a few years earlier at an NAACP meeting had shaken the rafters with his declarations that America could never become the great nation until it freed itself of racism which had kept it in bondage since the days of Reconstruction. Those words, however, were spoken when there was no mass movement of the Blacks striving to break that bondage. Now that Reuther was faced with the responsibility of taking a position in relation to a concrete mass action, he was silent. As one worker put it, "Reuther is going to India to sell our democracy. Why won't he go down South and sell some to the White Citizens Councils? How can he have much interest in the workers of India and forget the struggle of the Negro people here under his nose?"

The boycott was in Montgomery, but its influence was felt everywhere. And just how vital the independent movement of Blacks for equality was can be seen in an episode in a steel plant in Birmingham in 1956. In the steel mill there were Coke machines, and there was a policy that if you put money in the machine and nothing came out, you could report it and either get a refund or a Coke from the person servicing the machines.

When this happened to a Black worker and he reported it, instead of getting his money back, the white service man began to curse and use derogatory and insulting language against him. A fight broke out between them, and the Black beat the white man.

The steel company fired the Black, and for several months the union and company played around with grievance procedures. The Coke man was back to work, but not the Black steelworker. The Blacks were in the majority in the plant and after months of this footdragging by the company and union, decided to take their own action. They boycotted the Coke machines, and the action began to spread to other plants of the same company.

The company called a meeting for the Blacks to discuss the problem. The Black workers not only told them, they gave the company a certain date to rehire the fired worker, and said if this wasn't done, they'd spread the Black boycott of Coke throughout all of Birmingham. On the date they had set, the Black worker was back on his job. But the worker wanted full justice, and demanded that the company pay the worker for all the time he was off his job. The company paid him for every hour of lost time.

Northern Blacks, especially those who left the South in the '20s and '30s used to make statements and jokes about the backwardness and fear of Southern Blacks. When the boycott erupted, they were stunned, asking: "Who are these Negroes in the South, and where did they come from?" They never realized that the most oppressed people of any society are the most likely to revolt against it.

I was there, in Birmingham, the day the Supreme Court ruled that segregated busing was unconstitutional. The next day I was in Montgomery and I rode a bus. I parked my car, and with my sister's boy got on a bus. We sat in front, and I asked the white bus driver, "How do you feel now?"

He said, "Man, I'm so happy this thing is over I don't know

what to do. I had lost practically everything I had during the boycott. I went out and got a job in construction, and that work like to have killed me. I just couldn't do it. From now on, people can sit anywhere they want to...so long as they don't sit here." And he pointed to his own, the driver's seat.

He was friendly and jolly about it, but it was something he had learned. I'm sure he was among the drivers who passed Blacks by when the boycott first began, but that whole struggle changed the thinking of a lot of people. There was so much joy in listening to the Blacks talking when they broke the segregation. It was a new day. It was a new dawn on the horizon for them—just to sit anywhere they wanted to on the bus. And whites now would have to stand if they didn't get to a seat first!

I had a sister-in-law there. She was talking about being on a bus one morning and a white woman was standing over her. My sister-in-law knew that the white woman wanted so bad to tell her to get up so she could sit down...and my sister-in-law got the biggest kick in the world out of knowing she didn't have to stand up for her. It was the taste of freedom, a taste that was won after nine long months of continuous meetings and of planning and setting up a new transportation system for 60,000 Blacks in Montgomery. This was done while the constant terror, bombings, harassment, intimidation, firings and practically every form of inhuman treatment you can think of were thrown against the entire Black community in those months of struggle. That's what was so terrific—in the face of all of this, they fought and won.

Few can look out upon a calm sea and tell when a storm will rise and the tides will sweep all filth to the shore. No one can set the time, date or place for the self activities of the Blacks, as the Communist and other radical parties have always tried to do. They all cling to the conception of plan, and think that if they do not plan it for the Blacks, it cannot be done; and if a party leader does not lead the movement, that it is a useless movement.

This was, and is, also the line of the trade union leaders. These so-called leaders were completely blind to what was happening. They simply could not believe that Blacks in the South, where the whole social, political, legal and economic system was organized to keep them in bondage, could succeed in fighting against such overwhelming force. Because of this, they could not begin to understand the tremendous power and influence the bus boycott had among other Blacks in the South. This spreading courage and determination could be seen in a telegram sent by a group of Georgian Blacks to President Eisenhower early in 1957, asking him to send Vice President Nixon to the South, instead of to Europe and Asia where he was supposed to go to speak on American Democracy.

18.
LITTLE ROCK, GREENSBORO, OXFORD

PRESIDENT EISENHOWER GOT another message from the Black people later in 1957. This time it was from Little Rock, Arkansas, where the first public school desegregation plan ordered by the courts was supposed to go into effect.

The white power structure in the South, through legal maneuvering, had been able to hold off integration action for a few years, mainly because the 1954 Supreme Court decision had given a legal loophole in ordering school desegregation with "all deliberate speed." By the fall of 1957, the legal sidestepping was all over in one respect, but just beginning in another.

The plan to "desegregate" Central High School in Little Rock boiled down to this: nine Black students would be accepted. They were met by a shrieking white mob which would have killed them if they got the chance. Instead, they viciously beat the Black parents who went with their children to try to protect them against the white mob.

President Eisenhower, despite the fact that he opposed desegregation, was forced to send in federal troops to Little Rock to protect the nine Black students. Very few people understand just how much courage and bravery it took on the part of those Black students and their parents to stand up to the terror of that white mob. They wrote a very important chapter in the history of Freedom in the U.S.

The whole episode showed a lot of funny things, strange things; and one of them had to do with General Walker, the general in charge of the federal troops there. Here was a man right in the middle of one of the most historic civil rights situations in U.S. history, commanding troops sent to back up school desegregation. Yet, when he came out of the army, he became one of the most outspoken, one of the worst racists this country has ever seen.

Another aspect of that Little Rock situation was that once it settled down, the states in the South began desegregation of their schools for the most part, much more so than schools in the North even now. As a matter of fact, the northern schools didn't do a thing about desegregation. Instead, they took actions that resulted in more racial school segregation, not less.

I'm firmly convinced that if President Johnson had ordered troops into northern cities to enforce desegregation of the public schools that we'd never have had the situations develop where today, in 1978, we can still have such vicious racism in the school systems as are being faced in such places as Boston and Louisville. For those who are always shouting that this is a nation of laws, not men, it might be good for them to remember that the Supreme Court decision "outlawing" school segregation came down 24 years ago.

Black emotions for freedom were always growing. They had been able to force legal decisions outlawing discrimination in public facilities and in public schools through their mass actions. In the South, it became a question of the Blacks demanding enforcement of the law, and the southern white power structure opposing it. Every year, every month, every day the confrontations were going on—in the schools, in public places, on the job, in politics...everywhere in the South.

Just as nobody could predict the reaction to Mrs. Parks refusing to move back in the bus on Dec. 5, 1955, that resulted in the Montgomery Bus Boycott, nobody dreamed that when four Black students from the Agricultural and Technical College in Greensboro, North Carolina, sat down at an S.S. Kresge lunch counter on Feb. 1, 1960, and demanded to be served, that this action would explode into the Black mass revolt that would send the Black civil rights movement to every corner of the U.S. and throughout the world as nothing that had ever happened before. It was almost like every Black in the South had been set like a time bomb to go off when those four students sat down, because that simple act triggered a chain reaction throughout the whole South as Black youth everywhere began to sit in, picket and challenge the whole way of life in the South that denied them their freedom, their equality.

By Feb. 1, 1961, thousands of young Blacks had demonstrated in more than 60 cities in Virginia, North Carolina, Georgia, Alabama, Florida, Tennessee, Louisiana and Texas. Even in Mississippi, the most viciously racist of them all, while there had not been any sit-ins, there had been successful Black boycotts of stores with segregated lunch counters. These demonstrations sent signals all over the country, and there were thousands of whites, especially in the northern white youth, who got those signals and were answering them.

Many Blacks and whites who were dissatisfied with the NAACP's failure to get involved in anything but legal battles formed their own organizations. The Congress of Racial Equality (CORE) was one of these, and they organized Freedom Rides with Blacks and whites riding buses together through the South to desegregate the bus depots and break down racial discrimination.

There had been Freedom Rides before, but these had ended with the buses carrying the whites and Blacks being burned and the people inside beaten up. But when the Freedom Rides began in May of 1961, it was clear that now it was going to be different. The great bravery shown by the southern Black youth inspired white northern youth who began to get totally involved in the civil rights movement and joined CORE by the thousands—participating in everything from desegregating public places up North and demanding Black employment in formerly all-white jobs, to marching and volunteering for Freedom Rides in the South.

One of the earliest, and still probably the best, reports of what happened on those rides appeared in a pamphlet written by freedom riders themselves, and was called just that, *Freedom Riders Speak for Themselves*. Mary Hamilton, a co-author and a young Black militant, described the morning she and other freedom riders stopped in Jackson, Mississippi:

"We pulled into the Jackson station, Sunday morning, at 10:15. Everything was deadly still. Police were posted all over—outside the station, and inside the terminal. There were a few people standing around watching us. We walked very quietly through the Negro waiting room, and into the white waiting room. Some of the people took seats.

Police Captain J. L. Ray was there, and reporters, and plainclothesmen, and many policemen. Captain Ray walked up and said, 'Who's the spokesman for this group?'

We pointed out the spokesman.

He said, 'Are you all going to move on?'
Our spokesman said, 'Why must we move on?'
Captain Ray said, 'I said are you all going to move on? Move on, and move out of this here station?'
Our spokesman said, 'We're interstate travelers. What reason is there for us to leave the station?'
And he said again, he was very angry, 'I said you all move on and leave this here station.'
Our spokesman said, 'No. We will not leave the station.'
Captain Ray said, 'Does that go for all of you all?'
And we all said, 'Yes. That goes for all of us all.'
He said, 'Then you all are under arrest.' "

While the pamphlet goes on to describe the brutality of their treatment, one of the most important developments was the great role the Black women in Jackson played in trying to help the freedom riders and making them as comfortable as they could during their stay in prison. They called themselves Women Power Unlimited; and in the courage they showed in challenging the force of the police who tried to harass and intimidate them, they helped to lift the spirits of the freedom riders while they were in jail.

The pamphlet has some of the most profound ideas I have ever seen in print. It represented to me the same ideas as when Marx wrote in 1860, "In my opinion the biggest things that are happening in the world today are on the one hand the movement of slaves in America started by the death of John Brown and, on the other, the movement of the serfs in Russia...."

We could see the new beginnings with the Freedom Rides and the student sit-ins throughout the country. We were seeing at the same time new nations bursting out all over Africa, and a few short years before that we had seen the Hungarian Freedom Fighters in 1956 and the Montgomery Bus Boycott.

From the self-organization of the student sit-inners to the self-activity of the Montgomery Black Freedom Fighters who continued to get service at the us and train stations until they were successful, to the 30,000 youth who demonstrated in Washington, D.C. for school integration, all pointed to the dissatisfacion of people from all walks of life with the hollowness of U.S. "democracy." As one youth said, "We are not rebels without a cause!" They wanted to practice some of the freedom that was being talked about for the rest of the world.

When I heard the word freedom, I couldn't help but think of a white manager of a bus terminal in Birmingham, Alabama, who had been arrested four times for serving Blacks. I couldn't help but think of the politicians, of State Department officials yelling to the whole world that the American people were free and all those behind the Iron Curtain were enslaved. I couldn't help but think of the Black troops in West Berlin, told to be ready to give their lives to free the "slaves" from behind the iron curtain of East Berlin and other parts of the world. Why weren't the Black troops allowed to stand ready to preserve freedom in South, U.S.A.?

The southern power structure was hell bent to preserve but one thing, and that was the segregated life and culture of the South. Beatings, killings, floggings, harassment and intimidation were all let loose upon the Blacks and whites who dared to join them in their struggle. Congressinal hearings were held where Black and white freedom fighters testified to the brutality they had experienced in the South; reports of murders of civil rights workers made headlines. To all of this the Kennedy Administration asked for a "cooling off" period, for an end to civil rights demonstrations, so legal action could be taken.

What the administration didn't seem to realize, or deliberately ignored, was the overriding fact that legal action had been taken by the courts—by the highest court of the land, in fact—but that did not give a single Black in the nation any rights at all. It was the demonstrations, the demands for freedom the Blacks were backing up with their actions against violence and barbarism in the South, that had gained everything won up to that point.

The schools became one of the big battlegrounds in the struggle, where there were many examples of mass and individual bravery. Nobody will ever know how many thousands of Black youth were suspended or expelled from high school for participating in boycotts, marches and other demonstrations. There were no Blacks in the universities of Alabama and Mississippi, and that is why Autherine Lucey in Alabama and James Meredith in Mississippi are now a part of the civil rights history of the U.S.

In September of 1962, on the day when Meredith was to

enroll in Mississippi, the eyes of the whole world were focused on Oxford, where the university is located. Governor Ross Barnett, President Kennedy, federal troops, a mob of racist whites and Meredith were all involved. Before the night was over, a riot by the whites had exploded, resulting in the death of a French newspaper reporter who was shot in the back while covering the events, and in the burning, pillaging and looting by the howling pack of whites. The six-orbital space flight of astronaut Walter Schirra tool place at this same time, but that achievement was pushed out of the headlines by what was happening in Oxford. The race between the U.S. and Russia for superiority in space took a back seat to the fight for human equality on earth.

By the time the civil rights movement moved to Birmingham, which became the main target in 1963, Rev. King was leading it, and he was a genius when it came to the tactics and strategy he used to move the struggle forward. One of the things that was tremendous about the battle in Birmingham was the involvement of the youth. My sister lived there, and I remember one summer her son came up to visit us in Detroit, and he asked me if I had seen him on TV. I wasn't thinking very much about anything like that, and said, no, that I hadn't seen him, and asked him what he was doing on TV.

"Demonstrating! That's what I was doing. Demonstrating!" And he just shouted it out with great joy. He was proud of what he was doing, and I know all of the other youth were too. This is another side of the raising of the consciousness of everybody. There was no one who wasn't touched by that mass movement in one way or other.

In Birmingham, Police Commissioner "Bull" Connor's brutal attacks against the demonstrators were seen by the whole world on TV, as the camera recorded the full force of the fire hoses turned against the youth who tightly held hands to keep together and to keep from being knocked down, of the electric cattle prods pressed against the Black bodies, and of the vicious police dogs ordered to attack the marchers and tearing at the flesh of the youth.

I've never had a cattle prod put against me, but I've talked to many people who were shocked by them. Some of them will be marked for life. As many people know who followed those events, the cattle prods were jammed against the breasts and between the legs of women and young girls, and against the testicles of men and boys who were demonstrating for freedom.

One example in Montgomery was of a young Black man and a white woman who had come from the North to help. They were walking down a street together when cops attacked them. They pushed the white woman aside and started to mercilessly beat the Black youth as though they were going to kill him. The white woman threw herself over her Black friend to protect his life, and the police used the cattle prods against her. But she didn't get up, and probably saved the Black youth's life. And that was just for walking down the street together.

I attended the mammoth civil rights march on Washington on August 28, 1963. It was the biggest demonstration this country's lawmakers had seen to that point. No less than 150 Congressmen were there to make sure they were seen and counted by the more than 250,000 marchers and millions of others who watched on TV. This march was the first big one that had a large percentage of whites. It gave notice to the administration that they were dealing not only with Blacks, but also with many whites who felt none could be free until all were free.

There was a big difference between the enthusiasm and spontaneity of the southern marchers—many of them directly from jail cells to participate—and the delegations sent from the North. Some of the southern youth, in fact, never stopped picketing while they were in the capital.

By contrast, many of the workers participating from the North felt regimented by too much "central organization" and discipline from the labor bureaucracy. The feeling was very different from the huge Detroit march of June 23, two months earlier, where I had also been. There, the feeling and morale was so high that I felt as though I could almost touch freedom, and that nothing could stop this powerful force from winning.

At the Washington rally, the labor bureaucrats like UAW President Walter Reuther were saying the right words, but they were abstract. It seemed to me that the white leaders, with the help of some leading Blacks, were trying to submerge the Negro activity in a pure and simple class question along trade union lines. There was no question but that the support of whites was vital for success, but it was also clear that these so-called leaders were there for the sole purpose of controlling it.

The mammoth march down Woodward Ave., Detroit, June, 1963.

That's what made all the difference in the world when Rev. King spoke. He was speaking for, and from the aspirations of the Black masses—it was his famous "I Have A Dream" speech. This same feeling also came through when John Lewis spoke. He was a Black youth activist with the Student Non-Violent Coordinating Committee (SNCC) in the South. Lewis had planned to say that the Civil Rights Movement should march through the South like Sherman had marched through Georgia during the Civil War. But this reference created a lot of turmoil, and I know that Reuther and a priest from New York had threatened to pull out of the rally if Lewis' remarks weren't watered down, so, he took out the reference to marching through the South. Reuther and the others were showing great consideration for the feelings of the reactionary southern rulers, but Lewis was showing his concern for freedom and for human beings, and said we had to take our own actions.

The point is an important one, because when we win something for ourselves, it cannot easily be taken away. This is just the opposite of looking for a Moses to lead a people out of the wilderness, because a Moses could lead them right back again. As a matter of fact, the whole pack of would-be Moseses at the rally did change the rally. It was supposed to have been a more direct action and demonstration rally aimed at the administration, but was turned into a rally to hear speakers.

But the labor movement had money, lots of it, that they could give to the movement. Though they never came out and said it, the money always had conditions put on it. Things had to be done the way the labor leaders wanted things to happen. At the big mass rallies throughout the South, union representatives were sent to speak. But those same representatives were also getting information about the directions the Black leaders were moving in and reporting back to their own union leaders.

I remember a rally and march during the later years held in New Orleans, which was followed by a conference in Mobile that I attended. At the conference was UAW representative Oliver, a real Uncle Tom for many years, who had been sent to the New Orleans march. He gave a complete report of what he was going to be telling UAW President Leonard Woodcock and the top UAW leadership when he got back. This was the way they operated—to try to make sure they would be able to head off any development they opposed.

A few weeks after the March on Washington, what has to be one of the worst dehumanized actions of the racist South occurred. On September 15, four young Black girls in the 16th Street Baptist Church in Birmingham were blown to bits as they were changing into their choir robes by a bomb thrown into the church by racist whites. To this day, 15 years later, only one person has been found guilty of that outrage, and that was this year, 1978. No one else has been brought to justice for most of the other murders during this whole period.

A document, put out by The Council of Federated Organizations which was conducting a program called Freedom Summer in Mississippi, dealt with 37 bills introduced in the legislature of Mississippi in its 1964 session. It gave me the same feeling I had when I read reports of the extermination camps of Hitler. How inhuman people can be to people. Keep in mind that these bills were proposed to become laws of the state. It relates not only to Mississippi, but also to the South as a whole, to what the U.S. was, and to the thinking of all of those who were yelling for states rights, including Barry Goldwater, then the presidential candidate of the Republican Party. Goldwater was trying to tell the Black people that he was for civil rights, but that changes would have to come from a "change of heart" of the people. He couldn't have been talking about the Black people, because they had made very clear where their hearts, and heads, were.

The report by COFO, and the laws themselves, did clearly show where the hearts and heads of the racist power structure were.

Mentioning a few of the 37 bills will reveal just what was involved:

An "Anti-economic Boycott Bill" would outlaw economic boycotts by *Negroes* against white businesses which discriminate against Negroes. Another bill prohibited the distribution of leaflets calling for economic boycott. Another allowed the police to restrict the free movement of individuals and groups, and established curfews without formally declaring martial law. Two bills revoked the charter of Tougaloo College (a Black college) and would drop it from accreditation.

One bill was designed to pay the cost of county registrants and circuit clerks convicted under the Civil Rights Act, that is, those who refused to comply with Federal Court orders to register

Blacks on an equal basis with whites. Another reduced the number of Blacks on jury lists by changing the qualifications for jury members.

One bill sought mandatory sterilization for those convicted of a third felony. This was clearly aimed at Blacks and those whites who supported them, for no racist white in Mississippi had ever been convicted of any crimes committed against Blacks. Another bill sought to provide prison terms or sterilization for parents of illegitimate children. This was actually passed by the House, revised by the Senate and passed in a form that struck out the sterilization clause.

At least seven Blacks had been killed by whites in the first few months of the year in the South, but Federal agents in the states were unable to come up with any concrete "proof" against the murderers. This was the natural way of life in Mississippi. It was the natural way the U.S. government continued to operate in Mississippi—and the South as well. Even when white racists were caught, they were freed in the courts—and even given rewards. Three whites accused of the Birmingham church bombing were freed. Byron De La Beckwith, who murdered Black civil rights leader Medgar Evers, was not only freed, but was ridden around in police cars as a hero. When three young civil rights workers, Schwerner, Chaney and Goodman, disappeared from Philadelphia, Mississippi on June 21, 1964, and were later found murdered, other civil rights workers said it took 24 hours to even get the federal government to investigate. Civil rights workers constantly charged that the FBI would not come when called, and that they got nothing but obstruction from local FBI agents.

Nowhere was the corruption and hypocrisy more prevalent than in Mississippi. The white power structure there, frightened to its boots at the power of the movement and the support of whites it had won, showed the true face of what the freedom movement was fighting against. The civil rights fighters were not only challenging the way of life of white Mississippians, they were challenging the way of life of the entire U.S.

Obviously, there were race haters everywhere. A white southern worker told me of a vicious racist letter he had received from Indiana, which explained the "true" meaning of the civil rights bill to be a part of the Communist conspiracy to overthrow the U.S. and to mongrelize the white race, which was so pure.

That's what I mean about the '60s changing the thinking of almost everyone in the U.S. Practically every headline had something pertaining to the civil rights struggle. It could be reactionary thinking at times, but it was on an entirely different level than it had been before.

19.
THE FBI DOES NOTHING: THE MURDER OF VIOLA LIUZZO, THE BOMBING OF CHURCHES

ONE OF THE results of this period was that a lot of the smaller rural counties in the South separated from the bigger cities and were on the move. Places like Lowndes County in Alabama. When the marchers went through Lowndes County in the 1965 march from Selma to Montgomery, they changed the entire history of the county and raised the level of consciousness of the Blacks like nothing that had ever happened before. Up to that time, there had never been a single Black who had registered to vote. And not one Black in Lowndes County, everyone I talked to said, took part in the march.

The whites had the Blacks in Lowndes County so suppressed that they told them if they tried to join the march, they'd be run off the land and out of the area. The Blacks who owned their own land were threatened too, but the whites didn't try to stop them from going up to highway U.S. 80, the route of the march.

I had a cousin there, and I always thought he was an Uncle Tom because he was so submissive to whites. After the march to Montgomery, he told me, "When I stood there and looked at those people, hundreds and hundreds of them, coming up that road, something just came over me and you know, I said, 'they're doing this for me too.' And you know something, ever since that moment, I swore that I would die before I would take what I took before."

I just looked at him and said, "You Sanders?" And he said, "I'm with them 100 percent."

After he took his stand, none of the white families he used to work for so faithfully even talked with him. But Sanders doesn't care—when he became a part of the movement, he was a part of something great, and he knew it.

From that point, the march from Selma to Montgomery, the Blacks in the whole of Lowndes County began to organize—in that same week. They had a hard time. They were run off the land by the whites they worked for, and whites bought up the property that Blacks owned to drive them out of the county.

One of the things that happened during the march was that people would be sent ahead to find a place for the marchers to stay for the night. A Black man, Snap Dudley, had worked for a white man, Edward Meeling, for many, many years. Snap was considered to be a "house nigger," a person the landowner could trust completely.

As it happened, Snap met with these advance marchers and told them that they could stay at "his" place for the night. But the truth of the matter was that Snap didn't "own" anything; and to top it all off, Meeling was a Ku Kluxer and one of the most vicious racist bastards you could ever meet in your life.

Anyway, when the marchers got to Snap's "place," they pitched their tents and set themselves to stay for the night. Somebody told Meeling that the marchers were camping on his property, and at first he just couldn't believe it. But just to make sure, he went down to check. And sure enough, there were the marchers, camping on his property. He almost went crazy, yelling at the marchers to get off his land. One of the guards told Meeling that they had been given permission to stay there, otherwise they certainly wouldn't be there. After a big hassle, with Meeling calling the law and a whole bunch of arguments, the marchers moved out.

Later that night, when Meeling learned that Snap was the one who had given the marchers permission to stay on his property, he died of a heart attack. As for Snap, he said, "I've been working on this land all my life. If I didn't own the land, I sure should've owned it." The people of Lowndes County are still talking about this one, and will be talking about it for a long time to come.

When the marchers were evicted from Meeling's land, they went down the road a few miles to a place owned by a Black store owner, Rose Steel, and she let them stay there.

There are many store owners like Rose in Lowndes County, who make their living by selling to Blacks mostly. These store owners got their goods mainly from Montgomery, and when Rose let the Montgomery marchers stay on her place, the white suppliers to these Black stores decided they'd teach her a lesson by cutting off all her supplies.

The week after the march, the white supply driver drove on by her place, and didn't stop to take her order as he usually did. The next store up the road was Cosby's. When the supply man passed on by her place, Rose went to ask him if the supply man had stopped at his store. Cosby told her he had stopped, and Mrs. Steel told Cosby she thought the supply people were trying to squeeze her out, to punish her for allowing the marchers to stay on her place.

The next week, the supply man again passed by Rose's place and went to Cosby's with his big order of supplies placed the week before. He went into Cosby's with both his arms full of supplies, and just as he was about to put the order down on the store counter, Cosby yelled at him. "Hey! Just a minute there. Don't put that stuff down there. Hold it just a minute."

And there you really had a scene. There was the delivery man, standing with his arms loaded down with the order, and Cosby asking him questions.

Cosby said, "Did you deliver an order to Mrs. Steel?" The man said no, and Cosby asked him why. The man answered with, "Well, it's not me. It's my boss. I've got my orders, and my orders are not to deliver anything to her."

To that Cosby said, "Well, you can take your damned delivery and put it back in your truck. And don't deliver me anything else until you start making deliveries to Mrs. Steel. And besides that, you'd better not deliver anything else to any store in this county, because I'm going to go to every Black store owner in the county to tell them you're not making deliveries to Mrs. Steel because she let the marchers stay on her property."

"But it's not me," the supply man said, "It's my boss...."

"Well, you tell your boss," Cosby shot back, "that I'm returning my delivery right now, and next week you won't have a delivery to make to any Black store owner in this county unless you deliver to Mrs. Rose Steel."

The next week, the first place the supply man stopped at was Mrs. Rose Steel's. She told me he came in so polite that morning, saying, "Hi, how are ya? How ya doin'? Is there anything you need?" And he just went behind her counter and started checking her supplies and gave her everything she wanted...and even more than she wanted. And on top of that, he bought some things for himself. He spent a long time talking to her, and saying "Let me have this " and "Let me have that ...."

When the supply man left Mrs. Steel's, he went on up to

Cosby's. But this time he didn't take any supplies with him, and walked in the store with his arms empty. He said, "Cosby, I've delivered Mrs. Steel her supplies. The boss man said to cut it out, and to make deliveries to her. And so I did. Now, do you want your order?"

Cosby told him, "Just a minute, I want to call Mrs. Steel to see how she's doing." He called, and she told him that, yes, the delivery had been made, and, on top of that, the supply man had even spent about $5 of his own money buying stuff from her store.

And that was that. What I'm trying to show is how the Blacks were all united against the tactics used against them, and how they fought back and won...in Selma and Montgomery.

The Selma to Montgomery march was one of the great high points of the struggle. During the time of that march, several whites and Blacks were killed. And it was when the Black marchers crossed over the bridge into Montgomery that they were unmercifully beaten by the police. This was something the world was witness to, as newspapers, radio and TV reporters described what happened there.

This was the time when Rev. King asked President Johnson to provide federal protection, preferably troops. But Johnson said he wouldn't send any troops. I clearly remember him saying, "I'm not going to be browbeaten into doing anything I don't want to do." That's when the appeal went out to whites across the country to help, and they poured in by the busloads from everywhere.

That's what I think was crucial to the whole situation. It wasn't just that Johnson couldn't take the thought that some more whites would be killed—especially after some had already been killed. I believe that Selma would have been the place where the revolution could have started. And I believe that Johnson knew that, and that's why he federalized the Alabama state troopers and sent in thousands more to protect the Selma marchers.

It was this march that inspired so many Blacks in Lowndes County. And when the Blacks learned after the march that Mrs. Viola Liuzzo, the Michigan wife of a Teamster union official who had come down to join in the march, had been murdered for joining in the freedom struggle, they just became transformed.

Nobody could see it then, but Mrs. Liuzzo's actions, aimed at trying to change the conditions in the U.S. so life would be based on human relations, was the same basis that produced the women's liberation movement a few years later.

A truckload of Blacks went to the Selma courthouse and demanded to be registered to vote. Included were many prominent Blacks in Lowndes County, who declared that they didn't want any more nonsense about how many bubbles there are in a bar of soap. (This was one of the questions asked of Blacks in Mississippi to disqualify them from voting.) And they registered, for the first time in Lowndes County. That march just put inspiration in their bones. Nothing could stop them now.

Blacks were organizing themselves in a number of different ways. One organization they formed was the Lowndes County Christian Association, which established important contacts with former Lowndes County people living in Detroit.

But the threats and intimidation kept on in Alabama. Meetings of Blacks were held in various churches, because if they met in one church, there was always the fear of the church being bombed. In fact, many churches were bombed where civil rights meetings were held. The Ku Klux Klan and White Citizens Councils had many bomb specialists.

There were many individual Blacks who showed great courage and determination, including deacons of churches. Many were so committed to the freedom movement that they would often give permission for meetings to be held in their churches without first getting approval from their preachers or board of governors. The first time many of the conservative Black church officials learned that meetings were to be held at their chuches was when a mass audience suddenly appeared. Like the deacons often said, "It's as much my church as it is any one else's." It just grew and grew, and got practically every Black church in open support of the movement.

The one exception was the teachers. They were frightened. They knew the county employed them and held that big sword over their heads. They were told: "You work for the county, and a white woman is the superintendent. If you go to a meeting and we find out about it, it means your job." So for a number of years, the teachers were pretty well kept out of the movement, even though some would have liked to have openly supported the struggle. They felt they had no choice. It wasn't until Blacks began to gain control over the political life of the county that the Black teachers began to come out openly for the movement.

When I went to Lowndes County in the summer of 1965, I couldn't help but think about the 1954 Supreme Court decision on school integration and the yelling by white Southerners that they were for equal but separate educational facilities. Many of the elementary schools were the same, if not worse, as when I attended them 50 years earlier. Some had not been repaired since those days, and there was not a single white school in this county that was as dilapidated as those shacks for Blacks they called schools. Most did not have a window pane in a single window. The holes were covered with cardboard. The ceilings were tied up with more cardboard.

I asked people what happened to the money the federal government appropriated for the schools, and where were the funds from the state to support the schools. One teacher said that the Negro who was the principal of the high school and the white woman who was the superintendent of the county schools get the money for the upkeep of the schools—and keep it themselves. She also said that nobody dared question them without risking being thrown out of their job.

Some of the teachers had to pay $6 a month from their own salaries to these two people. All the Black children who graduated from high school had to pay $20 to $25 for one day's rental of a cap and gown—whereas white students only had to pay $3.

The one elementary school that looked fit for children had been built by the Blacks themselves. They hired their own teacher and kept the school, a modern block building, in repair.

This was during the excitement generated by the Equal Voting Rights act, and the Blacks were vowing that one of the first things they were going to change with their vote was the educational system.

During this period there were meetings held at least once a week, sometimes twice, and even more, depending on what was going on. The meetings were usually on Sundays, and they were moved around, in part so the whites would see that the movement was all over the county and also to protect against attacks. There were always many Blacks with guns stationed around the church to guard the meetings.

The Ku Klux Klan and White Citizen Councils decided to bomb Negro churches where freedom rallies were held. Not when the meetings were going on, but afterwords. One week they bombed three Black churches. The fourth church bombed was a white church—a big, beautiful church near Bennon. That stopped the bombing of churches. Whites suspected that Blacks had bombed their church in retaliation for the bombing of the Black churches. Some thought the Ku Klux Klan bombed the church by mistake, or even to try to create more hatred against the Blacks. But nobody ever did know what really happened. Anyway, it stopped the bombing of the churches where Blacks were meeting, and the meetings continued to spread to some schools, too.

During this time when I was down in Lowndes County with my wife, Christine, whose story you've read about earlier, we went to visit my sister-in-law in Mississippi. When we got to Jackson, Mississippi, it was nearly night and we had a long way to go—almost all the way to Memphis. So I thought I'd ask around to find a decent place to stay for the night. I was driving down a street and saw a Black man walking by, so I stopped my car and asked him, "Say, is there a place, a motel or a hotel, where we can stay for the night?"

"Yeah," he said, "there's places you can stay."

"Where at?" I asked him.

He said, "Well, straight up this street ahead of you there's a hotel. And just before that, on the road to the left, there's another hotel, called the Downtowner. And for sure, you can get a place just a little outside of town called the Ebony."

"The Ebony," I said. "That sounds like a place that Blacks would usually stay in. Don't Blacks go to these other places you mentioned?"

He looked at me and said kind of slow like, "Yeah, there's some that do once in a while."

So the first one I went to, I waited for a while and finally the white hotel clerk behind the desk asked me if I had a reservation. I didn't have a reservation, so the clerk said there wasn't anything available.

I was tired and didn't want to get into any hassle with anybody, so I decided to go to the Ebony. We got back in our car and started out of town, then came to a red light. When I stopped for the light, I happened to look down the street and saw the other hotel there, and thought I'd give it a try.

I pulled into the hotel driveway, got out and went up to the desk and asked for a room. The desk clerk asked, "Do you have a reservation?" This time I said, "No, man. But I've been driving for a long time. Come all the way from New Orleans, and we're awful tired. I was at a conference in New Orleans, and one of the people there gave me the name of your hotel and said I could get a place to stay here."

"They were right," he said, "but you have to have a reservation."

"Well, I said, "I just didn't have time to call ahead to make a reservation."

"The thing is, he explained, "there's a ball game going on here tonight, and all the rooms are taken. But you can wait around, and if somebody calls to cancel a reservation, you can get a room."

"O.K." I told him, and started back to my car. I saw a Black bellhop, and asked him which way to the Ebony Hotel.

"The Ebony...but why?" he asked me. "What did the guy at the desk tell you?"

I told him what the clerk had told me, and he said, "Well, go ahead and wait around. We can't break this thing down if you guys from up North come on down here and keep runnin' away."

I caught right away what he was saying, and said, "O.K., but I'll have to move my car. It's blocking the driveway."

"Just you go in there and wait," he said, "I'll take your car and put it in the garage."

"Well now," I told him, "I don't mind waitin' around, but I sure don't want to be payin' a garage fee if I can't get a room here."

"Hell man," he shot back, you won't have to pay a damned thing. Just go in there and wait, and take your wife with you."

So I got Christine, and we sat in the lobby for a while. We had fought for freedom in the North, and weren't going to stop just because we were down South. About three white people came in while we were there waiting, and they were registered. Just about the time the bellhop came back with my car keys, the desk clerk called to me.

"Well, it looks like you're in luck," he said. "A party just called in cancelling a reservation, so I can give you a room for the night."

We registered, and when we got to our room, the bellhop explained that we could call room service and have our meals sent up, but then he added, "Only I hope you don't. I hope you'll go down to the dining room and eat there...and get a seat by the window. One more thing. In the morning when you're ready to leave, ask for this bellhop." And he gave me a card with a name on it.

I've been in this line of work myself, and I've done the same thing. So I thought he was referring me to a buddy of his.

We went down to dinner, and saw right away what the bellhop meant by sitting at the window, because it was a great big one that covered the whole dining area and faced on to the main street. We got a table there, and while we were eating, saw another Black couple drive up and register for the night. And I'm sure they came in because they saw us eating as they were driving down the street.

The next morning when we got ready to leave, I called the desk and asked for the bellhop whose name was on the card. In a little while, there came a knock on our door and in walks this bellhop. Only he's not Black, he's white. He asked, "Did you call for number 63, my number?" I said yes, but didn't quite know what to make of it.

It was when I got to my car that it suddenly hit me, and I said to my wife, "You know, the Negroes here are smart as hell. When that bellhop gave me that number, he knew what he was doing. He knew that if I called the desk, the desk clerk would send up a colored bellhop, and it would look like a Black bellhop working for Black people. But this way, it was a white bellhop working for Black people. And if that white bellhop's daddy would have seen that, he'd have dropped dead."

This was the kind of spirit that the Blacks were showing to change the whole South. That Black bellhop was doing what he could to break down discrimination in his own way. It was no leader telling him or the millions of other Blacks what to do. They were doing it on their own, and the changes they were making were already a part of their thought and actions.

It was also true in the shops and the mills. I know several workers in a big pipe shop, the CIPICO plant, in Birmingham. One of them was telling me about the time, in the late '60s and early '70s, when they first started to make Blacks foremen. Some whites accepted it, but there were others who would almost rather die than work for a Black foreman—like the two white Ku Klux Klan members, and everybody knew it, who swore they would never work under any Black.

The way the work was set up, each morning the general supervisor would get all the workers together and assign them to work with various foremen. One day he called out the names of the two KKKers to go with the Black foreman. When all of the other workers moved on to their jobs, these two didn't, and went up to the supervisor and asked him who they were going to work for that day. The supervisor checked his list and repeated that they were to go with the Black foreman. They asked the supervisor if there wasn't some way there could be some changing around so they wouldn't have to work under the Black foreman, and the supervisor said, "No, I can't do that. You're going to go with that man if you want to work. In case you don't know it, they have a civil rights law on the books, and we're not going to be fined a lot of money just on account of you all." Many workers standing around who heard this began to yell, "Ku Klux go home!" It was almost more than the Ku Kluxers could take, but they did take it, and did work with the Black foreman.

20.
STOKELY CARMICHAEL IN LOWNDES COUNTY

WHEN THE CHURCHES were being bombed in Lowndes County was about the time Stokely Carmichael began to go into that area. He was already known, and was the one who first used the slogan "Black Power" that became a battle cry of the civil rights movement. He had led many important struggles and inspired many Blacks and whites with this bravery and courage. Nobody could deny his dedication and commitment to the movement. Unfortunately, his philosophy was only that "power comes from the barrel of a gun."

I talked with the people too, and said that armed struggle was all good and true when there is a revolutionary situation; but I didn't think the situation existing then called for the "barrel of a gun," and I didn't think it would solve anything. So Stokely and I had some sharp differences in Lowndes County, with him yelling that he had led many battles against the whites and that he knew the best way for them to go. We came to real verbal blows, as Stokely urged the Blacks to take up arms to gain their freedom, and me telling them to fight as they had been doing with their mass demonstrations, boycotts and marches.

I told them that while Stokely had done many brave and good things, nobody could say for sure where he was going. He didn't have to live in Lowndes County, while the Black people there, on the other hand, did not have any place else to go. They had to stay there; their homes were there. And whatever freedom they were winning, and would continue to win, would have to be defended by them on their own grounds, in their own way, with their own methods. My own conviction was that power did not come out of the barrel of a gun, but out of the mass power and reason of the people organized to win and defend freedom. I believed it then, and I believe it now.

I repeated that if it took a Moses to lead them out of the wilderness, that same Moses could lead them back into it again. But if they struggled and led themselves out, then nobody could

lead them back, unless they wanted to go back themselves.
Stokely always accused me of wrecking what he had done in Lowndes County, and looked at it like it was a personal wrecking of what *he* had done. I thought about the great difference between what Stokely said and did, and at how Rev. King acted and what he said: he insisted that the progress and achievements made were due to what the Black people had done, not what he had done. It wasn't that Rev. King always followed the masses, but he knew that they were the ones who made him great, and not the other way around.

Stokely left shortly after this. He made a big name for himself in Lowndes County—that's where he got the most publicity. I felt he was just using the people. I'm not saying he wasn't serious or dedicated in what he did, but his "Black only" policy had the result of isolating the Black mass movement from the white revolutionary element. He was the SNCC leader who led the move to exclude all whites from Black SNCC activity. His policy was that whites should work in white areas to break down discrimination, and Blacks in Black areas. This line led to the eventual downfall of SNCC, because the issue was not white on white and Black on Black, but the changing of the whole society.

And when Stokely kept running around in his own tracks peddling his Black Panther Party, he began to realize he wasn't going to get very far with it there—especially with me opposing him. And when he left, the Black Panther Party left with him. This says about as much as anything about his philosophy and the policies that flowed from it. They couldn't sink roots in the minds or activities of the people, and when he left there was nothing permanent left behind to build on for the future.

With Bobby Seale and Huey Newton in San Francisco, the Black Panthers did get a national name for themselves, but many paid a terrible price. I know that every mass movement in history takes its toll in human lives. I've been in a few. But the tragedy so often is that many lives are lost in what people believe to be a revolutionary cause and organization, one that will create a new free society. They want a revolution, but not by being ordered by some elitist group to show that power comes out of a barrel of a gun.

Blacks in Lowndes County organized themselves in March of 1965. By June, there were 17 Blacks registered to vote, and the movement gathered momentum. With the help of SNCC workers in the area, they began to tackle all the problems of civil rights: school integration, Black representation in the farming areas, better schools for Black children. There were about 600 organized in that group—which is tremendous for such a rural area.

In the November county elections that year, Blacks were chosen for offices that had always been held by whites. Those elected gave the farmers in the county the allotment of land they were permitted to cultivate each year. The federal government allocated so many acres to each state, and it was the county's job to distribute them. Before this time, white farmers were asked first how many acres they wanted, and acres were cut from Black farmers to make up what whites wanted. The quotas sent to the federal government never revealed that Blacks were systematically robbed of many acres.

In the November election, seven Blacks were elected to the 11-member group. It was an historic first, and was done despite the fact that the whites put 25 to 30 Black names on the ballot to try to divide the votes. They even gave some Blacks the wrong ballots to mark.

Many said there had never been so much progress in so short a time in a KKK stronghold in the South. After the election, the retaliation by the Klan began. Many of the white landowners ordered their Black tenants and sharecroppers who had voted to move. They tried to force them out of the county so they could cut down on their voting strength.

I took a trip to Lowndes County in March of 1967 and got further evidence that the Black Revolt in the South had not stopped. The enthusiasm at the meetings was not quite like it was before the defeat of the Black Panther Party in the November 1966 elections, but the people in the rural areas were not quitting. The best way to describe the situation is "in action"—this was the characterization used at one of the mass meetings they held while I was there. Their firm and bold determination to speak out on the problems that affect their lives gave proof of how people transform themselves when they are caught up in a revolution and become a part of it.

As one said, "The Negro Revolution meant that we destroyed the old, and replaced it with something new. This is our aim in this country, and when it is completed, everything will be new, including our lives."

They held their meeting on the outskirts of Hayneville, one of the hot-beds of the KKK in the state which has a history of flogging and murdering of Blacks. The fact that Blacks would hold a civil rights meeting in that county at night was something so new that it alone made you appreciate what the Negro Revolution had done.

At the meeting many questions were discussed, questions like: What is the road from here to complete freedom? What can we try now that "Black Power" seems to have failed?

Many factors helped defeat the Black Panther candidates. Some Blacks were forced to vote as their landowners demanded in order to remain on their farms. Racist whites intimidated many voters. Other Blacks even failed to register. There was also much confusion because some "outsiders" came waving a banner of support, but it turned out that they came not so much to support the movement and work with the Blacks, as to lead and capture the movement for their own purposes.

At that time there were five families still living in the Tent City that was born when Black families were forced out of their homes by the white landowners two years earlier because they dared to register to vote. I read about Tent Cities ever since the first one was formed early in the 60s by Black farmers who had been evicted en masse. I saw pictures of the Tent City in Mississippi that was called "Strike City" because those Blacks were evicted for their activities with the Mississippi Freedom Union. I had organized drives to send food and clothing and money to all of these places. But to actually see the conditions under which these people live with your own eyes gives you a feeling almost impossible to describe.

When I drove up Highway 80—Jefferson Davis Highway— and cast my eyes upon the side of a hill in a pine grove, with bare earth all around it, and five or six ragged tents propped up against sticks, I felt sick in my stomach. Here we were in the richest country in the whole world with a government spending millions of dollars a day on a war in Vietnam, and here were Black Americans, cast out of society and living like animals in a jungle for committing the crime of crimes—registering to vote.

There was one outhouse which they had built themselves some 25 yards from the tents. There was one wooden cook stove

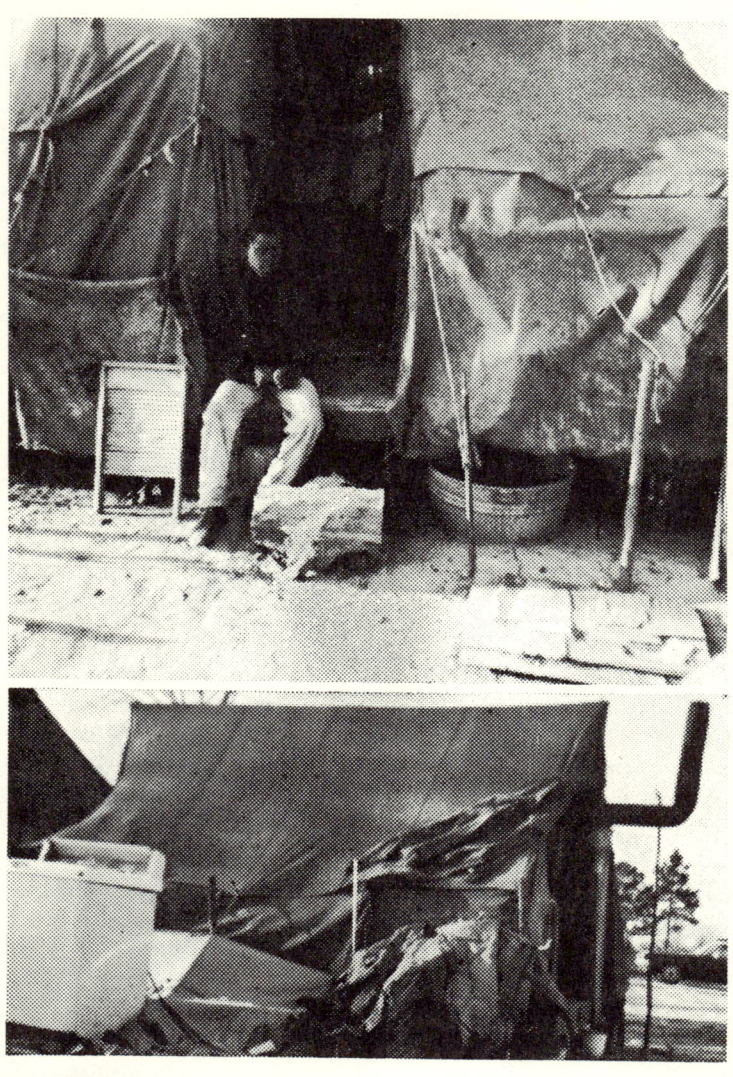

Tent City in
Lowndes County, March, 1967.

for all the families some ten yards from the tents in an open space. When I asked them how they cooked when it rained or was very cold they said, "We don't; we send some of the younger ones to the store to get cheese crackers and pop—if we have enough money." At night they had to stay on guard to keep the KKK from putting the torch to the tents, and guard the open well where they got their drinking water.

But more important than the sacrifices these families were making by having to live under those conditions, was the fact that they did have some place to go, and they weren't driven out of the county by the whites. And it was not only those families; it was any Black family that might be threatened for registering to vote and any Black who fought against oppression there. But they needed help and it was this kind of awareness that led to the establishment of the Detroit support group of the Lowndes County Christian Movement for Human Rights.

One of the main goals of the Detroit group was to buy 200 acres of land for Tent City, and in February of 1968 I went with a group from Detroit to pay off the purchase of that land. It had not been easy because as a result of the Montgomery But Boycott of 1955-1966, all whites in Lowndes County signed some kind of agreement among themselves that they wouldn't sell Blacks any land, on any terms, or at any price. It became possible to get this 200 acres from a white owner because he did not know he was selling it to Blacks until after it had been paid for. It was kind of historic in the sense that before now whites had not sold a single acre to a Black. When Blacks tried to buy land, the whites said they would not sell an acre for $1,000, when the going price was from $75 to $100 per acre.

Now, there were 200 acres that could be used to take care of Blacks or their families; they could not be driven out of Lowndes County. How important this was can be seen from the change in the population. Before Blacks could vote, they represented 85% of the population. Under the whip of the repression, this figure in two years dropped to a 65% majority.

In addition to the repression and intimidation, many young Blacks went to cities for work, leaving the county. Another major factor was that many whites moved from Montgomery and Birmingham into the county to live in trailers and after six months could claim county citizenship and register and vote.

They had their jobs and homes in Montgomery or Birmingham but so long as their trailers were in the county and they claimed they were living in them, even if only during weekends, they were considered registered citizens of the county.

So the buying of the 200 acres to guarantee a place to live for Blacks facing harassment was important for many reasons, not the least being that Blacks had found a way to break the white power structure's grip on the land in Lowndes County.

There were similar organized freedom movements in practically all the rural counties in southern Alabama. The oppressed Black farmers mobilized, and the KKK and White Citizens Councils knew this meant the end of their power if the movements couldn't be broken, because the Blacks were the overwhelming majority in almost every rural area of the deep South. One of the big landowners in Lowndes County told the Blacks after the election that the time had come for the Blacks and whites to try to understand each other because they had to live together. One Black told him that his parents, his grandparents, and his great-grandparents all had wanted to live in peace with the whites, but the whites would not accept the Blacks as human beings—and that that was still the problem.

The handwriting truly was on the wall, and many whites were supporting the Blacks. In almost all of the mass meetings and demonstrations, more and more whites were showing up. By 1967 the progress in Lowndes County seemed to be moving more swiftly than in most other rural areas. There had been integration of a previously all-white high school, and white teachers were teaching in the Black high school.

I happened to be there the day a special news bulletin announced that the sheriff of the county had resigned. He gave as the reason the fact that no crimes were being committed. I thought this strange, because reports had indicated that the crime rate was higher than it had been, and I believed this to be true, even though they tried to make it appear that Blacks were mostly responsible for crime. The announcer said the sheriff stated that he received a small salary from the state and county and that he got his main income from the arrests he made. But since there was no crime in the county, he was not earning a living; so he had to look for other employment.

At a mass meeting held later, a leader of the freedom movement said that what the sheriff said was partly true. But it was not that there were no crimes in the county. They were the same as before. But the big difference was that the sheriff could no longer walk into a Black home when he felt like it, ransack it, arrest the Black on trumped-up charged and throw him or her in jail. He now had to bring a warrant and have a reason to search a home. He could no longer arrest a woman for wearing slacks and lipstick as he did five or six years before. He could not arrest the family that lived nearest to a "moonshine" still found in the swamp or hills. The movement had forced the whites to apply the law somewhat equally. So it was true that the sheriff was not making the arrests and the money he did before, and he never would if it depended on running the office like it had been run in the past.

By 1971 the Blacks were able to elect their first public officials, and I had the opportunity to attend their inauguration. It was an historic occasion in every respect, especially for those who remembered that a few short years ago they couldn't even register to vote.

The oath of office was administered in Hayneville, the county seat, in the center of the village. There are about eight or ten stores and a few other businesses in a square of about four blocks, with a small park in the center. When I got in sight of the square, it looked like one black spot covered every inch of the park and overflowed into the streets. Some said over 2,000 Black people were there, and there may have been more. The courthouse, including the aisles, was jam packed. It was the first time I had ever attended a meeting where they didn't even have seating room for their guest speakers. But they seemed too happy to worry about that.

Saturday is the business day for the white merchants, but practically every one had closed up and gone. A few whites attended, including the judge who administered the oath and a few reporters. A reporter from the *Los Angeles Times* said he had been sent there about five years earlier to cover a story about the white minister who had been killed. At that time, he said, the attitude of the whites nearly frightened him to death, and he swore he would never be seen in Hayneville again. But when he learned of the election victory of the Blacks, he decided to return. After he left Highway 80, fear gripped him again, but as soon as he saw the square and all the Black people laughing and talking, his fear disappeared.

Dr. John Cashin, the organizer of the new National Democratic Party of Alabama, brought the house down when he spoke. He stood at the judge's bench and said he spoke from there because he knew that more Blacks had been railroaded to prison, and some to their deaths, by the racist judges who had sat there than from any other place in the county. He was there to let this judge know that his time was out, that the people would take over his seat and elect a judge just as they elected other Blacks who would serve all the people justly and equally.

We saw some Black hunters sitting in cars around the square. They said they had stopped hunting to see what was going on. But they were there from beginning to end—with loaded shotguns.

What was amazing to many of us was seeing several white women walking and holding hands with Black men at the inauguration ball. One man said, "I'm happy to see this change. Six years ago, only five miles from here on Highway 80, Mrs. Viola Liuzzo was shot to death for having a Black boy riding in the front seat of her car with her. Today these couples are walking around as if this has been a way of life since the beginning of time. Brother, we sure have come a long way."

When the Black movement continued to make political inroads, teachers and professionals came rushing in. They said they had the brains and the know-how to lead the Black masses to complete victory, and began calling the shots. They took over all the leading positions on the NDPA, and set up a steering committee to screen candidates.

During the primaries, they met with white leaders of the Democratic Party and agreed that they would leave some Black candidates off their slate if the whites would do the same. They agreed to support each others' candidates. When this became known, it created a great outcry from the grass roots. They asked: Why make such a deal when we have 80% of the votes?

Students at the high school had been raising funds for an athletic program, and a Black teacher was in charge of finances. Prior to the election, there were rumors that he had given money to support white candidates. Black students demanded that the money they had collected be turned over to them that very day, and began rioting when the teacher bolted himself in his office. But he had to write a check for every dime the student secretary had on his books.

Out of the eight Blacks running, only one got elected. The Superintendent of Education was the one position the Blacks wanted most—and they lost that. The one Black who did win credited it to the fact that a white democrat and a white republican were running for the same position.

When I was there for the Christmas holidays, many Blacks were still upset. The basic reason they lost, I was told, was that they had turned away from the grass roots to the professionals. In doing this, they forgot that the all-important foundation of the freedom of the individual had been the key to past success.

None of the Black candidates lost by more than 300 votes. There were 1,000 Black youth between 18 and 21 registered who were so fed up with the mess that they did not vote. Many of the grass roots people stayed home in disgust, and some of the professionals on screening committees voted for white candidates.

A Black man said, "We had the ball and sure were moving downfield, deep in their territory. But we fumbled it away and they (meaning the whites) have recovered it. The only thing left for us to do is to go back and try to organize all over again. We have to bury ourselves in the grass roots people, and let them and the youth take the lead, because I do not think they will trust us again."

Lowndes County is where I grew up. I return there every year, and have been a part of all of the events that have been described. With other Blacks living in Detroit from Lowndes County, I helped organize support for our brothers and sisters, many of whom had been thrown out of their homes for daring to register, and forced to live in the most primitive conditions of tent cities thrown up to try to keep them alive. They finally succeeded, not only in voting, but also in electing one of the leaders of their own movement, John Hulett, as sheriff. It was a great victory.

In 1974 to the shock of almost everyone there and in Detroit who had worked together for so long, Hulett came out endorsing Alabama Governor George Wallace for re-election: Wallace, the arch enemy of desegregation, the one who had stood in the doorway of the schools in Alabama and declared, "Segregation today, segregation tomorrow, segregation forever!"

Black people know this Wallace. When I heard about Hulett coming out for Wallace, I remembered a rally held for Wallace that I had attended back in 1968 in Cobo Hall in Detroit. I felt it was a must for me to be there to see the action and reaction to him. As soon as I entered the building, I could feel and sense the tension. You felt like you were sitting among a jungle of wild beasts and that if you did not quickly transform yourself into a ferocious beast or escape from this meeting, that you would be caught and destroyed as soon as this man got in the position to do it. You could see these beasts putting fear or trying to put fear into anyone who opposed Wallace. This was the tone of those who spoke before Wallace came to the platform.

Long before Wallace came to the platform, some of his supporters attacked a group of protestors. A huge Wallace supporter hit a small woman in the face with all the force he could, while another Wallace supporter cheered him on. When the police finally came, you could see they were on the side of the Wallace supporters. When Wallace finally came out to speak, reports said he received a seven minute ovation before he could get started. The truth is that that boos were so loud and long that his supporters were yelling to try to drown out the boos.

Wallace said the same things he had been saying from the beginning of his campaign. I wondered what was making these people who were supporting him tick. Then I felt, "This is fascism." These were the people who were yelling with happiness when the dogs were tearing the insides out of the Black people in Birmingham in 1963, under the direction of George Wallace. They were screaming and yelling when Wallace police and state troopers on horses, with swinging clubs in their hands, had the blood of civil rights workers running in the streets of Selma, Alabama.

There was a large group of Black and white protestors in the balcony, and I noted carefully that no Wallace supporters or police attacked them. At first I thought that the overwhelming majority of the people in the hall were Wallace supporters, but there were protestors all over the place. When Wallace began to speak, many young whites tried to drown out his words, and their boos and yelling were so long and loud that few words of what Wallace said could be heard. It was nerve-wracking, listening to what Wallace said. He would yell at the demonstrators, telling them to have their fun now, because after November they would be through in this country. Nobody could mistake what he meant would happen to them if he was elected. He yelled about law and order, his kind of law and order, but never once used the words freedom or justice.

Several weeks before the rally, I had heard a Black speaker say there were records proving that over 25,000 Black people had been lynched in this country since 1865, and not one white lyncher had been convicted. All during this long span of time, there was not this cry of law and order. What kind of law and order was Wallace crying for, except for more of the same?

Wallace said that if elected he would support South Africa and Rhodesia because they were friendly countries. What he should have said is that these countries' racial policies were the same as his: that there is no such thing as freedom or justice for any Blacks or whites who would oppose him. What so many racist white workers who supported Wallace did not realize was that he would put the white workers in concentration camps along with the Blacks if they ever opposed him.

But it's one thing for white workers to be fooled by Wallace; it's something else for someone like Hulett, who's from Alabama and who knew what Wallace stood for. It amounted to aiding and abetting the racist Wallace and Wallaceites, who were saying, "How can I be a racist when some of your own Black leaders are endorsing Wallace?"

It was not only in Alabama that this happened. Black Mayor Charles Evers in Fayette, Mississippi, whose brother Medgar had been gunned down by a racist white a few years earlier, came out with a stronger statement supporting Wallace. What I couldn't help wondering was if Evers was playing politics with Senator Edward Kennedy, who in turn was playing with Wallace.

As a result of these clear betrayals, the Black masses were questioning all of their so-called leaders, from Andrew Young, who went into Alabama to oppose those Black leaders who had capitulated to Wallace, to Julian Bond and John Conyers, Black legislators who continued to fight racism. To all the people I talked with, it looked like these leaders were going in for "big politics" to solve the problems, instead of using mass demonstrations which had won the victories.

We were sad to hear someone like John Hulett, who had been such a strong fighter against Wallace, trying to explain his actions by saying Nixon had made it impossible to get funds for Black clinics without having to go begging to Wallace. But it felt good to hear that many Blacks in Lowndes County opposed Hulett's actions. They were saying, "Why in hell didn't he call a meeting to hear what we had to say?" And Hulett himself reported that the great majority of Blacks in the country voted against Wallace.

Some said it was only opportunist politics that caused the revolutionary leaders of that period to turn into their opposite. I believe it was more than that. It was a question of losing faith in the masses in action as force and reason. Once you have lost your philosophy of liberation, which is based on that, you almost automatically end up wheeling and dealing.

At the same time in Detroit, at a meeting of the Coalition of Black Trade Unionists, the biggest ovation was given to William Lucey, president of the American Federation of State, County and Municipal Employees, when he blasted Wallace as being the same racist he had always been, noting that Wallace had not said a single word against President Nixon or indicated any regrets for his previous actions against Blacks. Lucey got a standing ovation when he attacked Michigan AFL-CIO Black president Tom Turner by name (and Turner was in the audience) for suggesting that workers support Wallace.

The Black workers were saying: If you don't stand up for the principles of freedom, for uprooting this capitalist society with its unemployment and racism, we will remove you from office just as easily as if your face was white.

A week before the 1974 election, I received a call from Dr. Cashin, the Black leader in Alabama. He confirmed that the Black leaders were involved in political deals with Kennedy and Wallace, but said there was much more than that. He said that Black leaders opposing Wallace were being harassed, and that the Internal Revenue Service had been brought into the act. This is what Cashin told me:

"We have been pushing for a voter drive concentrated here in Alabama for years. The idea would be to concentrate on one state at a time, rather than spread our efforts out. With the reapportionment since 1969, we've put 15 Blacks in the legislature so far. If we all work together, we could put 60 Blacks in the Alabama legislature.

"John Lewis (then director of the voters' registration drive) has been telling us since January that they had the money for the drive, but they've been dragging their feet. They just now had to admit that they did not have the money, because the Ford Foundation had reneged on their commitment. The IRS investigated Lewis the day after he was in Selma, speaking out against Wallace.

"Those white folks in power just manage to keep us busy defending ourselves all the time. When they have all the power and force, what can one do? They are trying to kill us off. Not everybody is killed the same way. They killed Martin Luther King with bullets, but there are other ways of assassinating people.

"Those Black mayors from Alabama, Ford from Tuskegee and J. Cooper of Prichard, and Evers of Fayette, Mississippi, are all Kennedy disciples. They are trying to make Wallace respectable to Blacks. But we know he's the same Wallace he always was.

"Kennedy came to Decatur, Alabama last July 4 and asked some of us Black leaders to sit on the platform with him. We rejected the offer because of Wallace, and some of us boycotted the meeting. We know the whites are only playing with us so they can keep power in their hands. It is time for Black folks to appraise where we are. When Kennedy starts playing around with Wallace, it's time for us to start playing a new political game."

This report from Cashin helped fill in a number of suspicions I had about what had been going on, and I later learned that Cashin himself had been continuously harassed by the IRS, with many charges brought that he had to take a lot of time and expense to fight against.

21.
THE ANTI-VIETNAM WAR MOVEMENT AND THE 1967 DETROIT UPRISING

ONE OF THE most important developments during the Civil Rights Movement was the stepped-up war in Vietnam. As the U.S. got deeper and deeper into the war, the idealistic white youth became more and more opposed to it. Many who had been active in the civil rights struggle left it to devote time to the anti-war movement. There's no doubt that many Blacks, and especially those in the South, felt betrayed by the desertion of the white youth. They felt their war for freedom in the U.S. was more important than opposing a war many thousand miles away. It was this situation which Stokely and other Blacks could point to when they demanded separation from the whites. Many Blacks agreed with them, but what also happened was that the real enemies of civil rights took advantage of that development to drive a wedge between the Blacks and whites who were trying to work together.

When the Black community in Watts, California exploded in 1965, it was clearly Blacks against "whitey," and that same Black-white confrontation carried through in most of the other cities that saw Blacks moving to burn down their ghettoes and demanding Freedom NOW! It was true of Harlem, Washington, D.C., Cambridge, Md., Atlanta, Chicago, Cleveland, Kansas City, St. Louis, Buffalo—and all points North, South, East and West. But when it hit Detroit in August 1967, it had changed, and changed tremendously. In Detroit the revolt was primarily against the police and shop owners—large and small—who were known or believed to be gouging Blacks and poor people. The Black ghetto along 12th and 14th Streets and many business places were torched, and there was a lot of looting. But it wasn't Blacks looting alone. They were joined by many whites. In many places it looked like whites and Blacks were shopping together—only they weren't paying for what they got.

One woman I know took a TV set from a store, went home with it and plugged it in—and the first thing she saw was a TV newscast showing her taking the TV set out of the store. But that's the way it was, and while there were some elements of racism in the situation, it was mostly on the part of the police against the Blacks. Insofar as the large majority of the Black and white community was concerned, it had become a question of class, of the establisment, not of race.

The fact is that to this day the damage that was done has not been repaired. Anyone can go up and down many streets that were hardest hit by the fires and still see buildings boarded up or empty lots where buildings once stood.

Even though there was martial law and curfews and warnings for people to stay at home for the two weeks the insurrection continued, I only missed about three or four days of work. Things got pretty quiet after the federal troops were called in. I know the first day I returned to work, the troops stopped me and the guy I was riding to work with. They asked me where we were going and we told them and showed them our work badges. They still made us get out of the car and searched us, then finally let us go on. But they were very nasty and harsh in their treatment.

Specialists in every field are still analyzing the Detroit insurrection, as well as other revolts on other cities. All of these intellectuals are trying to find the root cause of these outbreaks, the root cause of the Black frustration in the ghettoes, the Black attitude toward society, their city and state. These same studies were going on during the actual rioting, but no sooner did they begin to dig into "facts" in one city than another one was suddenly aflame.

One thing never exposed was that there wasn't any blame placed on the power structure, the police or national guard. I have read some reports of what happened during that period. In their monthly newspaper the New Jersey branch of the American Civil Liberties Union did report on the unconstitutional and inhuman acts by the police and national guard against the Black community. They stated that while they were going through Black homes searching for weapons, without warrants, they wrecked practically every home they entered, tearing up and scattering belongings all over.

They told about how the police drove up and began shooting into homes. A Black woman in her home heard the shots and ran to get her baby who was playing in front of her house. She was shot to death with the baby in her arms. The article also reported how they made a Black man take all his clothes off and run nude down a street. Another Black man had to kneel down and kiss the feet of the police. The curfew applied to only Blacks, and the police had young hoodlums helping them beat up Blacks. These actions were not so hidden that the federal experts could not have found them; they couldn't help but know them, in fact. They just keep these facts quiet.

A young Black worker was telling me what he felt, "Man, I don't dig this separation that those Black Nationalists are yelling for, but I dig what Stokely Carmichael said. For years and years my father, grandfather and great grandfather all tried to be friendly. Now I stand in a situation where the whites appear to be friendly by passing a few laws, but my basic situation gets worse and worse. They really don't mean to change anything. They really don't mean to accept me. I don't want them. No matter what they do, I don't like them."

He showed me the daily paper, carrying a report of Detroit Prosecutor Cahalan clearing policemen and national guardsmen of killing seven or eight Blacks. The prosecutor said it was all in the line of duty. My friend then said, "My house is filled with holes now where those sons-of-bitches shot it up. My family and I had to sleep flat on the floor at night, and they kept yelling at us 'turn those damn lights out.' But I didn't move from the floor for those blood-thirsty hounds to kill me. A Black barber shop across the street from me had lights on. They shot all the glass and lights out of it. You know as well as I do that this would never happen to white people anywhere in this country. And this same action is what we had to live through down South all our lives. There is no difference in policies here. All cities and all their leaders know this. The state and federal governments know that this is how the white power structure works."

I told him a story of a white minister in Detroit who said he walked into one of the police stations during the rebellion. The cells were packed with people as close as sardines in a can. All were standing, men and women. In the lobby they had a bunch of Blacks standing against a wall with their hands above their heads. One woman pleaded that she was pregnant, felt faint and might be having a miscarriage. She asked to please be allowed to sit down. The police never looked at her or said a word. The white minister said he felt the desk sergeant looked more humane, so he went over and asked him to let the lady have a seat. The sergeant angrily said, "What have you to do with it? She is not a lady, she is a Nigger woman rioter." The minister left and came back later. The woman was lying on the floor groaning.

They released some prisoners that night, after curfew was in effect, so that they could get shot or re-arrested on yet another charge. Not only did the whites keep their mouths sealed about this, but so did the so-called Black leaders in all the cities. "Why should we listen to them?" my friend said. I don't want to see them, or hear anything they have to say. They're all Uncle Toms, just sitting and waiting to get some appointment to a federal or state job from the actions and struggles of the ghetto Blacks."

I had written of those events in Detroit in a worker's paper I edited: " 'Law and order' in Detroit has meant federal tanks and troops, national guard machine guns and cops' revolvers. 'Law and order' meant 43 lay dead, over 1,500 wounded and 4,000 more jailed with such huge sums of bail demanded (up to $100,000) that there were no constitutional rights.

"To try to deny the new stage the Black revolt has reached in Detroit—to make the revolt appear purely racist—the power structure, from Democratic Vice President Humphrey to Republican Governor Romney, has had to quote Stokely Carmichael. But he was in Havana. The action was in Detroit. He was talking, not acting. In Detroit, those who were acting were saying loud and clear: Down with the Black slums! Down with two nations, one filthy rich and the other miserably poor! Let's have one nation with totally different, truly human relations!

"Blacks have always been the touchstone of American civilization because they have always exposed its Achilles heel—racism—and have always been in the vanguard of the nation's forward movement. Today, the vitality of the Black people has attacked only the symptoms of oppression—the white landlord in the slums, the white merchant, the white middleman.

"This is not because they do not know who Mr. Big is. It is because they don't see white labor ready to join them. They know better than the elitist leaders that, without white labor, the system cannot be torn up by its roots."

The next year, 1968, Richard Nixon was elected on an openly racist platform, and began to move to destroy the gains made by blacks. But too much had happened for the movement to be halted quickly. Gains that had been so bitterly won were not going to be given up very easily.

I was one of the thousands of Black "observors" who attended the first National Black Political Convention held in March 1972 in Gary, Indiana. Some reporters estimated the number present to be 5,000 to 7,000 while others went as high as 10,000, which I am inclined to believe. There is no doubt that the fact that so many thousands of Blacks could come and assemble for the expressed purpose of trying to work out the economic, social and political future of Black people in America was of the utmost importance.

Preparations for the Convention had been going on for some time, and I immediately tried to get a briefing on what was going on and what had been concretely proposed for the Convention. Every delegate I questioned said nothing had been done and that everything was in a state of confusion. When I located the Michigan delegation, which consisted mainly of Black labor leaders and Black city and state officials, I found them dickering over the preamble, trying to figure out what they could change, what they could live with and what was impossible for them to accept.

The Convention, scheduled to begin at 10 a.m., wasn't called to order until 2 p.m. The auditorium, said to seat 4,500 people, was filled; but a huge platform had been erected in front of the speakers' platform for newsmen and TV reporters, and some 30 to 40 were standing on it, blocking the view of delegates sitting on the main floor.

Michigan Congressman Charles Diggs, chairman of the first session, was trying to introduce the first Black mayor elected in the U.S., Richard Hatcher of Gary, when the chant went up: "We can't see!" The chant grew louder and the Louisiana and South Carolina delegations marched up to the speakers' platform saying, "Move these people so we can see, or there won't be a Convention." At this point Rev. Jesse Jackson, a former aide to Rev. King when he had been assassinated in 1968, rushed to the microphone and said they would be moved and moved right now. As every reporter and camerman got down from the platform, a huge yell went up, "All power to the people!"

Hatcher stated that the Convention was calling for the unity of all Blacks, regardless of political affiliation, ideology or philosophy. He added that they had tried to get Angela Davis to be there, and much of his speech surprisingly seemed to be in sympathy with the Communist Party line, the Maoists and the Black Muslims. Then I realized why there was such mass confusion among the other state delegates, and especially the Michigan group. The Maoist Blacks, Stalinist Blacks and Elijah Muhammad's Black Muslims knew what they wanted out of the Convention. They knew the line they wanted to set, and they achieved at least part of it.

Saturday's principal speakers, Mayor Hatcher and Rev. Jackson, were moving and dealing with the plight of the poor, Black and white. The biggest ovation was given to Hatcher when he mentioned organizing a Black police force in every city, to deal with ridding the cities of harmful drugs and dope that the white power structure profits from.

At the end of the Saturday session, with Diggs still in the chair, nominations were submitted for Diggs, Hatcher and Imamu Amiri Baraka (Leroi Jones) to be members of the Rules Committee. Hands went up for several other delegations which wanted to nominate other candidates, but Diggs recognized a delegate who moved to accept the three names and vote on the motion. A big yell went up, "No! No!", but Diggs called for a vote and about one-third voted for the motion and two-thirds opposed it. When Diggs declared that the motion had passed, a huge protest went up all over the place, with people yelling, "You call this democracy?" "The motion was defeated!" and "Steamroller!" At this point, someone threw an apple at Diggs, and he came back and rescinded his decision. Even the Michigan delegation said it was the biggest blunder of the Convention.

The Michigan delegation called a strategy session to discuss whether or not they could accept the preamble, what changes, if any, could be made, or whether they would be forced to walk out. They were caught in a squeeze. Their incomes came from the white power structure in the labor movement and in city and state politics. They knew it would be impossible to sell the preamble to their white counterparts, and they also knew they were dealing with a forceful agenda as it related to Black masses, Black politicians and United States' society as a whole. They walked out.

Although Mayor Hatcher was talking about giving the

Democratic Party one more chance, others were demanding a Third Party. A few quotations from the Black Agenda were:

"Americans cannot hide. They can run to China and the moon and to the edges of consciousness, but they cannot hide. The crises we face as a Black people are the crises of the entire society. They are the natural end products of a society built on twin foundations of white racism and white capitalism."

"A Black political convention, indeed all truly Black politics, must begin with this truth: The American system does not work for the masses of our people, and it cannot be made to work without radical fundamental change. (Indeed, this system does not really work in favor of the humanity of anyone in America.)"

But there was one paragraph I thought would raise objections, one asking to: "Recognize the importance of the Chinese model for fundamental political and economic transformation of African and other Third World societies." I was talking with some workers soon after President Nixon made his statement on his trip to China, and they said they wouldn't be surprised to see Black Maoists here in this country asking other Blacks to vote for Nixon during his election campaign.

I was not there when the resolution on busing came up, and I was somewhat surprised to learn afterwards that those opposed to busing carried the votes. In fact, I believe that the newspapers actually gave a misleading report on what happened. From what I'd heard, there were several resolutions adopted, and also several amendments. The resolution against busing from South Carolina condemned the idea "that Black children are unable to learn unless they are in the same setting as white children." Instead of busing, they wanted "quality education in the Black community through the control of our school districts and an equal share of the money."

But the New York delegation proposed an amendment separating the Convention vote from anything related to President Nixon's opposition to busing, and the Alabama delegation proposed another amendment supporting busing "in cases where it serves the ends of providing quality education for Black people." They passed without opposition.

The simple fact is that Blacks who oppose busing do so for different reasons than whites. Where whites oppose busing because they oppose integration, many Blacks have just given up on integration. Others have fear for the safety of their children. Some see it as getting control of their community, where they, the Black leaders, will be in control of the money.

Nobody knew where the Black Convention would go, but there were signs clearly seen by many that too many conflicting forces were pulling for their own positions that did not permit the kind of unity to carry the Convention further. It simply died a stillbirth, although many thought it was headed toward the organizing of a Black third political party.

Few things in the history of the U.S. have ever divided the minds and thinking of the American people as much as the Vietnam war, especially the positions of Nixon and Agnew about people who opposed the war. The Birchites and KKK who infiltrated all the law agencies were more than willing to carry out the hints that Agnew and Nixon threw out their speeches against student dissent. Nixon opened the floodgates of hate when he called the student protestors against the war "those bums in the colleges," and said the only good young people were the boys in Vietnam, that they were the only ones "standing tall."

There were about 20 workers in one group in my shop who work the same job. The majority were Black, but there were also several young whites who most Black workers felt were racist and supported Nixon's policies—until one of the young white workers came in and told us one of his younger brothers had been killed in Cambodia. One of the Black workers said sadly, "Will Nixon say his death was because he was standing tall?"

The worker said that his mother received the news while she was in a hospital. He said, "She used to oppose those who demonstrated against the war. She resented hippies. She always talked of how proud she was of her son in the service. But now she said that if my two younger brothers are called, she may take them to Canada, or let them take their chances in prison, instead of wasting their lives for nothing."

All workers in the department pitched in and collected money for flowers for the family; and when the worker returned after the funeral, he shook every worker's hand and thanked us all warmly.

When Nixon had been campaigning for the presidency, he kept yelling that what this country needed most was a leader who could pull the people of the country together. What he did not say was that he wanted to pull them together in line with a fascist philosophy. He said he had a plan to end the war in Vietnam. One of the workers in my shop said he had read an article that words would not have any meaning by 1978, and another worker said that Nixon had beaten the gun, because his words didn't have any meaning then. Workers called Nixon the greatest liar who had ever held office.

When the news broke about the murder of the four students at Kent State University opposing the U.S. invasion of Cambodia, and we learned that they were white students, Black workers were predicting that the next demonstration of Black students would be mowed down. When the news broke about Jackson State, where two Black students were shot to death and 15 others wounded, we knew that the blood-thirsty cops in Mississippi had got the Nixon-Agnew message. So had the KKK cops in Georgia, who killed six Blacks and wounded 25 more, shooting them all in the back to show how brave they were.

Several weeks before the invasion of Cambodia, Nixon had said he was not going to send troops there, nor even supply that country with ammunition. After the American people revolted so strongly against his decision, he said the Army was there to protect Cambodian neutrality. How can a country be neutral when it is being torn to pieces, when thousands and thousands of innocent people are being killed...and most of them by an armed force that was sent from ten thousand miles away?

Nothing pleased Nixon's administration more than driving wedges between white and Black students and pitting racist whites against white radicals. The racist white construction workers in New York must have given Nixon great joy when they attacked both young peace marchers and Blacks demonstrating for an end to employment discrimination.

I know that all white workers don't feel like those white construction workers, just as I know that Nixon feared an alliance of the anti-war youth with the working people. That kind of unity would have stopped Nixon in his tracks.

I was in Montgomery, Alabama, shortly after the celebration of the 20th anniversary of the historic bus boycott that launched the new stage of Black revolt in this country and turned around a way of life in a history written in blood. I was surprised to find that the same bus company that was the target of the boycott then was the target of a strike—this time by Black and white drivers together.

What was so impressive about the anniversary celebration was that it made no separation between all the issues facing Black people in this country today—whether it was full employment, or school busing for quality education and political empowerment, or the harassment of Black movement activists by agencies like the FBI. It was at this anniversary celebration that Mrs. Coretta King made a moving speech blasting J. Edgar Hoover for his role in the long campaign to "take Dr. King off his pedestal" and reduce his influence. In fact, all the speakers had something to say about Hoover and the Senate Intelligence Committee's exposure of the FBI programs that one senator called "a roadmap to the destruction of America."

It was not that I did not long ago learn that men like Hoover were the real subversives in this country, but I was still amazed when I learned the exent of the FBI's dirty tricks on the American people. Years ago, when I read about Hitler's Gestapo, I felt I would not be shocked at anything they would do. But I could not believe that the FBI would stoop to their tactics.

For a long time the FBI and its bulldog director, J. Edgar Hoover, supposedly represented law enforcement and crime fighting in this country. But in recent years their public image had been deteriorating. By now many people are convinced that the front page reports of the hundreds of illegal FBI burglaries conducted against dissident American groups between 1942 and 1968 is just the tip of the iceberg.

Black people caught Hoover's real number long before most other Americans did. Files stolen from an FBI office in Media, Pennsylvania in 1970 showed how the Bureau planned to infiltrate Black organizations throughout the country, and Hoover's attacks on Rev. King just confirmed what Black people had been saying about him for a long time. This country prides itself on race-hating.

What bothers many Black people now are the questions that have gone unanswered about the murder of Rev. King. How was Earl Ray, a stranger to Memphis, able to pick the one place where a sniper might shoot Dr. King, and have a chance to escape? They have glossed over how Ray was able to find Bessie

Brewer's rooming house, the perfect place from which to shoot King, when Ray said he had been in Memphis only two and a half hours. Where did Ray get the money he spent from the time he escaped from prison until he was arrested in London—after traveling through five countries? Whose clothing was it that was found in his luggage? The lawyers claim that Ray could not have gotten his big toe into it.

Most Blacks agree with Rev. King's family when they ask for an outside investigator to look into the whole assassination, because the Justice Department cannot be trusted to find the truth. It was the good "liberal" Attorney General, Robert Kennedy, who gave the FBI the first O.K. to bug Rev. King's office and home.

One of the most sickening revelations in the investigations was the report by Gary Rowe, a former FBI agent, about how the FBI not only did not try to protect the civil rights people working in the South, but actually agreed to give the KKK a specific amount of time to beat them up.

A young friend of mine, who had been an activist in the South in the '60s, began to shed tears when he read the report. He said one of his friends who had been a Freedom Rider had been beaten so badly he suffered brain damage that destroyed his whole life. "It's ironic," he said bitterly. "There was a popular song we used to sing: 'Brother Bob (Kennedy, of course), Where are you?' Now we find out that it wasn't just that the Justice Department wasn't there, but that there were actually agents plotting the killing and maiming of civil rights workers and reporting it all to the FBI. It makes you ill when you realize the full depth to which this country has sunk!"

The blame, however, does not belong all on the FBI for the dirty tricks that are its trade. The Presidents of the U.S. were every bit as much to blame, if not more so, with President Nixon the most dangerous violator. There's no question that he was the single most powerful influence at work consciously trying to destroy the gains of the civil rights movement. He never missed an opportunity to lash out against Blacks. He was elected on a platform of racism, and the one thing that he did keep his word on was to do all he could to crush the Black freedom movement. It was under his "leadership" that the racist northerners got their greatest support and encouragement to resist civil rights for

Blacks. A chief issue was busing of students to achieve integration, and under Nixon this was transformed into "forced" busing. It was never "forced" busing when Black students were truly forced to be bused many miles to maintain segregation in schools; it only became "forced" under Nixon when white students were to be bused to desegregate the schools.

As for President Gerald Ford, he followed pretty much in the footsteps of Nixon on the race issue. At some times he was just as bad, if not worse, in his support of white racists opposed to busing. This is not too surprising, especially when you stop to recall that in the 25 years Ford was in Congress, he never once sponsored a progressive piece of legislation. There are some who say that he was an honest president. But what does that mean? If you're an honest or dishonest racist, the result is that you oppose equal rights for Blacks. I'm sure Ford was appointed vice-president by Nixon because Nixon believed Ford would carry out his policies, and he was approved by Congress because the Democrats believed that he was so incompetent that he wouldn't be any threat to the candidate they'd be running in the 1976 election.

22.
WATERGATE AND THE COMMUNIST GIANTS

THE WHOLE WATERGATE affair that seemed to shock so many in this country did not come as any great surprise to the Blacks. There were many discussions among workers and housewives during the live TV coverage of the hearings, and practically everyone I spoke with during that time said they believed, from the very beginning when the seven "burglars" were arrested, that Nixon was either involved or knew all about it.

After listening to the testimony, they were completely convinced that it had been planned by the highest officials in the White House. As one housewife said, "How is it that every one of the men that testified can remember everything that does not connect them directly to the Watergate conspiracy, but on questions along those lines, they always state that 'to the best of my memory, I do not know'." Even those who claimed to be friendly witnesses used the same tactics. All of them were supposed to have brilliant minds, but they suddenly went blank when questioned.

Some workers asked why there was such silence from the world's two Communist giants, Russia and China. A few years before, they would have had a field day over such a scandal in our "decadent capitalist" country. Instead, Brezhnev, the Russian Communist Party chief, said it was the reactionary elements in the U.S. that were trying to discredit Nixon!

As one worker put it, "I guess the only people that are communist these days are those that are fighting a civil war in their country and fighting for their own freedom." In Russia, as in Czechoslovakia and other countries under Russian control, workers were, and have continued to be, in revolt against their own repression and conditions of labor. In China, Mao was forced to launch his Proletarian Cultural Revolution to head off mass revolt. But even this couldn't stop the movement for true freedom—even in China.

What many people even today in the U.S. don't really know is how close we came to a real totalitarian government under Nixon, how he had used the tremendous power of the U.S. government to crush opponents in his efforts to create a one party state here. He came very close to succeeding, and the crisis conditions that allowed that whole situation to develop have not disappeared. They are still here, and the threat from a police state is far from over.

Jimmy Carter won the election, but the surprising thing isn't that he won, it is that he won by such a small margin over Ford. It's true that one of Carter's first appointments was that of Andrew Young as ambassador to the UN. Young, a Black militant with a long history in the civil rights movement, knows very well that if there is one position that must support the policy of the U.S., it is the one he is in as UN Ambassador. He can't play an independent role there. He's already found out that every time he's tried to express the truth—about British imperialism and the racist nature of most established governments—he is jumped on with both feet. And he is keeping in line, and making excuses for the excuses he's making for supporting the imperialist foreign policies of the U.S.

The one president, outside of Roosevelt, that Blacks felt would be a good one was Kennedy. And there were many vast disagreements with him, too. Take for example the 1963 March on Washington. President Kennedy tried everything he could to stop the march, and didn't even show up there. After the march, he seemed to be supporting the movement again, but it seemed to be very meager support. But that's the way it always is: the political leaders wait to see how much support you have, and then decide how much to support or oppose you if you don't go along with their plans. There were reports that Kennedy wanted King on his staff, but that King declined the offer.

Both President Kennedy and his brother Robert, who was the attorney general, were pressuring King to try to pull him away from the Black masses. Some rumors were going around that Kennedy was thinking of King as his vice presidential running mate in the '64 election. And when President Kennedy was assassinated in 1963, the same story went around that President Johnson had feelers out for King. But this cooled when King came out against the Vietnam War and began to move toward labor to link up the struggle of the Blacks for freedom. It was when King was directly involved in the strike of the Memphis garbage workers that Johnson pulled off protection guarding King. And there are many people today who believe that the reason King was assassinated was because Johnson cut his protection.

We know how strongly Blacks felt about King's murder, because they exploded all over the country in their anger. Many Blacks were killed, and almost all Black leaders had to come out to try to calm the rioters down. There's no question that many Blacks were willing to die in their protest against what they believed to be a conspiracy to kill Rev. King.

But there were exceptions. In Detroit, for example, there was a group around the Black Rev. Cleague, minister of a church called The Shrine of the Black Madonna. They had often been critical of King, and they felt that he was just dead and his dream died along with him.

ANGELA DAVIS

One of the most important Black issues in the U.S. erupted in 1972 when the authorities in California arrested Angela Davis, an admitted Communist Party member, for conspiring to get guns in to several Black prisoners who became known as the Soledad Brothers. The case drew world-wide attention and support, especially by the majority of Blacks in this country. Most felt she was being prosecuted mainly because she was a Black woman, and because of her political beliefs.

Hers was one of many political trials, including the Spock trial, the Chicago Seven and Berrigan trials. It was clear to most everyone that these were nothing but trumped up charges brought against people to try to intimidate anyone who dared challenge the social order. The Nixon administration had for a long time made a mockery of the notion of patriotism by identifying it with support for his foreign policies, especially the Vietnam War.

In discussing the Angela Davis case with some Blacks, I found that many, especially older Blacks, did not agree with her political beliefs. Some younger Blacks did support her beliefs. The big difference was that the older Blacks remembered only too well the betrayal of the Black struggle in this country by the

Communist Party during World War II. They remembered how the Party had betrayed the "Double V" movement (victory abroad and victory at home), and the March on Washington that brought in the FEPC. They also saw the CP crush the Hungarian workers' revolt, killing thousands and imprisoning many more. Angela said she was a Marxist. But the philosophy of Marxism is as far from Russian state capitalism, which they call Communism, as the earth is from the sun. Angela stated that she would work to free political prisoners all over the world. There is no better place she could have begun than in Russia, where there are more political prisoners than in any other country.

While Angela was on trial and being persecuted by Nixon, he was off to China, sipping tea with Mao Tse-Tung. He followed this up with a trip to Russia and champagne toasts with Brezhnev. And in neither country did any of them tell how they were planning to sell out North Vietnam. The North Vietnamese were supposedly Communist, yet here were the two giant Communist powers who certainly could have come out in principled support of North Vietnam, but instead permitted the greatest capitalist power on earth, the U.S., to senselessly slaughter the Vietnamese people.

I was discussing this with some younger Blacks, who said they didn't believe there would be such a massacre if the Vietnamese people were white; they saw racism as one of the most important aspects of the war. So disgraceful were Nixon's policies toward Africa, that they were denounced by two former secretaries of state, 12 former U.S. ambassadors to African countries and a former U.S. representative to the UN.

These were the objective conditions that Angela found herself caught up in and a victim of. I know I was amazed when she was freed by a jury and gave credit to the Communist Party for freeing her. The simple fact is that it was the mass Black support she got throughout the U.S. that freed her, not the CP.

When she was freed and a citizen of Czechoslovakia tried to get her to sign a petition opposing the jailing of political prisoners in that country, she wouldn't even look at him. This is like President Carter talking about human rights all over the world, but not speaking out against the inequality here in the U.S. As murdurous as Uganda dictator Idi Amin is, he can still attack Carter by simply saying, "Why don't you so something about human

241

rights in your own country?" And Carter can't answer him.

What Angela did was talk about human rights in the abstract, but her concrete actions exposed her for all to see. The point is that there are thousands and thousands of Blacks and other poor people throughout the country who suffer from race and class injustice. The same thing applies to the so-called communist and socialist countries, and just because Angela doesn't know it, doesn't mean that the majority of people in the world don't know it.

Angela also had a lot of things to say about Cuba, after she cut some sugar cane and had many pictures taken of her "joining in" with the ordinary Cuban workers. What came to my mind when I saw all that was the statement from the Black woman who asked the question about the Cuban revolution that is at the heart of any revolution that will ever happen. Her question was, "After the revolution, when I put down my rifle, will I have a broom pushed into my hands?" This is the question that has to be answered before, not after, the revolution. Because after it is too late.

You don't have to be a worker to understand the working class, but the working class can always tell, and expose those intellectuals like Angela Davis who claim to speak for workers with their words, but whose actions show that they are against the workers.

I felt special sympathy for a Black Vietnam War veteran from California I read about, a sergeant who had come back and wanted to get into something to help the Black people here. He joined the Black Panthers because he believed their "barrel of a gun" method would answer the problems, and rose to a high position of leadership. He was arrested on trumped up charges of murdering someone who was found dead 200 miles from where he claims he was, and his lawyers said it could be proved if they could get access to the FBI and CIA files from the Nixon period.

There are many like this ex-sergeant in jail; and you also have some of the top leaders, like Eldridge Cleaver, who has come back to the U.S. and says that he is transformed. He says he is now a disciple of God, and it is sickening to see how low some people can sink to find a way out. There seems to be so much emphasis on religion in this country that almost anything can be forgiven in the name of religion. But I don't believe the Black people believe what Cleaver is saying. But I think it is his method, his way of getting the capitalists in the U.S. to accept him and to avoid punishment for what he's done in the past. By making his public repentence, he hopes to be welcomed back into the fold.

I remember a friend of mine from California telling me the story of a group of youths that Cleaver organized to hold a demonstration in the State Capital, Sacramento. They all had guns and were flashing them, and when they got back to Los Angeles, the police went after them and trapped them in a house.

They were surrounded but decided to go out, only Cleaver told them they'd all be shot if they went outside. He said that the way to avoid that would be for all of them to strip naked and walk out with their hands over their heads so everybody could see they weren't armed. That way, if the police fired, it would clearly be murder. One youngster was timid about going out naked, but he was finally convinced to strip and go out. But once he went outside, he apparently felt so overcome with being there naked that he started to run. The police opened fire and cut him to ribbons. It was quick thinking by Cleaver, and it was also vicious murder by the police, but some Blacks were critical of Cleaver for the youth's death.

There may be pros and cons about specific incidents, but there was no doubt in anyone's mind Cleaver's life was in danger every minute, and he had no illusions about "justice" for himself in the U.S. That's why he left the country when the police moved to arrest him—he knew his life wouldn't be worth two cents if they imprisoned him.

This is his background, the kind of history he knew and helped make, that he is turning his back on when he says he has "seen the light" to save his own skin. Before, the picture the people had of him was that of a Black fighter. Now it's one of a Black beggar.

Cleaver says he's been in and seen what they do in communist and socialist countries, and that U.S. capitalism is better than all of them. These kinds of statements tell a lot about where his thinking is at and what his philosophy is. In the first place, there are no communist or socialist countries in the world. There are those who call themselves communist or socialist, but that doesn't make it so, any more than them calling themselves Marxists makes it so. They use the words of Marxism, a philosophy of liberation, but act the opposite and practice repression and exploitation. If Cleaver had his philosophy of freedom clear, he could never be caught in the trap of "choosing between two evils." And instead of begging forgiveness from the U.S. capitalists for his revolutionary past, he would continue to fight against all oppressive systems everywhere in the world, whether that be state capitalism in Russia or China, or the more private capitalism of the U.S.

23.
CHALLENGING THE BUREAUCRATS

AS A BLACK worker involved in political struggles, I began to think about the problems at the work bench and discuss them with fellow workers in the auto shops. It was clear to see that all auto workers, whether they worked for GM, Ford, Chrysler or American Motors Corporation, all faced the same dehumanizing conditions of labor on the production line.

At the same time, I was talking with workers in other industries—coal and steel—as well as white collar and professional workers. The more we discussed, the clearer it became that all of us were suffering—some more than others—from the impact of automation, and all of us were fighting in our own ways against its domination of our lives.

Out of these discussions, the idea grew that we should combine our experiences and publish a pamphlet, which we did in 1961, called *Workers Battle Automation.* I edited the pamphlet, and became the editor of a workers' paper that followed the same principle involved in the pamphlet of providing a forum where workers could speak for themselves.

Those pages were full of their ideas dealing with every theoretical and practical problem of the world. Nothing was alien to them, whether it was how to fight speed-up and harassment on the line, racism, war and peace, economics, politics, parties or philosophy. The paper, *News & Letters,* was published by an organization of workers and intellectuals basing their thought and activity on the Marxist Humanist philosophy developed in the two primary works of Raya Dunayevskaya, *Marxism and Freedom* and *Philosophy and Revolution.*

There were many things I said about the changes in the union when I wrote the first part of this book in 1952. What had been feared then has become oppressive reality today. We could see the role the bureaucrats were playing then, and the union is now changed so totally that it is in absolute opposition to the workers and their struggles in the shop.

I have been involved in many strikes, walked many picket lines. But none seemed to show such great determination on the part of the company to break the union as did the Square D electric company in Detroit in 1954. The workers, represented by the United Electrical Workers Union, had been on strike for 80 days. At one point in the strike, it looked like an agreement had been reached. But the next day, the courts ruled that the Communist Party and communist dominated unions were outlawed. And the UE, which had been expelled from the CIO in 1948 for being "communist dominated," now came under new fire. When that ruling came down, the company demanded that there be a "no-strike" clause in the contract, which meant giving up everything, giving the company all the power and right to discipline and fire workers as they wanted to. This was a test of the law outlawing the communist dominated unions.

The daily papers, radio and TV started to scream about these "communist" workers and their union. The company immediately started a back to work movement without consulting the union. U.S representative Clardy, head of the House Un-American Activities Committee at that time, was shown on TV saying he would be in Detroit to investigate every worker on the picket line or taking part in the strike. The UAW officials didn't say a word, and the press and radio were reporting that the leaders of the UAW were not supporting the strike. At the Labor Day Parade that year, Square D workers flooded it with thousands of leaflets asking workers for their support. This put the UAW on the spot. They could only say it was too bad that the workers were caught between the company and the Communists, and that they should join the UAW.

But the ranks of the picket lines began to swell with workers coming from all over the city, many cursing the UAW leaders, many asking serious questions about why they couldn't support the strike and the Square D workers even if some of the leaders were Communists. Didn't the UAW leaders realize that if the company could break that union, the UAW would be next?

The company had put all of its office workers on production, claiming that the workers were with them and were walking past the picket lines back into the plant. The police were mobilized with tear gas and machine guns, hundreds all around the plant, and many carloads standing ready several blocks away. They were determined to crush the strike and break the union. They attacked, with mounted cops riding their horses onto the sidewalks into the pickets, clubbing the heads of the workers in one of the most brutal assaults I've ever seen. A horse stood on a woman's foot and, as she struggled to release herself, the mounted cop kicked her in the stomach. It was like strikes in the early days of organizing. A dozen cops caught a Mexican worker and beat him unconscious. He was hospitalized for several days. Other workers were carried off to jail. This brutality by the company and police enraged the workers, and put the UAW leaders over a barrel. The following morning, many union officers with their flying squads were there, completely ignoring the court order prohibiting mass picketing. Before this, only five workers could picket at a time.

The company began to back off a little. They began to slip scabs out early and bring them in early, where before they had the police boldly march them in at regular starting and quitting times. The majority of the workers were women, and their role in the strike surpassed anything I had ever seen. Women workers, along with many youth on the day of the biggest fight, were throwing bricks and stones at the cops—with many landing on target. They forced the police to retreat and kept them from smashing the picket line.

One worker said his wife tried to get him to scab because of their desperate situation—losing their car, home, everything they had. But the day after the battle, he told his wife what had happened, and she joined the strikers and was ready to wreck the place.

The workers finally forced the company to bargain. It was a great achievement for American workers. Some leading Communists tried to take credit for the victory, as did UAW leaders. But the fact was that the anti-communist law was aimed at destroying the American workers and their unions, and it was those Square D workers and their supporters who stood the test and refused to allow it to happen.

Back then, you could bring enough pressure on the union to get them to solve some of the problems in the shop.

The year 1954 was also when an executive at Ford first coined the word "automation" to describe what the workers were wildcatting against. Reuther refused to support the workers. He told them they "must not fight progress." The coal miners were the first to face this "progress," in 1949-1950, when the coal operators first put in the continuous miners that the miners called "man-killers," and threw hundreds of thousands of miners out of work.

Automation was introduced in Chrysler in 1956, two years after Ford and GM. They had the time-study man sitting there figuring every angle. We used to see the time-study man once a year, now it was 40 times a day, standing over workers all day long. I'd actually caught these guys standing behind a worker with stop watches behind their backs clocking the worker.

Before automation at my Chrysler Mack Plant and UAW Local Union 212, if you had a set quota and if you got that many jobs out within the hour, nothing was said. You often could get a few minutes an hour to rest. With the time-study, it was designed to make you work every second of every hour. You worked there, grinding your life away. What it actually meant was that you were coordinating the movements of your body to match that of the machines and the speed of the line. The machines were running the workers.

A line I was working on moved so fast that they had a buzzer sound every time the line moved. When that buzzer sounded, you'd better move and move fast, or else you could get hurt bad. Behind me, just a few feet away, there was a water fountain. I wanted a swallow of water so bad, and I thought maybe, if I worked as fast as I could in between the buzzer sounding, that I'd be able to jump back and get a drink of water. But no matter how much I tried, I never could get it. That swallow of water was so close, but it was like being on a desert.

The newest machine they added actually chained a worker to the machine. A maintenance man told us about it. He said, "A man has to be handcuffed with heavy leather straps and a steel cable—I'm sure that cable is what used to hold up the old welding guns—runs from the leather cuff up his arms to under his armpits and comes over his shoulders from behind. They say the breaking point of this machine is about 10 thousands of a second.

You should see how this thing cuts. It cuts foward and backwards. It works with electric eyes. The worker puts the metal to be cut in the machine. As soon as the metal gets into the machine—no buttons need to be touched—the machine comes down and cuts. This machine works so fast it isn't humanly possible for the worker to pull his hands back out of the way fast enough before it cuts. With these cuffs around the worker's wrists, at the point where the machine breaks and comes down, his hands are automatically jerked out of the way to keep him from getting them cut off."

He went on to tell us that there was such resistence to this machine that no worker would work on it. So the supervisor put the cuffs on the foreman. It takes two workers to work the machine because the one who is handcuffed to it doesn't have room to turn around. He only drops the metal into the machine. After they ran two or three pieces, the foreman begged them to turn him loose because he had to go to the rest room. He was so scared that he was pissing in his pants!

There were many ways of seeing how the separation between the union leaders and the workers continued to take place. In the 1954 Chrysler contract, for example, the production workers got a one cent raise, while workers in skilled classifications and white collar workers got more. It was based on their pay. In fringe benefits, the skilled and office workers got twice as much as production workers for sick pay and death benefits.

Soon after the official strike, a wildcat strike hit the Motor Products Corp. over disagreements with the contract and company work practices. The company had tried to speed up production, and several workers, backed by their stewards and committeemen, refused. The company fired a bunch of them, including the stewards and committeemen. The reaction was a walkout, and practically every worker on the first shift went out. When the second shift time rolled around, the UAW leaders were there with the company, trying to force the workers to cross the picket line and go to work. In the negotiations that followed, the union reached a new low by allowing the company to get away with putting the fired workers back in lower classifications than they had been in before they were fired. It was clear that not only the company, but the union also, didn't want representatives who would really fight for the workers' grievances.

In 1955-56, Chrysler merged its Conner and Mack plants, with all workers transferring to the Mack plant where I worked. The workers in the Conner plant left caucus joined those of the left caucus in the Mack plant, where the Reutherites were in control. Reuther had eliminated most of his CP and other left opposition. I've often been told I was lucky that they didn't get me, because Reuther was out to eliminate all his opposition.

When the Conner workers came in and joined us, everything changed. Workers began to rally to us. The first big challenge was the election for delegates to the 1957 UAW Convention. We had 14 delegates from our local, and the Reutherites had consistently won these elections during the previous few years. For the first time, our left-wing caucus ran a full slate of candidates. We didn't have enough well-known people to run for the 14 positions, so we just put up a few rank-and-file workers to fill out the slate, even though we knew they didn't have a chance to be elected.

But so deep was the disgust of the rank-and-file with the Reutherites, that we won every delegate position. Just how much of a defeat it was for the Reutherites can best be seen from the fact that every one of the unknown rank-and-file delegate candidates on our slate got more votes than our Reutherite union president.

The total defeat the rank-and-file workers handed Reuther's "Green Slate" in that election left the bureaucrats gasping. They couldn't believe it happened to them, after spending ten years to build a machine which they were positive would control and dominate the workers forever.

Before the long GM strike of 1946, there were two political factions in the UAW. One was the Thomas-Addes faction, with Thomas the president and Addes the secretary-treasurer of the union. They held the leadership, supported by the Communists and other radicals, with Communists holding top leadership in many local unions. The other faction was led by Walter Reuther. Neither faction could feel sure of how the workers would vote in any election, and the workers used one faction against the other to get their grievances settled. At that time, the faction who fought hardest to represent the interests of the workers were the ones usually elected. There was no solid bureaucratic machinery because the porkchoppers and opportunists wanted to stay in the good graces of both factions so that, depending upon which way the workers turned, they would float to a job on top.

Reuther was the leading GM negotiator during the 1946 strike; one of his demands was for a 22½ cent an hour wage increase, which was won. He also won the 1946 UAW International election for president, campaigning on the claim that the rank-and-file workers were betrayed by the left wing communists who had settled for an 18½ cent raise on the West Coast.

Several years earlier, however, when Reuther appeared to be a close sympathizer of the Communists, he had stated that any member who red-baited another would be brought up on trial for conduct unbecoming a union member. As soon as Reuther became president, red-baiting became his number one weapon.

When Reuther won the presidency, many International representatives began to float to his side. He began to take control of local unions, workers began to support him, and at the 1947 convention he won full international control. Within a few years he had solid control over the very large majority of local unions.

That's when Local 212, my Local, also became a Reuther-Mazey union. The workers supported them, and defeated or eliminated every splinter caucus that tried to emerge by red-baiting (this was when the cold war was very, very hot between the U.S. and Russia), by threats of firing (and actually firing) opponents, and by buying off others. A lot of rank-and-file resentment was beginning to show again, but there was no organized opposition.

Then the Reuther political machine turned against the workers. Membership meetings were solidly controlled. Everything was planned, geared and timed in advance. Mazey or Ken Morris or the local president laid down the line. Rank-and-file workers were squelched and quit going to meetings. After every wildcat strike, a meeting would be called at which the main point was the president's request for more power to handle the next wildcat, and the machine voted this power to him. Many workers were fired, as many as 20 or 30 at a time, for strike action. Chief stewards among the Reutherites often identified striking workers for the company to fire, naming the first 20 or so who punched out and labeling them as leaders of the wildcat.

The trim department, never completely dominated by the Reutherites, began to oppose the Reuther machine. They threw out their Reutherite chief steward, but that was an isolated thing and the local officers still felt secure. Then a few workers called a meeting to form an opposition caucus. Only eight workers attended out of a plant of 12,000. After several meetings, they grew to fourteen members. The Reutherites paid no attention. As one said, "They're too small to see."

But as small as we were, we were what the majority of the workers were looking for. The first shock came when these fourteen members, calling themselves the Rank & File Caucus, ran three candidates for the Election Committee against the all-powerful machine—and won. At that point, many of the old, dead opportunists came to life and joined the opposition. This the Reutherites could understand. They moved quickly with daily leaflets in a red-baiting campaign—to no effect. They called us gangsters—to no effect. We couldn't reply with our own leaflets because there were no funds, hardly any membership, no really organized caucus. But about 200 workers attended our meeting a week later.

After sweeping the delegate election, it was clear that the caucus was now in a position to wipe out the Reutherites. After the convention was over, we began to make plans to take over the local union completely. But what we did not know was that Reuther's big guns had already begun to make deals with our caucus leaders, Smokey Woods, Charlie Gassam, and a few others. We later learned that Ken Morris had made a deal with Smokey at the convention, and the results of that deal were soon seen in the politics of the local union. We should have won every office in the local union at the next election—but we didn't. Smokey Woods was elected president, however.

One of the big issues in the election Smokey won revolved around a Black woman, Marian Hunter, who had been working in the Local 212 office. She was the only Black woman on the local staff, and she had been fired—and out of seniority at that—by the previous president, Tony Cherwinski. Smokey said that if he was elected he would make sure she was rehired, and that she would be his own executive secretary. He got the vote of practically every Black in the shop.

After his election she was rehired, but not as his executive secretary. Smokey kept putting her appointment off, until one night Marian, another worker and I went to see Smokey at his home to find out what the score was. Smokey told us that Gassam, Sam Marcus, and some other caucus leaders warned him that there was a lot of talk about him being in his office all day with a Black secretary, and were pressuring him not to appoint her. At that time, all the top caucus leaders and top union officers were white.

The way that Smokey tried to get out of it was to appoint Layman Walker, a Black man, as his secretary. We put a picket line around the union hall to protest Smokey's not keeping his word to appoint Marian, but Smokey kept Layman on for about six months, until he completed his deal with Ken Morris. The deal was this: that the Reutherites would support Smokey for president of the local for as long as he wanted the position, and would give Cherwinski, whom Smokey had defeated, a job with the international union. But if Smokey didn't agree, they would keep Cherwinski in the plant and use all their power to defeat Smokey in the next election. Smokey bought the deal, and when the workers found out about it, they were all through with the Rank & File Caucus. That was its death blow. The workers had put their trust in the caucus, only to find out that the leaders couldn't be trusted.

A big issue came up in 1962 over the attempt by the International to raise our union dues. Nobody supported the dues increase. All the labor bureaucrats running for office came out against it, because they knew the rank-and-file opposed it. A meeting was called by the International bureaucrats of our Local 212 stewards to "explain" the reasons for the dues increase. The meeting was televised, and I watched it. What I saw I couldn't believe. The camera played over the audience, and it looked like the hall was completely full.

I knew something was wrong about that, because we had twice as many stewards when we were with Briggs than we had when Chrysler took the plant over, and we never had as many stewards as there seemed to be in the hall. So I kept looking, and every time the camera went to the audience, I looked closely at the people I saw, and then it all began to fit together. Most of the audience, about ninety percent in fact, were bureaucrats working at Solidarity House, the UAW headquarters. They had been ordered to attend the meeting to make it look like the "stewards" were for the dues increase.

The TV cameraman was a real genius, the way he played the camera, first on Mazey, then on the audience, and framing everything just right. All of it was nothing but a bunch of visual tricks to make something look like it wasn't. I thought that football players, who always depend on how tricky they can be in making their plays, could sure learn a lot from these people. Mazey ended up by saying that what was being proposed "Was not a dues increase, it was an investment in the union."

About a week later, I was working on a job that was a real killer. It was so hard, you just couldn't do it. I looked over at a guy who was sweeping and after talking with him for a minute, found out that he had wrenched his back on the job I was doing, and that's why they had him sweeping. They had him doing some work to keep a lost-time accident off their records, which would keep their insurance from going up.

I thought to myself, "It's no damn wonder that he's hurt with this job the way it is. But this isn't my job, and I'm not going to do it." So I started to raise hell with the foreman, and told him that I wasn't going to do the job, that I was going home. The foreman put another man on the job to help me, but it was still too much even for both of us. And the thought that went through my mind was, "How did one man do this job?" Why did he try to do it, and mess himself up the way he did?"

The job was so tough that the guy they put with me was really mad doing the job. I knew what he was feeling and said, "You know, a guy can get so mad about doing a job that he's mad at everybody."

He said, "God damn! Who in hell do these people think they are? What the hell do they think we are?" And he started to God-damn the union.

At that point I said, "Hell man, don't be cussin' the union. The union didn't do this , it's the leaders. They're running the show now. Why just a few days ago I heard Mazey telling our stewards on TV that we weren't getting a dues increase. It's an investment in the union."

The worker looked at me real mean and asked, "Do you know Mazey? Do you ever see that son-of-a-bitch?";

And I told him, "Yeah, I know him, and I see him every once in a while."

"Well, the next time you see him," the worker shot back, "you tell him for me that from the amount of union dues they're taking out of my paycheck, and the kind of work they expect you to do in these hell holes, I'm not getting a damn thing out of my investment. So far as I'm concerned, the union is bankrupt, and it's no place to make an investment."

He was right. He wasn't talking about the financial condition of the union, he was talking about the fighting condition of the union, which wasn't doing the fighting it was being paid to do for the workers in the shop.

By the time we had our Chrysler contract of 1962 to ratify at our local meeting, the deep divisions between the rank-and-file and the union bureaucracy were even more sharpened. Both Emil Mazey, then and now secretary-treasurer of the UAW, and Irving Bluestone, then Reuther's assistant and now the UAW's GM chief negotiator, were trying to sell us on how great the contract was that had been negotiated. Our local union president read the contract provisions, and was followed by Mazey and Bluestone. When our president read the contract provision pertaining to the relief time of women, he read it like it had been in the previous contract. That is, that the women had a fifteen minute work break in the morning and in the afternoon. Mazey and Bluestone talked about how great the wage increases and fringe benefits were.

When I got the floor to speak, I pointed out to our president he had left out a big difference in the present contract compared with our last one, and that was that the women would have their fifteen minute break periods in the morning and afternoons only "when and if it does not interfere with production." I said that women have many problems that men don't have and that clause killed everything they had before, because to the company production came before anything else. It was a very important clause, and he knew what he was doing when he did not read it all, because there wasn't a person in the hall who wouldn't know what that clause took away from the women.

I also pointed out that the great profits the corporation was making, which everyone had talked about, were going back into machines, into automation to make us work harder. It wasn't just a question of labor, I said, it was a question of the labor*er*; and I knew the company understood that very well, because they always kept putting more and more into the machines, and nothing for the human beings. Karl Marx, I said, had been the one to first point this fact out, a fact that every worker knows very well without having a long explanation about it. It meant that dead labor, the machines, were always on top of living labor, the workers. And if anybody wanted to find out the truth about that statement, all they had to do was go into any auto shop in this country, and they'd find out about it soon enough. In the shop, it's not a question of theory, it's a matter of fact that every worker knows: every year the machines are improved to run the workers more and more, to get as much out of them as possible.

As far as the union leaders were concerned, I said, they reminded me of a story I remembered about a lion and a jackass in the African jungle. The lion was old and feeble, and was having a hard time making it on his own any more because he couldn't run down game to eat. Then one day the lion came across an old jackass going through the jungle, and spoke to him, calling out his name. The jackass looked around, and at first was scared to see the lion, but then asked, "Do you know me?"

"Sure," the lion answered. "We grew up in the same area of this jungle. I used to chase you a lot of times."

"So you're the one," the jackass replied. "But I wouldn't recognize you as skinny and as bad off as you look now."

"Well," the lion said, "it's because our diets are different. You can eat a lot of things because you don't have to hunt, but I've got to have meat, and can't hunt for it like I used to." The jackass was sympathetic, and asked if there was anything he could do to help.

And the lion said, "Come to think of it, there is something you can do." He called the jackass over to a deer trail and said, "At the end of this trail there's a water hole where the deer go to drink. Near the water there's some thick underbrush, and if you'd hide there and yell—like I know you jackasses can—you'll frighten the deer, they'll run by here and I'll be able to reach out and grab one."

So the jackass went to the underbrush and began to bray. It wasn't just any ordinary bray. It was long, deep and powerful, and so strong the underbrush shook. And sure enough, the frightened deer ran up the path and the lion picked off two young ones. When the jackass came up to the lion and asked how he had done, the lion said, "Oh, you did wonderfully. But you know, you sounded so frightening when you were yelling, that if I hadn't known it was you, I'd have run away myself."

I told the union bureaucrats that that was the relationship between them, the company, and the rank-and-file workers. The bureaucrats did a lot of yelling, but the company knew them for the jackasses they were and wasn't frightened by them; and the workers knew the bureaucrats played the same role with the militant workers, singling them out for the company to pick them off individually to fire.

From the yelling that followed—hand clapping, foot stamping and whistling—it's clear the workers knew exactly what I was talking about. And after that demonstration, the bureaucrats turned off all of the microphones that had been set up throughout the hall and behind which workers were lined up to speak. And to this day in my local union, they've never set up microphones the way they used to at contract ratification meetings.

Another example of how much automation had changed everything in the shop was seen in the mechanics. Before, when there was a machine breakdown, there'd be a few minutes of rest that workers would get during the time it took a mechanic to get to the machine and fix it. We had three of them in our area, but with automation they watched those machines like a setter pointing to a covey of quail. All day long they'd do nothing but watch those machines, and when a machine so much as made a little noise out of the ordinary, let alone break down, they'd be there in a flash to check it out. All the workers saw this, and just shook their heads.

One day I asked our mechanic, "What would your wife say if you paid as much attention to her as you pay to these machines?"

The mechanic looked at me kind of surprised, but after thinking for a few seconds, he laughed and said, "You know something, if I did that, she'd probably divorce me. She'd think I was some kind of a damn fool."

I laughed and said, "You know something, she'd be right... and all of us here think exactly the same thing."

Even though there was a lot of disgust among the rank-and-file workers with the union leaders, Black workers sometimes did support Blacks who were in leadership positions or who were trying to get into the leadership. One Black leader was Jack Edwards, who had quite a few workers around him.

The thing you have to understand about this situation is that

Blacks can be just as opportunistic as any white...and make no mistake about that. And Blacks who had positions of leadership were challenged by other Blacks. They were after each other's jobs, and the higher you were, the more competition you got.

During the time Reuther was waging his campaign against the "Reds" and radicals, there were many Blacks who were with Reuther. But Edwards wasn't. He was with the left-wing caucus, specifically the CP. Reuther eliminated the CP as a force in the union, but knew many individuals were effective, and tried to win them over to his caucus.

Black workers, meanwhile, were always asking why there were no Blacks in real leadership posts in the UAW. All Blacks working for the International were on a white leader's staff, and had no real authority. The agitation for Black positions of leadership continued, and Rev. King, who spoke in Detroit on several occasions during this time, raised the question of Blacks in the UAW leadership. Reuther's answer was that he'd appoint one when he found someone who was qualified—and we'd heard that one for a long, long time from everyone who tried to duck the issue.

But the pressure never let up and, in fact, kept growing. In 1960 Horace Sheffield, a lower-level Black bureaucrat, began to put the word out that Reuther was going to appoint a Black to the Executive Committee of the UAW...and thought he was going to be the one appointed. Only Reuther didn't appoint any Black to his executive committee at that year's convention, and he didn't do it at the next UAW convention either.

By 1967, however, the pressure had become so great that Reuther couldn't avoid the issue any longer. Sheffield, feeling certain that he was going to be appointed, had his acceptance speech all ready. Instead, Reuther appointed Jack Edwards, and that blew the situation wide open. Sheffield and Buddy Battles, another lower-level Black bureaucrat, began to attack Edwards from every direction: he wasn't qualified, couldn't do the job, others could do it better, he was a Black stooge for Reuther. Edwards then began to really build up his support, and started to attack the Trade Union Leadership Caucus (TULC), a Black labor group in Detroit headed by Sheffield and Battles.

It was when this was going on that the election for mayor of

Detroit came up, with incumbent Mayor Louis Miriani being challenged by Jerome Cavanagh, a lawyer nobody had heard of before. At first, the UAW didn't endorse either one of them, but as election time got closer and every poll and report indicated a landslide for Miriani, the UAW came out for him. Al Barbour, head of the Michigan AFL-CIO, also supported Miriani. Sheffield and Battles came out for Cavanagh. Edwards, quiet for the most part, did have to come out for Miriani on the orders of the UAW—it was his job.

One example of how the UAW required its staff people to toe their line can be seen in the example of John Conyers, Sr., a Black UAW staffer whose son, John Conyers, Jr., was running for Congress in a Detroit congressional district in which the UAW was supporting another Black candidate, Richard Austin. Conyers, Sr. had to work against his son's election; but his son won anyway, despite the UAW's opposition, and is a leading Black now in Congress.

In this election, to try to guarantee his winning even more, Miriani turned the police loose on the Black community, and they instituted a real reign of terror with arrests, harassment and intimidation. Sheffield and Battles tore into Edwards for his support of Miriani, especially after Cavanagh was elected in one of the biggest election upsets Detroit had ever seen. One of the main reasons was that practically every Black in Detroit voted for Cavanagh.

The sparring continued for a few years more between Sheffield, Battles and Edwards, but eventually they patched up their differences. Later, when I got to know Edwards, he told me about struggles he had with other Blacks, especially Marcellus Ivory, another International UAW bureaucrat. Edwards was in charge of a district in Detroit, and Ivory began to build a base for himself in the district. Edwards was smart enough to know what was going on, and at a conference held in New Orleans, he got Reuther and Ivory together and bluntly asked Reuther what he was trying to do. Reuther said that Ivory and Edwards should make their own decision about what to do, and that he would accept it. Edwards then told Ivory that if he was going to try to take his district, he'd have to fight for every inch of it, then went back and told Reuther that they had settled nothing and repeated what he had said to Ivory. Reuther told Edwards to pull in his horns, that he could have the district.

Sheffield had been on the UAW staff of Roy Reuther, Walter's brother, and when Roy died, Sheffield transferred to Edwards' staff at the UAW. When Edwards was killed in 1976, Sheffield thought he'd take his place. As a matter of fact, he called me and asked me to talk with the president of my local union to try to get his support. But Sheffield was from Ford, and another Black candidate, Marc Stepp, was from a Chrysler local. Also, there was another candidate from Cleveland who would most likely win the spot if Stepp lost out, so my president supported Stepp. Sheffield was very upset when he didn't get Edwards' job, especially since he was the highest Black on the UAW staff and had been Edwards' assistant. Sheffield later went to President Woodcock's staff.

Battles has also been an opportunist UAW politician. Like Sheffield, he was at Ford, and ranted and raved against the company and the UAW bureaucrats. But when Ivory had a leg amputated and felt he couldn't get around like he wanted to, Battles was appointed to replace him as head of a Detroit area UAW district. Battles then shut up just like all the others did. The pattern is the same for all of them, Black or white.

Under the impact of the civil rights movement, many blacks in the shops were able to get into supervisory positions in the plants. Some called it upgrading, but I call it downgrading, because a boss is a boss no matter what color the skin is, and a boss is there for one thing. And that's to get out production. This was proven very quickly when Blacks became foremen and, as a matter of fact, some of them were as bad as any white foreman— sometimes worse.

With the union leadership being transformed into its opposite and doing nothing to fight for workers' grievances, in conjunction with the great power set in motion by the Black revolt of the 1960s, a completely new stage of Black activity moved directly into the factories. But this has to be seen as part of a continuous development, one that I was a part of from the first time I worked in auto.

An earlier stage of Black workers' revolt, in fact, arose because we began to realize that we would have to fight the union bureaucracy as much as we had fought management up to then. This unrest was what led A. Philip Randolph to organize the Trade Union Leadership Council in 1963. What we didn't know then was that there was some sort of "gentlemen's agreement" between Reuther and Randolph.

UAW members, and especially the Blacks, all over the country were attacking the union bureaucrats. Randolph came to Detroit to his little convention and ran it just like the UAW conventions, "from the top," evading all the questions the rank-and-file wanted to discuss.

After the convention, we kept pressing Randolph about the question of discrimination in the shop and he told us plainly that this was not going to be an organization to take up grievances of Black workers on the shop level. All TULC was going to do, he said, was to raise the question of discrimination, but writing grievances would have to be done through regular channels. A lot of the workers said, "Hell, this is what we've been doing all the time, and nothing had ever happened." But, because they made a big splash in the papers, many Black rank-and-filers came around, in the beginning.

The leaders always emphasized that it was not a "Black organization." Yet that is just what the Black workers wanted to make it—not by excluding whites but by Blacks controlling it, for themselves, not the UAW. As TULC developed, it played around more with community problems than shop problems, and when it did raise shop questions, it was more concerned with the building trades or things outside of the UAW than inside it. Reuther had always been a master of substitution—and he managed to teach Randolph the same trick.

24.
DRUM, ELRUM, FRUM, AND THE STINGER

AFTER TWO YEARS there was a tremendous drop in TULC membership, and now, when meetings may be called, you seldom see a rank-and-filer around. In 1970 they called a meeting and sent letters to older Black activists, asking them to come to discuss how they could protect themselves against the "vicious racist extremists"—like the Dodge Revolutionary Union Movement (DRUM). But there were more young Black workers outside picketing the meeting than older Blacks inside attending it.

The whole situation was summed up pretty well when twenty-six young Black workers were fired after a wildcat strike at the Eldon Axle Plant and went down to picket Solidarity House early in 1970. The UAW sent a Black official, Sheldon Tappes, to meet with them. Tappes had to admit that if TULC had done what it was organized for, there wouldn't have been any such development as DRUM. And one of the young Black pickets answered, "And if Reuther and the other bureaucrats had done what the union was organized for, there wouldn't have been any need for TULC."

An entirely new stage was born with the appearance of groups like DRUM within the auto shops. While the UAW convention was being held in Atlantic City, DRUM was organized; it formed after Chrysler fired seven Black workers who had struck the Dodge Main plant the year before to protest a speed up on the line. In July, 1968, when DRUM called for a strike to support a list of demands against racism, both by Chrysler and the UAW, the call brought thousands of workers out of the plant and shut down production for two days.

Several months before the Dodge strike in Detroit, five hundred workers at the Mahwah, New Jersey, Ford plant had shut down production for three days after a racist foreman called a production worker a "Black bastard." Out of that spontaneous wildcat, the United Black Brothers of Mahwah Ford was organized. The caucus led many wildcat strikes over continued racism at the plant.

What was new about the caucuses was that they represented a much more basic opposition than Reuther had ever faced before. The UAW had, until the appearance of those new caucuses, pretty much eliminated any organized opposition—by any means, ethical or unethical. The bureaucracy had not really given a damn about rank-and-file problems in the shop for years. Now they were facing some real opposition, from below.

In the early stages of the Black caucus at Dodge, DRUM raised a proposal that amounted to "dual unionism." They proposed in their paper that all Black workers stop paying dues to the UAW and pay them instead to DRUM, to be used in the Black communities. Many Black workers I spoke with, who were very sympathetic to DRUM's activities in the plant, were opposed to this idea completely. They were all for a Black caucus that would fight racism and inhuman working conditions in the plants. They were all for militant Black workers taking over the leadership in the unions for the purpose of making a complete change at the point of production. But they became skeptical of the objectives behind a proposal like this.

Black workers at Sparrow's Point, a Bethlehem Steel mill in Baltimore, Maryland, on the other hand, formed a group outside the union, called the Committee for Equality, rather than forming a caucus within the union. They had a specific situation there, in which they could apply pressure on the government to end its multi-million dollar contracts with the company unless the company stopped discriminating. These workers felt they had to find some way to shake everything up—the racist company, as well as their racist union. And it worked.

The opposition of the Black workers was part of the opposition of the Black people as a whole to white racist America, a movement that had been gathering momentum since 1961. In 1964, a mass picket line of about five hundred got world headlines by surrounding the GM building in Detroit with signs saying "Racism Hurts All Labor," "Automation Layoffs—Lily White Departments—Slow Upgrading—What Is My Job Future?" The demonstration had been called by the NAACP and was distinguished from traditional labor picket lines by the presence of student youth and the singing of freedom songs. GM agreed to negotiate, and even without the threat of a demonstration, Chrysler and Ford did the same. What happened after the talks is another question.

In 1965, SNCC helped to organize a Mississippi Freedom Union and later a Tennessee Freedom Union. They had found, while trying to work on voter registration, that what Black people in the South wanted most was to do something about their three dollar a day wages and miserable working conditions. From organized labor all they got was evasiveness. Later that same year, grape workers in California began their strike for a farm workers organization with the help of CORE and other civil rights groups. By March of the next year, 1966, the Freedom Union idea moved North to the cities when CORE organized a pilot project in Baltimore—and the Maryland Freedom Union was born. The greatest victory there was the manner in which the unorganized Black women working in several nursing homes of Baltimore took matters into their own hands. They walked out first—and then called to tell the "organizers" to come organize them.

That same year, organized Black workers elsewhere were also taking matters into their own hands. When the UAW convention delegates met in Long Beach, California in the summer of 1966, they found Black workers from Local 887 of the North American Aviation plant picketing the convention to protest discrimination by their local union against Blacks, women and Mexican Americans. They said simply: "We've written lots of letters to Reuther. We even sent them return receipt requested. We have a pocketful of receipts. But no answers."

By September, these same NAA workers held the first "Civil Rights Strike" of its kind to protest the discriminatory practices of the company. They wrote me that, "One Negro worker who had been trying to be a drill press operator for two years was finally accepted the day after the strike. Another worker who had been told a few months earlier that he had failed (by one point) the test for machine operator's apprentice was told he had been accepted. Another was promoted to assistant foreman, whatever that means. And the company even announced that a Negro top brass was promoted to a $30,000 a year job. Long Live Tokenism!"

One of the most significant developments out of that NAA situation was the appearance of a mimeographed shop paper, edited by these Black workers themselves, which they called *The Protester*. In Detroit a group of auto workers at the Highland Park Chrysler plant had come out that same year with a mimeographed shop paper called *The Stinger*. Another *Stinger* appeared later at the Mack Avenue Chrysler plant.

The richness and diversity of the Black workers' groups was constantly growing. Moreover, there were significant differences between the various Black workers' groups that were springing up everywhere. The Mack Avenue *Stinger*, for example, though it was edited by Black workers, made a distinction between the "whitey" who is a rank-and-file worker, and the "whitey" who was either a company representative or union bureaucrat. The Black editor put it this way: "It's true that we're fighting discrimination against Black workers in the shop as one of the most important questions of our lives. But that isn't the only question. The reason many of the white workers in our shop also read—and even support—*The Stinger*, is that we are raising the question of the inhuman conditions of all workers in production. Automation speed up and the inhumanity of the company and union bureaucrats is against workers as a whole. That is what *The Stinger* is fighting, and why white workers have told us they are glad we are distributing it."

There is nothing more stupid than to think that all Black workers think alike, or that there is only one face to the whole new phenomenon of the Black caucuses. This was one of the most important points discussed at a conference held in Detroit in January of 1969, where Black youth, workers, women, and intellectuals had a chance to discuss with each other.

One Black auto worker at the Detroit conference felt that "too much of the activity of some Black caucuses is pointed to getting on supervision rather than elevating labor on the line. The company doesn't care whether it's a white man or a Black man as long as they get production out. The company is getting very expert using Black supervisors to fight Black workers."

Some younger auto workers felt that "trying to get a coalition with white workers is impossible because they are hung up in their racist bag." But a steel worker from the East described the Black workers' organization in his mill, which was so effective in ending some of the racist practices there that it was recognized by white workers who had their own problems with the union. When the Black workers invited a group of white workers to come with them on one of their marches, the same white workers who hadn't wanted to associate with "those raving Black militants out to destroy everything," suddenly decided maybe it wasn't such a bad idea after all, and couldn't wait for the next march.

The United Black Brothers at Mahwah had also made it a point to appeal to all the workers in the shop. A leaflet issued in their wildcat strike put it this way: "Why We Ask Your Support?—Because the same thing can happen to you. The company has been laying off men by the dozens, but the lines have not slowed up a bit. You have been given more work, and if you don't do it, you lose your job or get time off. The supervisors are harassing the men and calling them all kinds of names such as 'Dirty Guinea Bastard,' 'Black SOB,' and 'Stinking Spick,' to name a few... We, the United Black Brothers demand an end to this now and those guilty of these charges be removed.... We ask all of you to stay out and support us in this fight."

The greatest difference between the new caucuses emerging then and those that appeared before was that most of us who were in Black opposition groups up to that time thought that the most important thing to do was to throw out the leadership, or change the union structure, or something of that nature. The young people then weren't thinking that way. They were thinking in terms of complete change—of revolution.

They were just filled up to their necks with racism. And with the war. During the Black student revolt that occurred at Cornell, one professor reported talking to one of the Black students about their use of guns. He had sympathized with their demands, but he had been trying to point out to them how powerful this country is and to warn them that they were facing tremendous oppression if they continued using such tactics. The Black student just laughed in his face: "You're talking about oppression coming upon me? I've been oppressed all my life. It's you and the people who call themselves liberals who are going to feel the oppression that's coming." It shocked the professor because he knew the student was right.

Young Blacks then weren't joking about the complete change they were out to get. When the group at Dodge named themselves the Revolutionary Union Movement, it was very significant. Years before, if workers called themselves "revolutionaries", other workers shied away from them.

Nobody knew what would happen with the Black groups that existed throughout the country. But it was clear that no national caucus was on the horizon; and to give the impression that one already existed, much less to imply DRUM was it (as the left publication *Guardian* did in a special edition on the Black workers' revolt) was futile self-deception.

In later shop elections, DRUM lost badly at Dodge Main, despite the fact that the membership there was overwhelmingly Black. The union bureaucracy boasted that it had won everywhere against the Black extremists, but that wasn't true. At the Eldon Axle plant, where 65% of the workers were Black, ELRUM ran candidates for only a few positions and, although they lost, Black workers were in complete control of the local for the first time. Doug Fraser, then head of the UAW's Chrysler division, claimed that workers he supported were "moderates", but ELRUM also supported them.

The most honest way to judge the response of Black workers is to compare the manner in which thousands responded to DRUM's call for the wildcat strike the year before, and the way they reacted at a mass meeting called after 26 workers were fired at the Eldon Axle plant. The meeting was held in a large church and about five or six hundred workers crowded inside. The majority were younger workers, but there were many older workers too. The first thing that struck me was that those in control of the meeting were not workers in the plant—or in any plant.

The speakers on the platform went on at great length attacking white racism—with the most vulgar name-calling possible. They spent a lot of time clowning and trying to be comedians. Once in a while, they touched on a vital shop issue. Finally, the principal speaker was called. As soon as he got up, he raised his Little Red Book above his head and said, "My comrades of the Black Revolutionary Movement, how many of you have this book?" He had to ask several times before four or five raised their books. The speaker told the audience that this was what the movement was all about, and gave the address where everyone could go after the meeting to get a copy of

"Comrade Mao's Thoughts." When he went on to call Mao "our closest ally," many workers in the audience began squirming and I felt this sort of meeting was what the labor bureaucrats needed to destroy the movement.

One older worker sitting next to me from Dodge, an Old Communist Party member, said, "Man, this guy has just sounded the tocsin for the death of this movement, because this is all that Reuther has been waiting to hear. Now watch him move to break it up." And I knew it was true.

I had been watching the DRUM developments, and especially when people outside the shops began to come into the picture. Among them was Ken Cockrel, a young Black radical lawyer who yelled loudest and longest against the system (he's now a Detroit City Council member), and who became chairman of the group. The fired workers from Dodge were getting paid every week—from $125 to $150 a week—and I wondered where the money was coming from. They collected money at meetings they held, but it was nowhere near what was needed to pay those fired workers for as long as they did. A lot of the pieces fell into place at that meeting.

Black UAW International representatives like Edwards and Tappes, who had supported DRUM (though not openly), came out strongly against them after that meeting. The one thing the young Black workers did not fully realize was that every time a Black independent movement has appeared, the "politicos" who have rushed in to take it over have helped the reactionaries like Reuther to kill it before it can get off the ground. It was true of the first Black organization in the union I was involved with, as early as the '40s. There were about 200 of us, and we "stormed" Lansing and every Black worker I knew was enthusiastic about what we were doing. But the Communists and Trotskyists moved in and began a naked fight over control of our organization. It isn't so much that the so-called "radicals" come rushing in, but every time they come in they want to take over. The same thing was happening again, with the Maoists doing it differently only in that they sent in Blacks instead of whites to take control.

At first, DRUM did inspire other workers. Groups were organized in several plants, like ELRUM at Eldon Axle and FRUM at Ford. But they were all connected to the original DRUM group. Another thing they did that made many workers angry to use vulgar language in their publications. There's nobody who can cuss more than auto workers when they describe their working conditions, bosses or union representatives. But it's one thing to use that language in the shop, it's something else when it appears in print as an expression of an organization. At first, it may have had some shock value, but each issue became more vulgar and derogatory, and then became meaningless. You can't substitute vulgarity for serious analysis of the issues.

DRUM also caught the attention of workers in other parts of the country. I know that workers from Ford Mahwah came to Detroit to talk with DRUM people and had asked me how to get in touch with them. Later I learned that Reuther sent one of his Black representatives, Eccles, to Mahwah to help put the clamps on any further independent Black developments there.

Now the Black caucuses are pretty well out of the picture. DRUM was never any mass movement, but it did get a lot of publicity. And I know from my experiences that when rank-and-file workers come around to any radical organization—DRUM or any other radical group—they do so because they want to make a fundamental change in their lives. And as soon as they see that is not what is going to be done from their experiences with the group, they just leave.

Another example of workers' thinking could be seen around the issues raised by Ralph Nader when he exposed the safety defects in U.S. cars. Many workers were glad to see that he was making headlines in his charges, but many got to the real issue when they said there could be no improvement in the safety of cars so long as the rat race for production continued. Nader could yell all he wanted to about more safety features for the cars being built, but until the companies slowed down their automated lines and machines to the point where workers could turn out quality of work instead of quantity of jobs, workers knew that safety would not improve, but only get worse.

Every year it's the same. The company speeds up work and takes short cuts on production. It means steadily declining quality. Many workers in GM say they're afraid to buy GM cars, Ford workers are afraid of Ford cars, and Chrysler workers complain about their product. They know how bad the cars are they work on, and think that their conditions are so bad that it must be better at other plants. Nader was talking about safety belts and padded dashes, and they're important, but workers were talking about much more important things.

One worker I know was going to Alabama with his family for a visit. He had a new GM car, and after driving two blocks from his home, the motor dropped from the frame onto the street. He looked at it lying on the pavement, and when he said "Thank God," his wife thought he had gone crazy. But he said, "If we were on the highway and this happened, we could have been killed." Workers are convinced that many wrecks that kill people are caused by defects like this in the cars.

I was working in the frame department, and every day the defective parts got worse than the day before. Nobody in supervision seemed to care about it. Often when a frame was loaded to be put on a car, a worker would say, "Man, I hate to think about who will get this car." And another would chime in with, "And think of all the money people pay to buy this scrap!" The part of the car that used to be the biggest lemon was the motor. Today the cars are lemons from top to bottom, inside included.

Workers are facing the greatest challenge of their existence as a labor force. A white worker, an inspector, told me, "We older workers seem doomed so far as hoping for any changes in the production relations that have caused us so much misery and headaches because of automation. The only hope I see to this challenge is the youth, the younger generation.

He gave this explanation. At one of the plants where he had worked for a few weeks, the company had hired about 20 young workers in his department. The foreman, as usual, yelled at them that they had to work faster...to keep pace with the machines... that production was set and they had to make it each hour.

By the end of the first day, 15 had quit, saying it was beyond their imagination that a living human could be forced to work at such a pace. The following day, the other five walked off the job, saying, "The hell with it! I'd rather take my chances on starvation rather than be murdered by a machine."

I told the worker that I was sure he'd be very interested in a book that I knew very well, called *Marxism and Freedom,* that described exactly what he was talking about—the insanity of capitalist production. And not just how it is under automation, but how it had developed historically from its beginnings after the French Revolution. I told him that to me, the most important point of the book was that it always was looking at what workers were not only doing, but also what they were thinking, and how they expressed their thinking in their actions.

I said I understood why those young workerd quit because the work was impossible, but to say we older ones must bow out before there could be any change was taking a defeatist attitude. The great value of the book, I said, was that it showed a method, a way of looking at what was happening in the shops to challenge automation as well as the company and union leaders who seem to have combined to keep the workers in their place.

The book itself can't change the conditions in the industries. But it points out the road workers must take as clear as day, if we are to survive while facing the monster of automated production.

25.
WITH THE WILDCATTERS

SPONTANEOUS ACTIONS BY Chrysler workers in the summer of 1973 made national headlines and frightened the company as well as the UAW bureaucracy as nothing that had happened before. In July, two Black workers protesting against work speed-up locked themselves in the power room of the Chrysler Jefferson plant in Detroit and stopped the production line. The two workers refused to come out of the room, and when the company guard started to move in to throw them out, other workers spontaneously surrounded them and refused to let the guards get to them. The two workers demanded that two hated foremen be fired by the company, and that Chrysler management negotiate directly with them.

The workers remained in the room for two days, with the plant shut down. The circle of workers remained in the shop to protect the two protestors. The company was over a barrel, and despite the insistance by the union that they not negotiate with the workers, the company was forced to. They agreed to the workers' demands: they fired the two foremen, and promised no reprisals against either the two workers or anyone else who supported them. This action attracted the attention and support of workers throughout the whole Detroit area, and many would stop at the plant to picket with others.

When this happened, Doug Fraser became completely encouraged, and publicly blasted Chrysler management for not only agreeing to the workers' demands, but also for daring to negotiate with the workers, for letting them represent themselves. Fraser's line was clear: only the UAW had the right to represent the workers and to negotiate anything.

This question was the talk of the union bureaucrats for weeks because they knew their own authority was being threatened by this kind of independent action by the rank-and-file. They knew the danger to themselves very well, because this was the same way, with the same methods, that workers organized the unions in the '30s—when they were creating something new, their own organizations, the UAW, their fighting arm. The difference here was that a UAW existed. The workers were moving to create something new again to fight for them, and they knew they had to go outside the union structure to do it because the union no longer fought for them.

The smoke hadn't cleared away from this rebellion when another exploded at the Chrysler Mack plant of Tuesday, August 14, during my last year in the shop. Only this time, it wasn't two workers challenging from a power room, it was a spontaneous sit-in strike by many workers whose challenge to both the company and union was much more serious.

Some five workers were fired in the previous week for not keeping up with production standards. On Tuesday morning, several of these discharged workers sneaked into the plant and went to their jobs, saying no one was going to do their operation, no one was going to take their jobs away. They stopped the production line and then sat on their stools. Their foreman rushed up and, when he was told what was happening he ran into the superintendent's office and they called the plant guards.

They soon had to call the captain of the guards, who is a Black with completely "white" thinking. This guard's name is Prince, and the great majority of the 5,000 workers at Mack knew and hated him because of his past actions and attitudes against workers. He was responsible for more workers getting fired and disciplined than practically all of the foremen.

Prince rushed up and collared one of the workers and started to drag him. Another worker swung an iron pipe up against his head and he went down in a puddle of his own blood. Another guard rushed in and he was likewise put down with a pipe.

The news spread to other departments and floors all over the plant, and workers began rushing into Department 9780 to protect the fired workers and others. Management was so frightened that they began rushing all over the place, and started rumors that a bomb was planted in the shop which was supposed to go off in thirty minutes, in the hope that the workers would leave the plant.

Workers in Department 9780, where the rebellion began, declared they were staying there and taking the plant over. They were yelling for their chief steward and committeeman, but

The jubilant Chrysler workers after their sit-in at the Chrysler plant, Detroit, August, 1973.

none of them would come. But the police came into 9780 and saw there were more than 100 workers, Black and white, who were protecting the ones who were fired. The police looked at them and just left. They were scared too.

Most of us in the plant knew that it did not just begin on Tuesday morning. For more than a month there had been serious complaints about working conditions, speed-ups and foremen running roughshod over production workers. And there was not one damn thing our union steward or committeeman would say or do about it.

Several weeks earlier, the news reported that our local president, Hank Ghant, burst into the national negotiations. He started yelling at Doug Fraser, telling him that if something was not done over the conditions at the Mack plant, they were in for serious trouble. It had reached the point where a white woman worker had chased a Black foreman all around the department with a two by four, and other workers were trying to help her catch him. This foreman just ran over people, everybody was wrong but him.

The Mack plant was 80 percent Black, and the company had put on many Black foreman to pacify the Black workers, but we soon learned that there is not much difference in these foremen, only in skin color. Many Black foremen push workers harder than some of the whites. We have some SOBs, and we have to deal with the Black part of management the same as we do with the white. You could see the workers in Mack were beginning to do just that.

After the police left, some 200 workers sat down in the plant with the workers who were fired. The union and the company began to yell that they were all Communists. Some two or three sit-inners said they were members of the Progressive Labor Party, but most workers had never heard of P.L. or knew anything about its philosophy. But we all did know about the working conditions, the lack of safety and the speed-up in the Mack plant.

Doug Fraser went on TV and said it was all "outsiders" who were causing the trouble at Mack. This was ridiculous and the workers said, "Do you think that one or two men can control the thoughts and actions of 5,000 workers at Mack?"

None of these union leaders would come to the plant that

morning. Workers demanded that Hank Ghant come to the plant and discuss their grievances. After getting word that he was not coming, they formed a committee of their own and went to the union hall. They forced him to come to the plant with them to talk over their demands and grievances.

The workers who sat down held the plant for 30 hours. Chrysler had said they would not call the police to take them out. But Fraser and the rest of the International UAW leaders kept demanding that the police be ordered in. Finally, about nine the next morning we heard that Lynn Townsend, the head of Chrysler, made a call from Louisiana to have the workers in the plant driven out at any cost.

About 10:30 a.m., hundreds and hundreds of police began to arrive with paddy wagons. They stormed the plant and took the workers out, and arrested two they said were "the masterminds." There was a meeting of about 250 workers at the union hall right after the workers were taken out of the plant. There was a lot of yelling at Ken Morris when he got to speak, and finally several workers took the microphone away and repeated the demands of the strike. But what really finished these bureaucrats at the meeting was Joe Zappa, our Vice-President of Local 212. He said, "I heard you say the leadership is nothing without the membership. Maybe so. But don't forget that in this UAW the membership is nothing without the leadership. You can't do anything without us." After that, there was nothing else the leaders could do because of the commotion. Every worker voted to strike.

Here again, we had a repeat of so many things that had happened before. The workers exploding into action, the company and union trying to get them back to work but failing, the radicals rushing in and giving the company and union the excuse to accuse outsiders for the problems and turning attention away from the workers' grievances. But this time it was also different, because at no time for several decades had there been an actual sit-down of this magnitude to challenge the company and the union.

That's why the reaction of both the union and the company was so vicious. Following TV announcements by the International union telling workers to return to work on their regular shift on August 16, many went to the plant thinking it would be the same as a return to work after other wildcat strikes in the past. Instead, they found lines of city police, over 1,000 union representatives and officers, and about 100 hoodlums who never worked in any plant. All of them had small baseball bats or police billyclubs. They had forced the strike pickets about four or five blocks away from the plant entrances. Some Mack workers even had to go through a screening test by the company and union before entering the plant.

The fired workers and others were there passing out a leaflet. Some of the union-hired hoodlums went over to them and began beating them up. It was sickening to see five or six big men beating up a smaller worker. A woman went to try to stop them and she kicked them. They tore most of the top of her blouse off. Some of the local officers just stood there and watched the beating.

The retaliation by the company, which was without a doubt also demanded by the union, was very severe, with practically every worker who sat down being fired, as well as many others who didn't even take part in the sit-in, but had their picture taken by company and union stooges because they were near the plant out of curiousity. Many workers who were known militants, even though they had many year's seniority, were fired and never rehired again.

Many workers were also confused. They didn't understand how radicals operate or what they try to do, and got caught between the radicals and the UAW. The radicals yell that the only way out of the mess is to follow them, and the UAW says they have the answer. And if workers are not with either one of them, they are attacked by both. The real problem is that neither one can answer what the workers are fighting for in the shop.

Recently there have been a number of reports showing how many dangers workers face in the form of chemicals and other substances they breathe or are exposed to in the work situation. The reports are disturbing, but many workers have known this for years. Even after making occupational health and safety codes into law, the big question is having them enforced on the job in the plants. Any time a worker refuses to work a job because of a health hazard and that operation is vital to production, some worker will still have to do it or be fired.

Several years ago, workers struck over this issue at a Chrysler plant. The grievance of the Chrysler workers went to Federal Judge, Cornelia Kennedy. She ruled that a worker could not be forced to work under a job-induced threat to life and health, but workers have to have absolute proof of this before they can refuse to do work. One worker said, "What this really means is that workers have to get seriously injured or killed before they can refuse to work on a dangerous or hazardous job."

When the union actually represented workers in production, a worker could call the company safety man on some hazard, and if it was not corrected at once, the union would shut down the operation until it was corrected. Today there is no such thing.

Practically every worker who spends fifteen years or more in a factory contracts some type of occupational health disease. I have met and talked with many workers in the plants, mines and mills, as well as retired workers. Almost every one is suffering from some type of occupational disease. After fifteen or twenty years in a factory, the company has taken away the best of your health, body, and mind.

It was only in the '60s that the UAW began to move on occupational health issues. And this was because some foundry workers who had been fired and rehired by another company were given physical exams, and it was discovered that each one had very bad lungs from dust inhaled for over fifteen years, and many had only a short time to live.

Almost every month we read about some new chemical or health hazard that has been discovered endangering the health and lives of workers and their families. And still nothing effective is done about it. It has such a low priority for both the government and medical profession that it looks like it's going to be a long time before anything effective will be done about it.

I especially remember a vacation I took one year in southern Pennsylvania and West Virginia among unemployed coal miners. Things have changed somewhat for them in that there is not the unemployment there had been, but their health situation has not changed—except maybe for the worse. Since there's such a great demand now for coal because of the energy crisis, many safety provisions are being violated and ignored.

In Pennsylvania, I spent a week in a mining district. The vast majority of men there were unemployed—some for as long as five years. In talking with a white miner, unemployed for four years, he said, "You know, people in other parts of the country can read about us, see us on TV and hear about us on the radio, and many will sympathize. But no one really knows unless they live here or come here and be with us for a while.

"Long ago, I read of the problems colored people had, and sympathized with them. But I know now that I could not feel like them because I was not one of them and was not living with them where they were facing the problems of being permanently unemployed, of being degraded to the point where you do not think. I lay home in bed and sit around the house until I feel sick. Sometimes, you get a job for a day. They tell you what they will pay. Instead of finishing the job, you work on it two or three days—just to say to yourself, I have something to do tomorrow!"

One morning I saw a dozen men standing in an open field. Several were holding .22 rifles; all were laughing and talking. I walked up to them and asked where they were going. They said to hunt rats, snakes and lizards. Two of them had some kind of net, said they were hunting butterflies. I laughed. One asked if I was employed. When I answered yes, he said, "We're unemployed miners. We do this to keep our minds active." I never felt so bad in my life, and I apologized. The miner spoke about a college student wanting several different species of butterflies for her studies in biology. Even after he caught as many as she wanted, it seemed to occupy his mind, so he continued to catch them. He had hundreds of different species. If no one wants them, he will turn them loose and probably catch them again.

I was told of a miner some 25 miles away, a man I had not seen since childhood. In that area, practically all of the mines were worked out or closed down. Most of the miners there are old men, and all seemed to have asthma, with shortened breath. When I asked my relative about this, he said it wasn't asthma, it was silicosis. He drew a diagram of lungs, as a lab technician might do, explaining how much coal dust is likely to settle in the lungs each year. After 30 years in a mine, it is almost impossible to come out with no silicosis.

At one time, he said, miners died rapidly, but doctors had found ways to make you last longer—only there is no cure. The disease slowly clogs your breathing and smothers you to death. I thought of all the wealth these miners had produced, and the profits they had made for the companies, only to become forgotten human beings. As one miner said, "When we first were out of work, we were all afraid of hitting bottom. We felt we were as low as we could go. And after a year or two, something would come along and we'd be able to lift our heads up and have hope of going again. But we have wallowed in this bottom so long, we feel it's hopeless now. If the women here were not working, we would be like mad dogs."

I asked about the government commodities they were supposed to be getting, and he said, "Man, we are used to having some money of our own in our pockets. This food is the same thing every two weeks. After you eat it for a while, the taste leaves it. It never tastes like the food you buy. And you don't have any choice—it's just something to keep you alive. Your children ask you, 'Can I have an ice cream or pop?' You just don't have the money. You feel like you are nothing. They say when you hit rock bottom, the only way you can go is up. If I thought this was possible, I would feel better."

In West Virginia, the army of the unemployed was the same. My amazement was at the relationship between the white miners and their families and the Black miners and their families. I could not believe I was near the Mason-Dixon line. There was some prejudice there, but the attitudes of the miners to each other, their social relationships, were moving closer, drinking with each other, talking on the streets and visiting each other's homes. When I asked about this, one old miner said he believed that every miner for many years past discussed the conditions of work with his family, and helped them to understand that one miner's life underground depends on every other miner. He talked about the organizing days of the UMW, pointing out that the state militia and yellow dogs did not single out race to shoot, and if the white and Black miners had not fought together, the UMW never would have been organized.

He said, "When you're in the belly of hell and something happens, you don't think about Black or white." I thought about something I'd read written by a revolutionist: "A tickle affects different people in different ways, but a red hot poker affects all humans alike." And I also thought about how the coal industry was the first hit by automation in 1949-50, and how the number of miners was unbelievably slashed from about 450,000 working then, to about 120,000 ten years later. Here you could really see the fruits of automation, and I kept remembering how Lewis, Reuther, Meany and all of the labor leaders kept on declaring that you can't stop progress. To me, progress is when people live better lives, and there was nobody who could see those people and say that was progress.

26.
WORLDWIDE STRUGGLE FOR FREEDOM

LONG BEFORE THE word "revolutionary" became popular in the shops, workers were in constant revolt—not only in the auto shops, but in the mines and steel mills, and all basic industries. It wasn't only against management, but also against the union bureaucrats way back in 1953, and this was shown clearly in *Workers Battle Automation.* By now management and the union are so much alike that there's no difference between them when it comes to fighting for better shop conditions and grievances. One sign of the great separation between union leaders and ranks can be seen from the stepped-up picketing of Solidarity House, headquarters of the UAW, by rank-and-file workers. This was unheard of a very few years ago.

I wrote about this and the relation of Black workers to the labor movement in an article that was published as a appendix to *American Civilization on Trial,* which traces the historic roots of America's so-called civilization to the revolts in the factories as well as to the slave revolts. That revolution is still going on because it remains unfinished to this day. Workers are the key to the whole revolution, and in this country Black workers have been in the vanguard of every forward movement. But the Black Revolution has now reached the crossroad between nationalism and proletarian internationalism.

Blacks always have been important in the history of the UAW, from the beginning to the present. Because of this, I was very surprised when I read a recent book by Frank Marquart, *An Auto Worker's Journal: The UAW from Crusade to One Party Union.* I've known Marquart for many years, and always thought he was a Reutherite. A little left, maybe, but he always seemed to defend what Reuther did. So reading the attacks against Reuther came as a surprise to me.

It's also puzzling why Marquart doesn't even mention the one person who played the most important role in the organizing of the UAW—John L. Lewis. However, there is much valuable information in the book about the UAW's history and developments which transformed it from a fighting organization into a controlling one.

But more surprising was that he had practically nothing to say about the Blacks in the UAW—and he knew many in his long career with the UAW. To me, Marquart doesn't recognize the important influence Blacks had as much as old Henry Ford did. In his whole book, Marquart makes only passing reference to A. Philip Randolph, and says almost nothing about Blacks and the UAW itself.

The fact is that it would have been impossible to organize the UAW without the direct support and struggle of the Black workers. The companies planned to use Blacks to break the union organizing going on, and many companies did in fact bring up many Blacks from the South to do just that. Instead, Blacks joined with the white workers and that unity resulted in the victory of the union movement.

An important clue may be that Marquart was a member of the Socialist Party, which he describes in detail. I think that as a Norman Thomas socialist he accepted the position that there is no Black question outside of the class question. What that does is blind you to the fact that Blacks have many problems whites don't have, in and out of the shops, and that Blacks are necessarily forced to fight on both race and class lines.

Today, many civil rights leaders of the 1960s are either trying to get rich writing about "those good old revolutionary days," or running for some state or federal political office under the banner of the capitalist Democratic or Republican parties. At the same time, the economic crises get worse—not only in America, but all over the world. Automation keeps on throwing workers out of jobs, and speeds up those kept working beyond what a human can take.

Only now they've added a new dimension to automation, and are calling it unimation. I read recently where Unimation, Inc. of Danbury, Connecticut held an open house at their offices in Farmington Hills, Michigan to show customers how smart their industrial robots have become.

What concerns me most about that was how we felt when we first saw automation introduced in the auto shops over 20 years ago, and how workers revolted against this "man-killer." I know that automation has wrecked many workers' lives. There are thousands that are messed up from automation, and many have died as a result of it.

Now they have gone from automation to robots. The report is that the unimation machines they were referring to can weld along a continuous irregular path. Just the presence of a car body on the assembly line causes it to close in to make the welds as it moves by. The company president, Joseph Engelberger, said, "The human being is a magnificent creation and we are not going to replace him soon." But the article went on, "Maybe some humans will be replaced, since what the robots do, they tend to do quickly, efficiently, without deviation or complaint—not to mention without salary, fringe benefits or personal problems."

Sure, robots will eliminate some of the work force, but those who will remain will have to work harder to keep pace with this robot. As Karl Marx said, when capitalism gets to the point that it puts all of its best science, its best knowledge, into improving dead labor over living labor, for the purpose of exploiting the living labor, it is creating chaos and revolt in the workplace.

Engelberger said jobs taken over by the robots tend to be the most repetitive, dangerous and lousy jobs that the younger union members don't want. What he is really saying is that younger workers will be much harder to control. They do not accept jobs at face value. About 60 percent of the robots have been adapted for use in the automotive industry, Engelberger said. He predicts that the gradual replacement of people by robots in "dull" jobs through normal attrition will make auto plants more interesting places to work. It will eventually lead to job enrichment for the human who directs the work of the robots, and he said it would also improve productivity which could lead to the creation of new jobs.

All of this was said when they introduced automation. But it eliminated workers by the thousands, especially production workers. For those who were left, the machines changed their whole lives, and it was more miserable for most.

This is what I wrote in 1960 in my "Workers Battle Automation" pamphlet:

Death by Automation*
When you hear about Automation being a "man-killer" that's not just a figure of speech. That's what the wildcat strike at Great Lakes Steel was about.

After the 116 day strike was supposedly won by the men, the steel companies put on a new drive to put automatic processing equipment on the mill floor. From the strain of overwork, a crane operator fell from his scaffold and was killed. When the men went to his funeral they learned of three other operators who had died in the same week from the strain of the crackdown and speedup. That's what made the men mad. That's why they walked out.

As in the steel mills, so in the auto shops: as the speed from automation becomes more intense, safety conditions are thrown to the wind by the company. I can remember when they first brought those machines to our department. I don't know how many workers were hurt that first day: crushed hands, lost fingers. There are signs all over the department to work safely. Inside of a couple of hours workers wrote under these signs: "These machines are not safe to do it with."

February 10th of this year an auto worker got off the bus at the plant gate and fell dead on the pavement. He died of a heart attack. Workers said that he had repeatedly complained to the foreman that it was impossible to keep up with the pace set by time-study and the machines. His complaints didn't mean a thing to management. The union simply shrugged its shoulders.

On Wednesday, December 30th of last year there was a combined wildcat and lockout in one of Chrysler's assembly departments. It resulted from a worker being seriously injured on the frame job. Chrysler's mad rush for production and more production, with workers bound to the inhuman pace of Automation, is very dangerous to the lives of the men on the frame job. Workers have been severely injured by the cross bars flying out

---

*"Workers Battle Automation, published by *News & Letters,* Detroit, Michigan, in 1960 is out of print, but it is available on microfilm from the Labor History Archives of Wayne State University, Detroit, Michigan, where it is included with all of my other writings in the "Raya Dunayevskaya Collection: Marxist Humanism— 1941 to today."

from the frame before it can be welded. Minor injuries are a daily occurence.

On this last Wednesday in 1959, a bar flew out and struck a worker across his back and head, knocking him unconscious. After the unconscious man was rushed to the hospital on a stretcher, the foreman yelled for another worker to come and work the same job. The worker refused, saying, "You're crazy as hell! I wouldn't work there for double pay." This never happens when the machine is running at a normal pace.

To the production worker in auto, Automation means physical strain, mental strain, fatigue, heart attacks—death by Automation.

Urine As Red As Blood

It isn't only those who die. I have never seen so many workers sent home sick by first aid as I see now. There is hardly a job in any plant that is not against the workers' health in one way or the other. If they aren't sucking in too much dust in their lungs, they are getting too much smoke or too many chemicals or something. There's just too much of it that goes into their bodies and the older you get the lower your resistance gets. The sun hasn't shined on this job yet. Wait until it gets ninety degrees or ninety-five degrees outside.

One young guy, just about thirty, works on the heavy frame job, lifting the frames onto the machine. He came out of the wash room one day and told me he felt a sharp pain and his urine ran red like blood. These are everyday occurrences in automated factories today.

I received a letter from a worker who asked how much exhaust can a person's body stand. Three or four copies of the issue of *News & Letters* in which this question appeared were hung up in the washroom. The next day I received a few more letters, asking our medical columnist to answer. Here are both the question and the M.D.'s answer:

How Much Exhaust Can A Person Stand?

I would like to know one thing from M.D.—Just how much fresh air does a person require in the body every day? In an auto plant we don't get very much. We get dust and exhaust—just how much exhaust is a person's body supposed to withstand?

In a year's time what effect would this exhaust have on a person? And it's not exhaust alone, there's gas. You take arc welding—that rod is throwing off a gas and the machine is throwing off a gas. What does this do to people?

This job is going to get worse yet. The sun hasn't been able to shine on us yet. This summer they'll be able to see who can stand it. It may be that some of the younger people will but I know the workers over 45 won't be able to.

Summer is going to be tough. It was hot in there when the temperature outside was 25 degrees, what is it going to be like when it gets to be 95 degrees outside? The building is going to be even hotter than that. It is going to be murder all right. I would like to know what does all this do to people, if they can stand it?

The Doctor Answers

A Detroit auto worker asked what do gases, exhaust and high temperatures do to a person working under pressure. Physical fatigue and exhaustion from a driving belt line will decrease the reservoir of vital energy, and consequently make one more susceptable to the stress of poisonous chemicals. So will the stress of nervous tension, anger and frustration.

High temperatures require greater stores of body energy for maintaining a state of balance: excessive sweating causes losses of large amounts of fluid and salt. The increased heart rate and respiration in overheated atmospheres make for more rapid absorption of chemicals through the hundreds of square meters of absorbable surface present in the lungs in direct contact with the blood.

When welding is done at high temperatures in the adjacent area, the effect of the release of gases irritant to the lungs, as the oxides of nitrogen or metal fumes will tend to make the victim even more responsive to the damage of poisonous chemicals. The nitrogen dioxide gas, which is frequently liberated when metal is heated at this high temperature, is not only irritating to the lungs but it can have harmful effects possibly to the liver and blood.

Welders or those working near welders sometimes get what is called "a flash" from the welding arc. What is irritating to the eyes is ultra-violet light. It can and does burn the eye surface, giving an inflammation that is acute with red eyes congested, discharging and a feeling as though grit or foreign material were present in the eye.

How much of this can a person take?—I don't know. But one thing I am certain, that all of the gas from the combustion of petroleum is deadly to life. A small amount can sicken, and a lot can kill. Excessive speed of work, high levels of heat, and the action of other chemical irritants or poisonous substances in the work area will influence susceptability.

With carbon monoxide inhaled into the lungs in large amounts, acute poisoning and rapid asphyxia and coma follow. However, I have often wondered, as I pass through garages filled with dense clouds of auto exhaust, about the slow, chronic, insidious damage taking place over months and years as carbon monoxide, lead, arsenic and other products of oil and gasoline breakdown reach the lungs, the blood and blood-forming organs, and the sensitive spinal cord and brain centers.

I am sure that often symptoms and headaches, weakness, dizzy spells, nausea and indigestion, chest pains and other vague complaints are the result of such repeated exposure.

* * *

Nothing has been done to eliminate these dangers to the workers. If anything, they've gotten worse—which shows just how much management is interested in the health of workers.

On the other hand, we have the new robot of unimation. It is the last step of the capitalist's dream of replacing what Marx said was in the capitalist's view, the "refractory hand of labor." What they don't understand is that they cannot eliminate that "refractory hand," which is still the gravedigger of capitalism.

These developments are putting American labor at an historic crossroad, and the answers to these problems will decide which way this country will go in the future.

I have been thinking about the whole question of the Black dimension in the U.S. and how it is integral to the total idea of philosophy and revolution. Both thought and action came out of the history of the Black revolt, whether it was Marx looking at it in his day, the time of the Civil War, or today, especially in the civil rights struggles of the past 20 years, as recorded by News & Letters Committees.

But even before *News & Letters* was born, we started a new way of recording Black history as revolutionary, even when it was just a biography. I am referring to the first edition of this book, *Indignant Heart*.

First let's look at the most fundamental statement of Marxist Humanism, the book *Philosophy and Revolution,* by Raya Dunayevskaya with whom I've been closely associated for the past 30 years. The book, analyzing the 1960s at the very moment when the Black revolution both in Africa and America reached a higher stage in the world, points out that when Stokely Carmichael put forth his slogan "Black Power" in 1966, it marked the end of Dr. King's predominance in the leadership of the movement, as well as the beginning of a separation between the masses and all leadership, including Stokely Carmichael.

Both in the 1967 Detroit rebellion and in what I have written about it in my recollections in this book, our view of the revolution can be seen right at the point of production. As I noted, the most popular word in the shops was "revolution." Before then, even when we didn't parrot the union leadership and call workers "Communists," we would shy away from workers who declared themselves to be revolutionary. We were saying, "Why be for a foreign revolution? We need one right here, right here!"

As *Philosophy and Revolution* states, "The Black people have always been the Touchstone of American civilization precisely because they could expose both its Achilles' heel—its racism—and because they were always in the vanguard of its forward movement. It was so in the struggle against slavery when they fought together with the white abolitionists. It was so during the birth of imperialism when Blacks stood alone in their opposition. It was so when, with white labor, they reshaped the industrial face of America with the creation of the CIO. And it is so now when the Black Revolution has reached the crossroads between nationalism and proletarian internationalism."

One may ask what has happened to all our civil rights leaders of the '60s now that they are all looking for some state or federal job. Some have even come out in favor of right wing reactionaries like Wallace. They have turned their backs on working and poor people, even though these same people were yelling for a complete change in this society just a few short years ago. But their demand for change was not based on a philosophy of liberation, so they could take the easy way out, which means exchanging their principles for a high-paying government job or for a job with some establishment corporation that uses their talents and reputation to exploit the poor and working class Blacks and whites.

While these so-called leaders have been busy capitulating to the capitalist class, the thoughts and actions of the Blacks and workers are being sharpened in the experiences of their continuing revolts against their ever worsening social and economic conditions marked by speed-up in the plant, increasing unemployment and inflation.

A crossroads has been reached in Africa, too. And there is much Black Africans and Black Americans can learn from each other. In the early years of my life, it was a common thing among Blacks to discuss our relations with Africa. Many older ones would remember which tribe in Africa they came from, and the younger ones could not understand their dialect. But it was practically impossible for any Black not to have a feeling of close kinship as he or she sat and listened to the stories of slave ships the old ones told. I can remember my grandmother telling me about how people were put on the block for sale. She told me how she was sold in Virginia while her mother stood screaming. She never saw her mother again.

In my adult life the most outstanding events bringing Africans and Black Americans together were Mussolini's attack on Ethiopia, and the present revolution in Africa which has gained so many countries their independence. In the Depression I was traveling all over the country looking for work. So was everybody else I knew. Yet, next to the question of a job, what Blacks would talk about most was Mussolini's attack and how Africa was always getting the short end of the stick.

Somewhere between that period and the great independence movements of the Africans in the 1950s, the middle-class Blacks began to preach that Blacks were not really African. They didn't seem to be satisfied just to point to the obvious—that Blacks were American in language and culture and experience. No, they showed they were afraid of the African heritage by talking of Africans as backward, if not still outright head-hunters. However, as soon as the Africans began to win their independence, the tune changed. I suspect they found how great the African people were with the help of the State Department, because soon thereafter, in 1960 during the Congo crisis, the line between the middle-class and working-class Blacks became very sharp.

Where the middle-class Black was very quiet, working class Blacks first began to speak their minds during the assassination of Patrice Lumumba, lining up solidly behind him and his nationalist movement. The workers in my shop eagerly followed all developments, both in the Congo and the UN, warmly supporting the demonstrations before that body, and holding it responsible for Lumumba's murder.

One discussion had its comic aspects, since it showed that the workers in Detroit knew more about Lumumba than they did about their own trade union leaders. They were discussing conditions in the shop and how the leadership is always selling workers down the river. A white worker said it was all Meany's fault. A Black worker asked, "Who's Meany?" But the worker who did not even know Meany, president of the AFL-CIO, knew every detail of Lumumba's life from the time he organized the national movement for independence to his murder. The thing that irritated this Black most was that American trade union leaders were going around telling Africans how high the standard of living is in America, and how the Blacks here do not feel anything in common with Africans. What the bureaucrats fail to tell the Africans is that the car or home the Black Americans have puts them in debt for the rest of their life, and that in no case can they possibly mean that Black Americans do not feel a close relationship to the freedom movement of the Africans.

I am not saying that Black Americans would exchange life in America for one in Africa, though in America too, many live on welfare aid. I am saying there is a feeling of unity with African brothers and sisters, and a closer relationship is wanted. Unfortuntely, some African students here, even as some of the African leaders who come to this country on the invitation of the State Department, never get to see the rank-and-file workers. They associate either with the big shots in the government or in the trade unions or in the universities, but not with the Black people who are the true friends of African freedom fighters.

The experience the African people have made with their revolutions, and the problems they are still facing after all the great advance they made with "Negritude," have much to teach us here. We, too, are facing a new stage, and have much to learn.

I recently had a chance to talk for some time with two Africans, a young man from Nigeria and a woman from South Africa. Nobody has to be told that very deep changes are taking place in the thought and actions of Africans. We can see it in those who have gotten rid of colonialism, but most of all in the South Africans, where the actions are the most revolutionary.

The Nigerian said what practically every Black in U.S. industry knows—that skin color doesn't mean anything where the capitalists and working class are concerned. Just as a Black foreman or Black businessman can oppress and exploit the workers, so do the Africans in power oppress their own masses.

He pointed out that it is a very serious mistake to talk about Africans as though they all have one attitude. When colonialism went out the front door, neo-colonialism came in through the back door, and the economic ties of the earlier imperialist relations are still a noose around the necks of the African masses. The present oppressors have a Black face instead of a white one.

"There is a class in Africa," he said, "in whose interest it is to have neo-colonialism, for us to still be divided into tribes. There is an enormous gap in wages—you cannot fool the workers about whether you have a new society." He said that Nigeria has the most people and the most industry in Africa, and shows what will happen in other African nations if they don't act to stop the development of capitalist class relations.

The South African woman talked most about the youth in Soweto, but also about others in South Africa, and said nothing can stop them from gaining control of their country. Here too, she said, class not race is the main issue. But what hides the class relations, and makes it appear to be race, is that whites are the capitalist rulers, keeping control over the African majority through their brutal apartheid policies.

Instead of being surprised at the revolt of the Soweto youth, she said she had been expecting it. The way she expressed it, the youth of today in Soweto drank the ideas of revolt with their mother's milk. That's a measure of how long, deep and powerful the conscious thinking has been directed toward freedom, and the Soweto youth are acting on those ideas they have been getting since their birth. She said, "We can find parallels between what is happening among the masses in America and the masses in South Africa, in particular in Soweto, because in both we find the struggle to create a new world."

Just how vicious and almost overwhelming this battle for a new world is hit me again with great force when the reports came out on the horrible murder of Steven Biko, the young leader of the Black Consciousness Movement in South Africa, who had been tortured and beaten unconscious, chained naked in a cell, and driven 750 miles to his final death.

But even here, the revolutionary opposite comes through very sharply. Because nobody outside of South Africa had even heard of Steve Biko, and now the whole world knows about him. It reminded me of the quote from Wendell Phillips I used in the beginning of my life story: "Every true word spoken for suffering humanity, is so much done for the Negro bending under the weight of American bondage." The same idea is more real today than ever before, and goes around the world immediately.

It's what could be called the "shock of recognition"—when strangers from different countries react so much in the same way to ideas that they feel like they have always known each other. I know I felt this way toward Steve Biko, and know he felt the same way about Frantz Fanon, who he quoted on one of his last interviews. In that interview, Biko gave his ideas in Black Consciousness and referred to Fanon's idea on the internationalism of true revolutionary consciousness. Biko said:

"By Black Consciousness I mean the cultural and political revival of an oppressed people. This must be related to the emancipation of the entire continent of Africa since the Second World War. Africa had experienced the death of white invincibility.

"The Black Consciousness movement does not want to accept the dilemma of capitalism versus communism. It will opt for a socialist solution.

"As Fanon puts it, 'the consciousness of the self is not the closing of a door to communication...National consciousness, which is not nationalism, is the only thing that will give us an international dimension."

What both Fanon and Biko are saying is that the struggle for freedom has no national boundaries, and everywhere that you have a battle for human liberty helps the worldwide movement for freedom.

Just how important and widespread these ideas are is

emphasized in the Introduction I co-authored with Raya Dunayevskaya for the newly published pamphlet, "Frantz Fanon, Soweto and American Black Thought." In that Introduction we said:

"It is this, just this, type of affinity of ideas of freedom that led American Black youth to identify with Africa and Caribbean freedom struggles and thinking. Petty-bourgeois intellectuals may not have noticed this working out of a new relationship of theory to practice that is itself a form of theory, since *they* haven't done the 'theorizing.' But the American Black identification with Soweto and Biko, with Fanon and Caribbean thought, was precisely *that,* as Black and white American youth demonstrations against U.S. imperialism's heavy investments in apartheid South Africa have shown. Opposition to U.S. imperialism's propping up of Rhodesia while mouthing hollow words regarding 'Black majority rule,' words as false as Ian Smith's, is another such manifestation. Many are the ways the passion for freedom is articulating itself."

The ideas and actions coming out of the Black revolt in the U.S. and Africa are often sharper and easier to see than those of the working classes in every country, but they are all moving in the same direction.

I consider my life story as part of the worldwide struggle for freedom. As a Black from South U.S.A. and a Black auto production worker in Detroit, my experience has proved to me that history is the record of the fight of all oppressed people in everything they have thought and done to try to get human freedom in this world. I'm looking forward to that new world, and I firmly believe it is within reach, because so many others all over the world are reaching so hard with me.

AFTERWORD

YOU HAVE READ my book. My hope and wish is that rather than being an end, it will become a new beginning. I would very much like to hear from you, and welcome your ideas. My address is: Charles Denby, *News & Letters,* 2832 E. Grand Blvd., Rm 316, Detroit, Michigan, 48211.